Rich,

Your recent gift[s]
are making a real and
meaningful difference in the
lives of Music students,
Hispanic students & our CyberSe
program. Thanks so much
for your generous investment
in A.U. & our students!

Blessings,

John Pistole

May. '21

Dr. Barry L. Callen is Dean emeritus of Anderson University and its graduate School ofTheology. He is biographer of the university's former President, Robert H. Reardon, and of the primary pioneer of the University's sponsoring church body, Daniel S.Warner. He is author of the University's seventy-fifth-year history, *Guide of Soul and Mind,* and of *Enriching Mind and Spirit,* the history of all North American and Caribbean institutions of higher education related to the Church of God (Anderson).

Founding Editor of Anderson University Press and Aldersgate Press, Dr. Callen also is the longtime Editor of the *Wesleyan Theological Journal* and now of the *Connections* journal of the Wesleyan-Holiness Connection. Beyond being an educator, minister, author, and editor, he is Corporate Secretary of Horizon International (serving AIDS orphans in Africa) and Special Assistant to the General Director of Church of God Ministries.

John Pistole's father, Hollis, was a seminary teacher of Dr. Callen, and his mother, Elizabeth, an educational mentor of Dr. Callen's wife, Jan.

John S. Pistole

Searching for Integrity and Faith

Barry L. Callen

Emeth Press
www.emethpress.com

John S. Pistole: Searching for Integrity and Faith

Printed in the United States of America on acid-free paper

Library of Congress Cataloging-in-Publication Data

Names: Callen, Barry L, author.
Title: John S. Pistole : searching for integrity and faith / Barry L Callen.
Description: Dardenne Prairie : Emeth Press, Anderson University Press, [2020] | Includes index. | Summary: "This is a biography of John S. Pistole, from his humble beginnings to positions of national power, from a chat with his father to conducting briefings in the Oval Office with three very different Presidents of the United States, rising up through the ranks of the FBI to become the Deputy Director, then the Administrator of the Transportation Security Administration of the United States, and finally becoming the President of Anderson University"-- Provided by publisher.
Identifiers: LCCN 2020050742 (print) | LCCN 2020050743 (ebook) | ISBN 9781609471682 (hardback) | ISBN 9781609471699 (kindle edition) | ISBN 9781609471750 (paperback)
Subjects: LCSH: Pistole, John. | College presidents--Indiana--Biography. | Anderson University (Anderson, Ind.)--History. | Christian education--Indiana--History. | United States. Federal Bureau of Investigation--Officials and employees--Biography. | United States. Transportation Security Administration--Officials and employees--Biography.
Classification: LCC LA2317.P57 C35 2020 (print) | LCC LA2317.P57 (ebook)
| DDC 378.0092 [B]--dc23
LC record available at https://lccn.loc.gov/2020050742
LC ebook record available at https://lccn.loc.gov/2020050743

Acknowledgments

A special YouTube account has been created to make available videos highlighting John Pistole delivering key addresses, conducting pivotal interviews, and celebrating with students.

The address is **tinyurl.com/JPistole**. These videos bring to life what the best of words on paper cannot quite capture. Special thanks goes to John L. Wechsler, Anderson University Trustee, who provided the technical assistance.

Numerous quotations of individuals are found throughout the text. Unless indicated otherwise, these derive from recorded interviews conducted for this work between March and September, 2020.

Bible quotations are from the New Revised Standard or The Message versions unless otherwise indicated.

Although "Anderson College" was the institutional name when John Pistole graduated in 1978, it was changed a decade later and always is referred to herein as "Anderson University."

Select original photos and photo enhancements were done by George Abiad, longtime photographer of Anderson University.

The pointalist depictions of the five presidents of Anderson University appearing below were created by J. David Liverett, skilled artist long associated with Anderson University.

Gratitude is expressed to John Pistole who sat patiently through numerous interviews during which he shared frankly and in detail in response to all questions posed.

Select photos appear with the permission of Kimberly Butler of Impressions by Kimberly, Anderson, Indiana. Many others come from various members of the Pistole family.

Appreciation is extended to Mischon Hart, Director of Marketing of Anderson University, and other members of her superb and most cooperative staff, especially Michael Baker.

John Pistole's father, Hollis, was a seminary teacher of Dr. Barry L. Callen, and his mother, Elizabeth, an educational mentor of Dr. Callen's wife, Jan. Therefore, he was privileged and pleased to research and author this biography of John. Detail about Dr. Callen is found above.

John A. Morrison

Robert H. Reardon

John S. Pistole

Robert A. Nicholson

James L. Edwards

Dedication

This biography of John S. Pistole, current President of Anderson University, is dedicated to the four previous Presidents, John A. Morrison, Robert H. Reardon, Robert A. Nicholson, and James L. Edwards. These outstanding educators and church leaders of yesterday led in the formation of an institution that shaped the early intellectual and spiritual life of John Pistole. Now this same institution serves as the instrument through which President Pistole is seeking to shape new generations of leaders for the good of church and society. May God grant the grace necessary for such a worthy goal to become reality.

John S. Pistole has been on the move his entire adult life, from local lawyer to FBI field agent, from FBI Deputy Director to Administrator of the Transportation Security Administration, and now to the Presidency of Anderson University. Always he has sought to walk humbly and joyfully with Jesus Christ, his Lord.

Contents

Preface

It aired for decades on radio and then television. Each episode of this very popular Western was introduced musically with a rousing rendition the "William Tell Overture." The dramatic music was accompanied by these heart-throbbing words: "A fiery horse with the speed of light and a cloud of dust and a hearty 'Hi-Ho Silver!' On his magnificent white horse and with his faithful Indian companion Tonto, the daring and resourceful masked rider of the plains led the fight for law and order in the early American West. Return with us now to those thrilling days of yesteryear. The Lone Ranger rides again!"

Admittedly, I've never seen John on horseback or wearing a mask, other than to protect against the spread of Covid-19. However, John has led the fight for law and order, not merely on the plains of the West but all over the United States and even around the world. He's flown in countless white planes, if not at the speed of light.

In the 1500s a "pistol" was a French name for a Spanish gold coin. Pistols were minted in Ireland in the 1600s and in Scotland in the 1700s. The word eventually became military slang for a handgun. The contemporary John Pistole (with an "e") is hardly a gold coin or gunman any more than he's a masked rider on a white horse. Even so, there are some similarities, and so much about him worth knowing.

Was John once a skilled basketball jump-shooter in high school and college? Yes. But here's the more important question. Who *is* he, not only what skills does he have or what prominent jobs has he held? It's best to think of the presence in one man of the rare combination of disciplined reserve and decisive leadership. Think of a man often in the headlines who nonetheless doesn't have a bloated ego. John "is quietly bold because he knows the call of God on his life. He feels no need to try impressing those around him. He just is impressive."[1]

This is a biography of John S. Pistole, a man of high integrity and strong Christian faith, a man of transparency and truthfulness. He's a gold standard, a twenty-first century valuable coin of the realm. He's a simple Christian man, a respected national leader, a loved university president, a wise gentleman worthy of being followed in today's tribalized and power-crazed world.

An Alternative to Chaos

We can't say we weren't warned! It was announced long ago that "there'll always be wars and rumors of wars" (Matt. 24:6). This sad insight came straight from Jesus. In case you don't take this man from Nazareth as your authoritative source, it doesn't matter. Today's global events make his warning frighteningly real and completely obvious. Selfishness and greed, nationalism and tribalism, rebellion and terrorism abound.

The sad truth is that integrity and peacemaking often are pushed to the background. Jesus was worse than ignored. He was brutally crucified. These days "pistols" are everywhere and frequently aim deadly bullets at innocent people. However, there's a Pistole (with an "e") of a very different kind. He's named John and prefers to be loaded with religious faith, selfless public service, and Christian education as ways to "attack" the present and ensure a better future.

This biography offers a brief pause from the tragic and ongoing chaos of our contemporary world. Without apology, it puts forward the life of a contemporary peacemaker, a servant and educator. Your reading will bring you one more "Pistole," but not one that's threatening anyone. This tall and slender man is on the side of the law, in fact he's been the face of the law in the United States. He's handled human trafficking at its ugliest in Minneapolis and investigated the Mafia in New York City while assigned to an FBI/NYPD Joint Organized Crime Task Force. He's provided investigative, operational, and/or forensic support in at least a dozen foreign countries from China and Japan to Iraq, Saudi Arabia, Israel, and Italy. He's sought ways to control international terrorism whenever possible, all without firing a shot.

To be such an activist and visionary leader obviously requires intelligence, ego strength, personality, and perseverance. While these all are part of who John is, he never has exhibited an arrogance prepared to sacrifice others to gain personal goals. His highly successful leadership has been invested for decades in the federal government of the United States. Now, late in his career, he has shifted his life's efforts to Christian higher education, preparing new generations to pursue transformed lives that seek to make peace and not war.

This life story is about a highly successful and yet especially unassuming Christian man. He models well the advice St. Paul gave long ago to the Philippian believers. "Don't push your way to the front; don't sweet-talk your way to the top. Put yourself aside and help others get ahead. Don't be obsessed with getting your own advantage. Forget yourselves long enough to lend a helping hand" (Philippians 2:3-4).

The Floor of Heaven

Try looking into the sky on a very dark and cloudless night. It's been said that the maze of twinkling stars are really holes punched in the floor of heaven to allow the beloved deceased to observe and shower blessings downward. If that's the case, numerous shafts of blessing surely now are smiling on any person who takes Jesus seriously and tries to extend the healing influence of this Prince of Peace. Several shafts undoubtedly are focused on the subject of these pages.

Little boys ask questions. John directed this one to his father decades ago. "Are we rich, Dad?" Hollis Pistole responded gently and with rare wisdom. "Yes, John, actually we are, and someday we might even have money." That exchange marked little John Pistole for life.

There were values prominent in the Pistole household that clearly reflected Jesus. Hollis and Elizabeth were committed Christian parents, gifted servant people, natural leaders, visionary, strong and yet gentle people. While they sought no headlines, eventually they would see plenty featuring the name of their youngest son.

John would become much like his parents in key ways. From that yard conversation as a little boy in Anderson, Indiana, to positions of power in Washington, D. C., to meetings with national leaders around the world, and then back to a university presidency in his hometown, John Pistole would function with a level of integrity today's world sorely lacks.

One of John's Bible heroes is Joseph in the Old Testament. He would resist being compared with this great man of God featured so prominently in the history of ancient Israel. Even so, a few comparisons present themselves and are hard for a biographer to ignore. Like the story of Joseph told in Genesis, John would begin as a handsome young man much too full of himself. Big trouble would follow, as well as much blessing.

Both Joseph and John would rise to national leadership positions that were quite unexpected. Both would face and resist numerous opportunities for corruption. Then would come a time of great crisis for the people of God, famine threatening the survival of Joseph's family. In John's case, it would be the 9/11 terrorist attacks threatening his beloved nation that sometimes thinks of itself as God's contemporary chosen people. Genesis tells about Joseph's continuing integrity despite his privileged position in Egypt. This biography does the same for John as it reports on his privileged positions in the Federal Bureau of Investigation, the Transportation Security Administration, and Anderson University. While circumstances would shift dramatically over the decades, in the midst of it all, the integrity and faith of Joseph and John would hold steady.

When asked what the title of this biography should be, John's older brother David first thought of the word "Knucklehead!" When he managed to quit grinning, David switched his suggestion to "Straight Shooter." Why? Because that conveys much about who John turned out to be—transparent, decisive, believable, strong and yet gentle, always delivering the needed goods with honesty and integrity.[2]

Trajectory

This is John's story. Its trajectory runs from simplicity to complexity, humble beginnings to positions of national power, a chat with Dad in the yard to conducting briefings in the Oval Office with two very different Presidents of the United States and interviewing with a third. John was a student on the campus of Anderson University early in life and later would return as its President.

Through it all, John remained much the same, even if now a little worn looking on some of his most stressful days—and he's had his share.

The beloved Pistole parents are now long gone, having become new sources of those shafts of proud light raining down from the night sky. John's nation, the United States, should be more appreciative of its leaders than sometimes it is. Law-keeping can be a dangerous and thankless business. Politics is a difficult arena. Power doesn't always cater to the humble. Integrity is much too rare a characteristic of those in charge.

The halls of government too seldom are populated with those who are truly rich, although without necessarily having lots of money. Many seek to govern with personal interests dominating. John Pistole is an exception. He gladly reports that he knows several other exceptions who are his colleagues and friends in public service. They will appear in these pages and are much appreciated for aiding in the research that lay behind them.

Why emphasize the word "trajectory"? It's meant to convey more than John rising steadily upward through the ranks of the Federal Bureau of Investigation, arriving as its Deputy Director under one President and then being interviewed by another to be its Director. And more is meant than that John was chosen in the administration of still another President to protect the transportation system of the United States after the terrible terrorism of 9/11.

Over the years John's trajectory moved steadily from West to East. A generalization often made has real meaning. People in today's Western world focus on individual rights; people in the Eastern world focus more on community obligations. That was especially true of the Near Eastern world of Jesus. John became highly sensitive to the values of true community, be it family, nation, campus, or church. Very self-focused early in life, eventually the momentum of his Christian faith carried John far the other way. Man of the West, he would find himself living out his faith at top governmental levels in the Far East, Middle East, and "Third World."

The trajectory image also has reference to the spiritual journey of this exceptional man. It went from the downward place of a young party boy absorbed in some of the wrong things to a steady path upward, by God's grace and his increasing obedience. The journey now has arrived at an elevated position similar to the confession, witness, and urging of St. Paul. In chapter three of his letter to the Philippians, Paul makes something clear. Jesus people must choose carefully those things about which they dare boast.

John Pistole's life could be recounted with nothing but a series of stunning highlights. It won't be that way here because that wouldn't represent well who he really is. St. Paul's life might have been presented as a Hebrew among Hebrews, a top-notch teacher of God's law, someone unmatched in zeal, blameless when it comes to living as God's law directs. However, Paul's overriding desire was very different from such boasting.

The Apostle's desire was to count all seemingly justified human pride as quite secondary. Discount it all for what? He told the Philippians that it was "For the excellency of the knowledge of Christ Jesus my Lord who took the form of a servant and humbled himself, being obedient even to death on a cross" (3:5-7). He was anxious that such a humble mind also be in the Philippian believers, however elevated his own human status or theirs might be in the public eye (2:5).

John Pistole's human status became high indeed over the years, but all the justified pride that could come from that has been willingly subjected by him in favor of the humble mind of Christ. Accordingly, his biography needs to be weighted in the same manner.

Not Just One More Story

Dr. David Pistole pursued a distinguished career as a university professor and physiologist ecologist interested in various vertebrate species. His younger brother, Dr. John S. Pistole, is also focused on mammals, but of the more human variety. Some of his "specimens" have been members of organized crime or international terrorist groups, while others now are representatives of the younger and more innocent variety, the cream of new human generations studying at Anderson University.

Life stories are numerous, of course. Some are worth more than others, even if the headlines and sales numbers sometimes fail to get things right. John Pistole's story is a particularly worthy one because it's quietly loaded with what counts most in the long haul. John hasn't sought headlines, although he's been in many and deserves more because his focus has been on his Lord and not himself.

This particular Pistole is a resource for peace rather than a firearm dangerous to others. Let's learn from one life story actually worth knowing.

John himself would quickly add something if this were an autobiography. His life journey has been informed and enabled by that servant man from Nazareth whom John is convinced was God in human flesh, and thus wisdom and power and life itself. And one more thing.

Reports John, "I've been blessed to work and serve with many exceptional people." Some of them have been interviewed for this book. Their leadership positions in the United States have been in the Department of Justice, the Department of Homeland Security, the Federal Bureau of Investigation, the Transportation Security Administration, the Church of God Movement, and more. Others have been from the world of American higher education, public and private, from Anderson University, Grove City College, Geneva College, and Illinois Wesleyan University to Indiana University and the University of California. The names are found in the Index. They all speak with great respect and appreciation when the name John Pistole is mentioned.

John is hesitant about the writing of his biography. "If there is mere ego behind the writing, I wish it weren't done." What he prefers, and I hope is accomplished here, is for his life, whatever its prominent successes, to become seen as one lived in humble obedience to Jesus Christ, both in its personal and public phases. He wants his story widely known only if it brings glory to God and not to himself. May these pages serve that noble purpose.

Chapter 1

GOD'S PROVIDENCE

The journey of a thousand miles begins with one step. —Lao Tzu

He that takes truth for his guide, and duty for his end, may safely trust to God's providence to lead him aright. —Blaise Pascal

The ancient Chinese philosopher was right. A long journey always begins with its first step, likely the hardest one to take. What actually lies ahead can be much more than life's simple travelers could begin to plan, manage, even imagine. Wonderful eventualities sometimes just happen, or are they the byproducts of the grace of God's all-seeing and loving providence?

The first steps of the grandparents of John Pistole were modest indeed. Even so, they would lead to a future they could never have foreseen. St. Paul had it right long ago. "We can be sure that every detail in our lives of love for God has worked into something good" (Rom. 8:28).

The story John begins with his grandparents in the early twentieth century. The Divine surely was guiding them, although they had little awareness of it happening. By the early twenty-first century, that same hand from above also would be guiding their grandson John. As he would put it in 2020, "My being open to obedience to Jesus Christ and God's gracious guidance has led to what for me was completely unimaginable."

The Meanings of "T"

They had "Tennessee" in common from the beginning, long before they ever met. Hale Center and Muleshoe actually are in west Texas. Hollis was a Tennessee Pistole, actually from that state, and Elizabeth was a Smith ranch girl born in Hale Center and growing up in nearby Muleshoe, Texas.

The long distance between the Pistoles and Smiths would evaporate one day.

It's strange, or is it providential, how the shared "Tennessee" of these families one day would see Hollis and Elizabeth managing to meet and marry in Michigan, have their children while living in Ohio and Maryland, and live out their family and professional lives in Indiana. The youngest of their four would be John, and what a little Pistole he would be!

Elizabeth, the Texan, was born "Elizabeth T. Smith." At least that's what the original 1920 birth certificate said. It soon was altered slightly, however. The family story is that Missouri Tennessee Sanders, John Pistole's maternal great-grandmother, was upset that no one born into the family had been given her middle name. The doctor proceeded to alter Elizabeth's certificate since he said a middle initial wasn't good enough, and apparently he somehow was aware of Missouri's complaint. The "T" of this Texas newborn was extended on the certificate to read "Tennessee."

Sarah Waller Smith, Elizabeth's mother, didn't object. The doctor's change stuck until, as an adult, Elizabeth would decide to drop the extension and replace it with the initial "S" to honor her Smith family. She could be a firm and direct woman, as well as intelligent and compassionate. Missouri Tennessee Sanders had been honored long enough, and by then Missouri wouldn't know the difference anyway.

The sharing of "Tennessee" came from the fact that the Pistole family actually was from that state, even if none of them ever got named after it. One of the children, Hollis, was born in 1919, three months after the fighting of World War I. By the age of six he would be part of the family's move to Michigan in the mid-1920s. Before that, however, he had learned that his great-grandfather, Stephen, had been a Tennessee constable, his grandfather, James, a justice of the peace, and his father, George, just before the big move north, the deputy sheriff of Sparta, Tennessee.

Who could have imagined that, many decades later, John, son of Tennessee Hollis and Elizabeth, would also be in law enforcement work on a national and even international stage? Maybe it's in the family DNA. Hardly living in jail facilities in Sparta, as his Pistole grandparents once had, John's setting would be in the capital of the United States among the rich and powerful. There he would be responsible for more than the justice and safety of a small Tennessee town. His would be the gigantic task of helping to protect a whole nation from international terrorism, including responsibility for the entire transportation system in and out of the United States!

Hollis had "ordinary parents."[3] They lived on a farm that he remembered as "nestled among the red clay hills of Tennessee." The local Pistole roots went deep. The forefathers of young Hollis had helped found Pistole Baptist Church in 1851. When Hollis was five, he attended a revival service there and reports, "I was so stirred by the powerful sermon that I began to cry." George and Luella, his parents, countered his resulting inclination to make a religious life commitment. They said he was too young for that big a decision. A "yes" to Jesus would be a wonderful thing, certainly, but not yet.

They may have been right. If the boy had been allowed to yield all to Jesus in that revival service, it probably would have been mostly emotion. As Hollis would reflect much later, "I was always drawn toward spiritual things."[4] One day he would choose to make that critical commitment and become a dedicated Christian minister, although much would have to happen before that would ever be.

The Pistole's, whether on the farm or later living in small-town Sparta, had found life difficult. For a short time they actually lived in modest quarters right in the town's jail facility. Young Hollis was sickly as a child and later wondered if that didn't stunt his full growth—his brothers were 6'3" and 6'4" and he only managed 5'10." Tall or short, the life of Hollis wasn't destined always to be in Tennessee.

"Hillbillies" Headed North

Dad and Mom Pistole decided that it was time to move north, changing the family address to Detroit, Michigan. Unknown to them, of course, a similar relocation decision was being made in Muleshoe, Texas. Hollis Pistole and Elizabeth Smith always had been states apart. That was about to end. Two journeys north would be a new beginning full of destiny for thousands, maybe millions.

One could drop several Spartas, Hale Centers, and Muleshoes into Detroit and they would disappear in the mass of this large multi–cultural city. But size wasn't the point. The point of moving there was that work opportunities were assumed to be greater up north and the big moves of the Pistoles and Smiths would be well worth all the upset. Looking back now and seeing all that these struggling families could not see at the time, it appears that the providence of God was quietly at work.

The northward migrating families soon would be thought of as "hill-billy" new-comers, the Pistoles from Tennessee for sure and the Smiths at least having come through the southern hills to get to the northern factories. These two families were part of what's now called the "Great Migration." Especially during and after World War I, there was a huge demand for workers in the northern factories, especially in Chicago, Detroit, Youngstown, and Pittsburgh. Millions of southern Blacks headed north, with many poor Whites joining the flow.[5] The major migration included the Smiths and the Pistoles.

Little Hollis Pistole was in the second grade at the time of the move and would have to adjust to a dramatically new cultural setting. So would little Elizabeth "T" Smith, one year younger, who now would be in the same school and even local church with Hollis. George Pistole, the former sheriff from Sparta and father of Hollis, got a job in plant protection, a natural for him, maybe a foretaste of what his grandson John would do with a large part of his life much later. Price Smith, the rancher from Texas and Elizabeth's father, landed a job in a machine shop.

The Pistoles and Smiths had both traveled far to the north in the mid-1920s, unexpectedly enabling son Hollis and daughter Elizbeth to find each other and eventually become joint travelers in life. Once a new couple, they would begin in Michigan and then transit together to Anderson, Indiana, Oberlin, Ohio, Baltimore, Maryland, and finally back to Anderson for the rest of their family and professional lives. Son John would be born out East in Baltimore, grow up in Anderson, Indiana, return to the East for federal service, before also spending his later life back in Anderson, Indiana. He would judge in hindsight that it had been the providence of God behind it all.

Price and Sarah Smith

Sarah and Price Smith

Luella and George Pistole

Luella Pistole

Chapter 2

FOUNDATIONS FOR THE FUTURE

If we are to go forward, we must go back and rediscover two precious values, that all reality hinges on moral foundations and that all reality has spiritual control. —Martin Luther King, Jr.

Never be afraid to trust an unknown future to a known God. —Corrie ten Boom

The years of the Great Depression were hard for most people in Detroit, Michigan, especially for newcomers like the Pistoles and Smiths. They had found work, but it barely provided enough to get by. What they did accomplish, despite all the obstacles, was the laying of family, faith, and professional foundations for the future of family members.

These two new Northern families were sure that reality does hinge on moral foundations. Time also would show that, for the Pistoles and Smiths, their realities were under spiritual control. They hadn't been afraid to trust an unknown future to the God they knew.

Going Without

Young Hollis Pistole knew days when there was no food in the family home except bread and peanut butter. Sometimes his father, George, who had gotten work in plant protection at the Briggs Company, would come home in the evening having managed to buy a little something extra and special at the store. Even that changed when he suddenly died from a ruptured appendix in 1936, was buried back in beloved Sparta, Tennessee, and the family car was repossessed.

George had $300 to his name at the time of his death, requiring Hollis' mother Luella, "Mom Pistole" to her future grandkids, to take in boarders. Her three boys had to sleep in one bed—and the brothers of Hollis were big guys. They managed with what little they had.

Ironically, from these most humble beginnings, one of Hollis' two sisters, Carrie, eventually became an executive assistant at General Motors and married a professional truck driver, Jack Ott. Neither ever attended college. Nonetheless, after lives of great stewardship learned through those Depression years, and believing in the educational ministry of brother Hollis and that of his Anderson campus, one day they would leave a generous estate gift to Anderson University.

Hollis attended junior and senior high school in Detroit by walking miles each day. One special joy that eased this burden was the presence of Elizabeth Smith, the former Texan now in the same school and local church where each had their initial contact with the Church of God Movement, so important for their futures. Hollis and Elizabeth each graduated from high school in 1938. She went on to Anderson University in Indiana, the area school affiliated to their local church. Hollis would do the same, but couldn't right away. He had to delay college-going for two years in order to help support his mother's struggling family. Despite the unwelcome delay, rich educational and relational opportunities were ahead.

These two young people, immigrants from the South now with more in common than a Tennessee state designation, soon would migrate themselves, this time to Indiana. The "Ts" would evolve into a joint "AU" (Anderson University) that would last them a lifetime.[6] Once Elizabeth was off to college in Anderson in 1938, Hollis longed to join her, both for the education and the love he kept sharing with her by mail. All of his longings would be fulfilled in due time, although necessary sacrifices were first necessary.

Years later, John, youngest son of Hollis and Elizabeth, would look back on those hard Detroit years endured by his Dad and feel deep appreciation for the willing sacrifices. The work Hollis had found before college was on a dangerous and extremely loud assembly line of the Ford Motor Company. For this spiritually sensitive young man, there was no car. Instead, there was a long daily commute on buses and trains, and no safety equipment once he reached his job. No matter. Hollis would do what had to be done. He was setting the pace for his children to follow later on.

Becoming a Couple

Elizabeth Smith came home from Anderson to the State Fair Church of God in Detroit to marry Hollis Pistole on Valentine's Day, 1941. Their first residence together was an apartment with Mom Pistole in Detroit. Hollis would report in his autobiography that, after his relationship with Jesus Christ, he considered his marriage to Elizabeth the most significant decision of his life. He would describe his bride as a "vibrant personality, charming, free and confident, with a daring open spirit."

In a letter to Elizabeth on her eightieth birthday he would write this. "A darling little girl from the wind-swept plains of Texas, you made friends easily, did well in your studies, and found faith in God as a guiding force for all your endeavors." With God in the lead, Hollis and Elizabeth now were a loving team pursuing their educations and getting ready for a family and future of their own.

Back to the campus in Anderson they would go, now together, beginning life in a little apartment in the college's Old Main building that dated back to the early 1900s. The first years there were terrible war years worldwide. Hollis was spared direct military participation because of deferment as a quality college student and then his graduate ministerial studies. His two brothers, Lee and George, both saw military action, Lee with the Combat Engineers in Europe and George with the Eighth Air Force flying bombing missions, being shot down once but surviving.

These Pistoles and so many of their colleagues at war were supported in major ways by the industries in Anderson, Indiana. It was widely reported that Adolf Hitler kept a private priority list of American cities scheduled to be bombed if the opportunity came. Anderson, Indiana, wasn't far from the top. Guide Lamp and Delco-Remy produced lighting for tanks and military vehicles, cartridge cases, barrels for firearms and machine guns, and various parts for military vehicles and aircraft. That all would be stopped if possible.

In the constant swirl of war news, but with pacifist tendencies, Hollis began thinking about the possibility of becoming a military chaplain. He later would reflect in his autobiography about the military service given by his brothers in World War II and the extensive government service given to the nation by his son, John. Dr. Pistole would write this proudly about John in 2004: "He's doing his part for our nation's security with the FBI in his position with counter-terrorism and counter-intelligence." Much would happen before "FBI" would be letters with any personal meaning for the Pistoles, but they certainly would come.

The young Anderson University couple both had to work to help support themselves, Hollis at Delco Remy in Anderson and Elizabeth in an agency of the Church of God located adjacent to the campus. Despite all the distractions, once they got a chance to go together on a Christian Volunteer program in the Kentucky mountains where Hollis delivered his first sermons and performed his first baptisms. It surely felt to him like the hills of Tennessee and ministries he had seen performed in the Pistole Baptist Church back in Sparta, Tennessee. He was coming to find his vocation's true home.

Elizabeth completed her studies at Anderson University, receiving a B.S. in 1943. Hollis was two years behind, completing his studies with a B.A. in 1945. He felt called to Christian ministry, possibly to the Navy chaplaincy. That, however, would require advanced credentials from a recognized, graduate-level seminary. Anderson University was not yet accredited and would have no seminary of its own until the 1950s—a seminary that then would be central to Hollis' future. So, there would have to be a big venture eastward into Ohio.

Deepening Intellectual Foundations

The early Church of God Movement of the late nineteenth century tended to be hostile to church institutions in general, including ones of higher education viewed as "hotbeds of heresy" and instruments of continuing denominational divisions. When Anderson University was founded in 1917 as Anderson Bible Training School, many ministers reacted with caution, not wanting human "papers" and head learning to supplant the divine calling and gifting for Christian ministry. By the 1940s, however, a series of the most gifted young Church of God ministerial candidates were seeking seminary educations.

In 1961 Rev. James Earl Massey was a young African-American pastor in Detroit, Michigan. He had the same educational need that Hollis Pistole had just a few years earlier, and he made a similar decision. Massey chose Oberlin Graduate School of Theology in Ohio, a reasonable drive from his Detroit congregation. Part of the attraction for Massey was the prominence of this seminary educationally and its historic record of racial openness—it was a stop on the Underground Railroad.

Before the Church of God established its own seminary in Anderson, Indiana, in 1950, Massey recalls that "Oberlin had attracted and educated most of the leading Church of God ministers who sought a seminary education."[7] The list of these leaders includes Robert H. Reardon who would become the second President of Anderson University, Gene W. Newberry who would become the second Dean of Anderson's future graduate School of Theology, and Hollis S. Pistole who would join the Anderson seminary faculty in 1959 and serve until his retirement in 1984.

Reardon's 1943 Oberlin thesis studied changing patterns in the Church of God Movement and helped stimulate quite a stir among the Movement's ministers. It would be a tension that Hollis Pistole would know well for the rest of his life, as would his son John later on.

Oberlin stood tall in the background of some of the finest stances of the Church of God Movement. Robert Reardon would observe that "the place of women and Blacks in the Church of God Movement in its early days may have been encouraged by views assimilated at Oberlin by one of its students, Daniel S. Warner (d. 1895), primary pioneer of the Movement."[8]

That sensitivity to the values of a quality intellectual education and the importance of Christians championing social equality, racial and gender, also would impact a later Oberlin student, Hollis Pistole. In part through Dr. Pistole, that impact would be felt by coming generations of Church of God ministers, and certainly by the Pistole children. Cindy, the Pistole's first child, was born in Oberlin in 1946.

Judging from the standpoint of the Church of God Movement at the time, young Hollis Pistole found Oberlin to be "liberal." He was challenged to stretch his realm of learning, and he grew with the stretching. The opening new vistas to which he was exposed included the "higher criticism" of biblical study, which Hollis learned to appreciate. Also, with the help of Dr. Walter Horton, "I moved beyond the more restrictive concept of theological truths to honor the grandeur and greatness of God, and also acknowledge the mystery of things unknown."[9]

Part of what Hollis learned at Oberlin was a warning he often would quote, and that his son John would recall decades later. Originally it was D. A. Carson who said, "A text without a context is a pretext for a proof text." If, for instance, we don't know the context of a biblical passage, we easily succumb to the temptation to find in it meanings that do little more than support our feelings, opinions, and desires. This caution, this wisdom lies at the root of one main reason for Christian higher education. It's the enterprise of learning contexts that yield balanced, appropriate, and originally intended meanings. The ultimate context of all things is the grandeur and greatness of God. Decades after his father's Oberlin experience, John Pistole would find himself championing Christian higher education and repeating with deep conviction many of the things his father had learned.

Hollis had applied to Oberlin Graduate School of Theology with interest in its pre-chaplaincy program. World War II and the devastation of the atom bombs had impacted him greatly. In the midst of his really stretching classes, he also had served as a student pastor in Cleveland. In his youth group there were Robert Smith and Harold Conrad who later would join the Pistoles in providing key campus and church leadership back in Anderson, Indiana. The big venture into Ohio had provided valuable intellectual growth and key new relationships.

Enhancing Functional Skills

After graduating from Oberlin, the Pistoles, now joined by their daughter Cindy, spent the next three years pastoring a congregation in Marbury, Maryland, just thirty miles south of Washington, D. C. That proximity allowed a unique privilege. In January, 1949, Hollis and Elizabeth left Cindy with a trusted neighbor and went to the Inauguration of President Harry S. Truman. They managed a great spot only a short distance from the platform where it all would happen. They saw close-up the parade of national dignitaries, having no idea that years later their yet-unborn son John would be one such dignitary in another Inaugural crowd.

Carole, the second daughter, was born in 1950 while Hollis pastored the Marbury church. Their son David was born in nearby Baltimore in 1954. Finally, also in Baltimore, came John on June 1, 1956. John reports with a twinkle in his eye, "I was a total surprise. My folks thought our family was complete with the five of them." In those days a woman aged thirty-six was thought to be beyond a safe child-bearing age.

While not intended, time would prove that John was well worth the risk taken (or accident suffered) by Hollis and Elizabeth. John now puts it like this. "It was thought to be a perfect family when there were only four, the parents and the girls. Then David came along, and then me—forget the perfect family!"

David remembers vividly two posters that soon appeared on the wall of the bedroom the brothers shared when young, and he insists they were John's and not his. One featured a menacing gorilla with the caption, "When I want your opinion, I'll beat it out of you!" The other showed a poor man crawling on the ground with the last of his strength. High above in a nearby tree sat two observing vultures. One is saying to the other, "No more patience for me. I'm ready to finish that guy!" David and John were delightful boys, sort of.

Meanwhile, presumably aware of the posters, Pastor Pistole was beginning to appear on the radar of national church leaders. He soon was invited but turned down an opportunity to return to the Anderson campus to teach. He and Elizabeth also received an exciting offer from the Missionary Board of the Church of God in Anderson to become career missionaries of the church. The international offer was particularly tempting, although it came with a significant problem. The Board insisted that it would have to be a lifetime commitment.

Hollis and Elizabeth had the vision for such a big challenge but were concerned about their two little girls (David and John not yet born). They simply weren't prepared to venture so far into the unknown for the sake of Cindy and Carole. Instead, in 1951 Hollis accepted an offer to move to the leadership of a Church of God congregation in nearby Baltimore. It was a big change from the small town to a sprawling city, not unlike their parents venturing from Sparta and Muleshoe to Detroit years before.

For the next six years, while the boys were being born, Baltimore would be the scene of an excellent pastoral experience for the Pistoles. Elizabeth was active with special events at the church while Hollis planned the services, preached the sermons, ran the copy machine, and emerged as a community leader. Social problems surrounded the church and Hollis saw his ministry as bigger than the confining church walls. He found ways to prepare himself to better serve the needs at hand.

Hollis had studied earlier at Detroit Business Institute to gain a sense of the business world that impacts any church assignment. Now the church building in Baltimore needed major renovation, so he sought training as a fundraiser as a way to make that possible. He managed to secure a scholarship for a month-long seminar at Yale University on addressing alcohol abuse and other social problems. Reflective of the long history of police work in his family, Hollis even got himself elected to the state parole board, which brought him to one of the most unwelcome experiences of his life.

On one occasion Rev. Pistole was required to attend a state execution carried out by hanging! He was only ten feet away when the body dropped, twisted, and finally went limp. A sensitive and peaceful Christian man, that awful image would never leave him. Always afterwards, capital punishment would be something Hollis totally opposed.

Home Again to Indiana

The largest sporting event in the world is the Indianapolis 500 motor sports race. Before the roaring of the powerful engines each year, there always is sung the nostalgic "Back Home Again in Indiana." This wonderful returning reality would be the experience of many members of the Pistole family, including John later in his life.

In 1957 the general offices of the Church of God located in Anderson, Indiana, were calling back home its Baltimore pastor. Rev. Hollis Pistole's fundraising training in particular fit a pressing need for bolstering pastoral financial support of the national work of the church. Hollis accepted a two-year contract to move his family back to Indiana and assume the challenge. This decision understandably upset Cindy in particular. She was eleven, the oldest of the four children, and had many local friends she hated to leave behind. The youngest, John, was only learning to walk and just came along for the ride.

The Pistoles moved into what would be their longtime home on Walnut Street close to Anderson University and the national church agencies. Soon Elizabeth was serving as office manager for Park Place Church of God and Hollis was asked to teach a preaching course on campus. These were skilled servants who related well to a wide range of people. They remained attentive to Hollis' mother and Elizabeth's parents still living in Detroit and now attending the Woodlawn Church of God. Especially Cindy and Carole remember various family trips there once the family was relocated in Anderson.

When Hollis's two-year contract ended, at first he hoped to find another good pastoral assignment. Instead, a retirement found him heading up the young Board of Pensions in Anderson and continuing to teach the occasional course on campus. This Board role, however, soon proved a frustrating one for Hollis. The church's pastoral retirees had few benefits and many needs, with little funding available to address them. He began to feel like "a fish out of water," a man who really was cut out to teach and not be the administrator of a barely sustainable church program.

Soon Hollis was approached by Dean Adam W. Miller of Anderson School of Theology, the seminary that hadn't existed when those seeking such graduate education were now joining the Hollis Pistoles in going to places like Oberlin. The new Church of God seminary was seeking accreditation and needed a full-time professor of pastoral work and field education. This faculty addition, now being offered to Hollis, was enabled by funding from a Lilly Endowment grant to the Anderson campus.

Dean Miller persuaded Hollis in part by making this keen observation. "With the Pension Board you would be helping old men *out* of the ministry; with the seminary you would be helping young men *into* the ministry!" That did it. Without having to move the family again, and already having taught part-time since 1959, in 1962 Hollis became a full-time seminary professor and would remain so until his retirement in 1984. George Kufeldt had been added the year before in Old Testament and Boyce Blackwelder the year after in New Testament. Yours truly began his own seminary education at Anderson's School of Theology in 1963, with all three of these new professors esteemed teachers.

Now Hollis Pistole was an educator and his family of six well settled into their home at 616 Walnut Street, Anderson, Indiana, only two blocks from the campus. Outside the home Hollis had a basketball goal installed in the driveway. It was a magnet for the local boys. Inside there was concern that the presidential candidacy of John Kennedy threatened a national takeover by the Pope of Rome. That bias had its limits, however. Once son David inquired whether a girlfriend would go to hell because she was a

Catholic. The parental response? "No, God isn't like that. There's always room for growth in our intellectual and spiritual understandings."

Years later, David would learn this lesson dramatically. In 1997-1999 he would suffer from a gambling addiction that brought near financial ruin to his family through the loss of a substantial amount of money. They had to leave their home, only to have a generous neighboring family buy a home for them and act as their banker until they could get back on their feet. God was especially good to this family in their time of great struggle. The generous friends were Jewish, quite different from the Pistole family tradition, but nonetheless instruments of a gracious God.

The Pistoles Painted Green

One infamous event on the Anderson campus happened in a Christmas Chapel one year. Student clubs staged various seasonal skits to allow wide participation. Some were serious, some very clever and humorous. One suddenly was outside the bounds of acceptability. When the curtain opened, there on a scaffold hung by their necks life-sized replicas of a father, mother, and the children. The sign over the ghastly scene read, "The Hanging of the Greens." Wreaths and flower decorations, yes, but hanging people, no! The charter of the club was immediately suspended.

There's a much better use of the color green. Sometimes it's thought of as the "go" signal, forward encouragement, the growth-encouraging color. In this sense, the Pistole family, now arriving back in Anderson, Indiana, in 1957, was quite a green-oriented family. They were learners, educators, encouragers, growth-oriented, forward-looking people. It would be a good family setting in which the four children could grow to their very best potentials.

Chapter 3

GREEN INK IN ANDERSON

The philosophy of the school room in one generation will be the philosophy of government in the next. —Abraham Lincoln

We should not judge people by their peak of excellence but by the distance they have traveled from the point where they started. —Henry Ward Beecher

An old saying goes like this. "When ripe it rots, when green it grows." Maybe the initial reference was to apples and bananas. Too long a growing time and things can go bad. The saying also can have reference to traffic lights and the process of education. As opposed to the "stop" color red, green indicates "go" and youth, with education being the process of motivating the young to move forward, develop deeper understanding, stretch to reach maturity.

There was lots of encouraging green in Anderson, Indiana. It was the goal of the Anderson campus and the very culture of the Pistole household, where some things appeared on green paper and green ink was used by Elizabeth to grade student papers. This home was an encouraging classroom for learning and life. What was not known to the wise parents was that the positive nurturing of their youngest son John would one day, as Abraham Lincoln said, impact the government of the United States.

A Convincing Logic

Dean Adam W. Miller had worked a very green style of logic on Hollis Pistole, luring him into leaving the Pensions Board and joining the ranks of seminary educators—come and encourage the young. And that growth logic already was present in the normal workings of the Pistole family.

Mother Elizabeth would become a great teacher, earning her masters degree, and pursuing a career of counseling and teaching mostly at Anderson High School. She did her student teaching in nearby Alexandria High School under the supervision of Bill Gaither, a young teacher himself and head of the English Department.[10]

Daughters Cindy and Carole would follow similar paths in the Anderson public school system and on the nearby Anderson University campus where their father was a professor. They both were natural teachers. Carole started early by practicing on John, her kid brother. She taught him to tie his shoes and then tackled a bigger task. John had some trouble with the letter "L." A neighbor's dog was named *LoLo*. John would call it "*YoYo*." She drilled him on the difference, which he slowly learned. Cindy, ten years older than John and herself an educator, gladly left to Carole most of the needed fussing with the problems of the boys.

Son David, more the scientific type, would graduate from Anderson University, as did all his siblings, earn his doctorate, and be a university professor in Pennsylvania. Only the youngest of the Pistole kids, John, seemed to miss the family educational trait, at least at first. He would become a lawyer and then a servant of the nation's government before also finding himself an educator.

Mother Elizabeth practiced her educational instincts as a parent as well as in the classroom. There was that time when little John was in kindergarten at Park Place School. Occasionally he would become a handful for Norma Jean Rockwell, his teacher. One day the class came in from recess and soon Norma became aware that John was missing. A growing panic suddenly was relieved when John, his hand firmly held by his mother, walked into the classroom.

What had happened? Elizabeth was quick to explain that her little boy had become bored with the lessons of the morning and had walked from the playground to the family home that was only a short distance away. On arrival, he had announced to his surprised mother, with a bit of childish aloofness, that he already knew his name, letters, and numbers, the subject of the morning's lessons. So, John had reasoned, wasn't it obvious that staying longer would be a waste of time? He'd generously offered to come back to school the next year when there'd be more to learn!

Elizabeth Pistole, herself a wise educator, joined the relieved teacher in a creative plan, one that worked immediately. John, rather than being paddled, was assigned to a group of students who didn't know their letters and numbers. What about his being an educator himself? That seemed to make John, Elizabeth, and Norma Jean equally happy. Elizabeth left and John stayed willingly. Might John one day be in education himself? That day brought at least a bit of hope.

The ability to learn and an outgoing personality would go with John right into grade school at Park Place Elementary. John Johnson recalls vividly a scene on the school's playground. He had looked on with admiration, even jealously. Four slightly older students were playing together. They were smart, athletic, and very popular. John Pistole was with the very beautiful Jeannie Horvay and David Courtney was with the equally impressive Rhoda Freeman. Young Johnson watched these four at play, "all that's best in the world that I so wanted for myself."

These two Johns, the one watching and the one being watched, each had a father teaching in the graduate seminary of Anderson University just a few blocks from that playground. Years later, these Johns would travel the world, serving their common Lord in dramatic but different ways, and remain good friends. In grade school, however, it wasn't clear what John Pistole would become. There were some interesting hints that he might be something special, maybe.

John received a Christmas gift when he was in the sixth grade, a little toy oven into which a child could pour some liquid goop. Once heated with various molds and then cooled, there would emerge a range of pliable and scary-looking bugs, scorpions, spiders, whatever. John played with this amazing process for days. Then his enterprising "green" mind got to work. What might all this become?

He went back to school as a new entrepreneur selling the "Creepy Crawler" bugs to his friends. He soon got reported, scolded, and put out of business. His defense? "They never told me in kindergarten that there was anything wrong with entrepreneurship!" It wasn't clear if John could spell that big word. What he could do was implement it!

Young John was always good with money, both earning and saving it. His bedroom was above a set of carpeted stairs in the Walnut Street home. Once, when a little remodeling was going on and the steps were being recarpeted, a five-dollar and even a twenty-dollar bill were found here and there stuffed under loose corners of the old carpet. John had saved and hidden them, maybe his secret assets to launch an undetermined future enterprise.

The boy's saving instinct was one reflection of a dramatic experience in his young life. When John was five, the Pistoles took a six-week family vacation, hitting nearly every state west of the Mississippi River. They pulled a trailer in which they slept. Hollis, the professor father, would do some business with seminary graduates along the way. These weeks did more for John than inspire his love of travel. At points along the way various circumstances heightened the competitive rivalry between John and his brother David. It also awakened John's sense of conserving the earth's resources.

That impulse had been real for John since he was a little kid. He and his friend Dave Courtney were known to pull a little wagon around the Anderson campus. They were trying to fill it with stray pop bottles left by college students. Cleanliness of the environment wasn't their only motive. They knew that they could collect a deposit on each littered prize found.

One day the six Pistoles stood at the rim of the Grand Canyon looking downward at the slender little Colorado River slinking its way along far below. John heard one of his parents make the observation that there was a severe lack of water in the region. One day that could bring widespread environmental destruction and even human desperation. The Pistoles as a family had few of the extras in life. John thought, "Might the whole Earth be heading toward much worse if people didn't learn to live sensibly and conserve?"

When camped one day near the shores of Lake Louise in Canada, the Pistoles had eaten and gone to bed without cleaning up all of the food. The bears naturally came to do the job themselves, making noise that awakened the family. As son David recalls, father Hollis saying to the boys, "You loudly bang pans together and then I'll go out and retrieve whatever food's left!" Nothing should go to waste.

John determined to be a conserver, a good steward, and grow into being a particularly frugal man, including being a good steward of God's grace and gifts. Years later, soon after marrying Kathy, the young couple would fuss about whether to wash the dishes in hot or cold water. Kathy would insist on hot, but John, sensitive to the cost of heating it, would counter that cold was good enough to get the job done. Maybe luke-warm would be the solution for saving a marriage.

Many years later still, once back on the Anderson campus and living in the university's presidential home, John's conserving sensibilities would show up again. Before daylight on the typical morning, he would take his early morning "prayer walk" around the campus. If he saw a light on in some building, he would go in and turn it off. By then his strong sense of stewardship would have been deepened by his strong Christian faith. He heard that John Wesley had wisely advised Christians to earn all they could, save all they could, and give all they could.

Choosing Ink Colors

Jan Hitt (Callen) was a psychology student of Elizabeth Pistole at Anderson High School in 1970. Years later when they were teaching colleagues, Jan asked her respected mentor why all the students seemed to love her so much. The answer was so impressive that Jan, about to have a long teaching career at Anderson High School herself, always afterward tried to model her own student-relating style after Elizabeth's response.

Elizabeth explained that students seem to respect and appreciate two things that she did regularly. They were telling students the straight truth and then grading their papers in green ink. Students, she explained, appreciate a teacher's honesty and forthrightness, and they knew her intention with the choice of ink colors. It was to highlight the constant attitude of encouraging progress. Green is the "go" color and Elizabeth wanted her students to get themselves in gear and proceed actively forward with their learning and lives. When you're green you grow.

A "green-like" encouragement was Elizabeth's standard approach to students. She practiced this in the classroom where Jan was a high school student. Then later, Jan experienced them again. Since Hollis was a faculty member at Anderson University, Elizabeth was active with the campus organization of faculty wives. When Jan married a university professor, Elizabeth made sure she got involved with this organization of wonderful women. It was a great way to get acquainted and inspired, to get green herself.

It was a green "go" opportunity for Jan both on the campus and also back at Anderson High School where she began teaching in 1978 after her divorce. This was a very difficult personal time. Often Elizabeth would appear at Jan's door just to ask how things were going and offer any help needed. Jan recalls Elizabeth being "everybody's confidant since anyone could share their troubles with her and never be betrayed."

Jan later would get speech training and experience as part of her college years at Anderson University. On one occasion she and Elizabeth co-led a communications conference in Kansas City for Women of the Church of God. Elizabeth, as always, was forthright, a take-charge person. Since most participants were women, at break time the line at the women's restroom was very long, with virtually none waiting at the men's restroom door. Jan watched and was a little surprised—and amused—when Elizabeth stepped out of line, went to the men's door and announced loudly, "If anyone's in there, be aware that the women are now coming in!" Suddenly the women's line was cut in half, to the great relief of many of them.

He's Really Dead!

Back on the east side of Anderson, Indiana, the Pistoles were regular attenders of Park Place Church of God next to the Anderson University campus. In their home, the focus was on the positive, with lots of love, acceptance and forgiveness and a rare mentioning of the threat of hell. The green environment was much the same in the nearby Park Place Church where numerous professional educators were present and seminary seniors often were the youth leaders. Questioning of one's faith was welcomed and processed, not shamed.

Carole Pistole, six years older than John, recalls this congregation as a good place to learn and grow without constantly being judged. Once, for instance, she wanted to go to a school dance, something frowned on and even prohibited in many churches of the time. She went to the pastor of Park Place, Rev. Hillery Rice, to get guidance. He explained the problems usually associated with dancing, like smoking and drinking in the typical dance hall, then concluded with this. "If you are talking about a school event that is well chaperoned by caring adults, attend if you wish."

Dr. Hollis Pistole finished his doctoral program in Chicago in 1968 and continued as a professor of "applied theology." His wife Elizabeth joined other seminary faculty wives in an informal organization of the wives of male ministerial students. Their meetings were social but often also therapeutic since these young women felt isolated as their husbands were immersed in heady studies of hermeneutics and theology while they, knowing little about such things, were carrying heavy support roles in the homes.

In addition to not being part of the mind-stretching their husbands were experiencing, there was much anxiety about the roles they would be expected to play once their husbands graduated and took full-time church responsibilities. Mature and relationally sensitive women like Elizabeth Pistole were lifelines for many of them. Joining her was Arlene Callen, wife of Dean Barry Callen who later, after Arlene's death, would marry the very Jan assisted with her beginning teaching at the high school by Elizabeth years before.

Hollis was something of a "green man" himself. He functioned for many years in Anderson School of Theology (1959-1984) relating seminarians to needed field education as an extension of what he and his colleagues were teaching them in the classroom. Good as he was, linking theory and practice isn't always easily learned by the inexperienced young.

One day a recent seminary graduate called Dr. Pistole in Anderson with an emergency. "A man has died in my church and I have to conduct his funeral in three days. This is my first and I don't know how to do this. Time is very short. Can you help me?"

Responded the former professor, "Don't you remember our class in pastoral methods when we designed funeral sermons and discussed procedures?"

"Yes, but that was just a class assignment. You don't understand my circumstance. *This man's really dead!*" The former professor, smiling a little to himself, proceeded to offer the practical help needed.

John Pistole's mother and father were "green" people, helping others forward. In fact, much later the Pistole parents would deliver a team sermon at Park Place Church in Anderson. Hollis would stand in the pulpit and Elizabeth in the lectern. Their joint subject was the Christian fellowship that should characterize family and community. Suddenly Elizabeth delivered an unusual illustration. When their son John was a little boy, a neighbor lady a few doors down toward Eighth Street called her with an urgent concern.

The problem? John had climbed high up in their tree! Elizabeth's response was a "green" one, delivered in an effort to gently encourage the woman to take responsibility for the issue right in front of her.

"You're closest to him. Please get him down and I'll be there as quickly as I can." Little John was athletic and already a risk-taker, a challenger of frontiers. Caring for him and keeping up with him would take a village! He was gotten down safely and wondered at all the unnecessary fuss.

After years of service as a government administrator and then university president, what would others be saying later about little John? Time would tell. He'd still be up some trees and crossing some difficult frontiers. He'd still be a decisive risk-taker when necessary, although not often just because he wanted to. At least he'd not be caught again climbing with his brother David on the fire escape of the University's Old Main, not because he might want to but because the building would be gone! And with it would go the little pond near the eastside entrance. No more could little John and his friend Dave Courtney get in it and try to catch one of the goldfish intended to be admired only.

Apart from John's occasional childish misbehavior, in the Pistole home it was food and fun. In the 1970s the color green would even make it to the choice of paper. Elizabeth Pistole was an excellent cook and her two daughters soon gained interest and skill. They began helping their mother gather quality recipes. Elizabeth compiled and wrote the narrative for two cookbooks published by the Church of God. They included recipes "for tasty foods and hints for zesty living." The first edition was *Food and Fellowship in the Christian Home.*

The second edition in 1979 was co-authored by daughters Cindy and Carole who now were married, cooking in their own homes, and secondary and elementary school teachers. *Serving with Love* appeared beautifully and was printed on light green paper. How did the two Pistole brothers help with this edition? Green-like, the purpose of publication was to encourage everyone forward, including the boys. David, quite the young chef himself, would bring college friends home to try new recipes. He was a natural experimenter, a budding scientist. The Pistole home was gracious, articulate, and well-fed.

And John, the fast-growing and sometimes mischievous athlete? Well, the 1979 book edition reports that John "just loves to eat and pleases any cook with verbal appreciation." He would have many characteristics that would stand out in public, but arrogance wouldn't be one of them. John Johnson, a good friend later in life, was two years younger and a great admirer of John when they were kids. While he never got into John's inner circle of friends, he always knew him to be friendly and personable. John had that green color all over him—always on the go and encouraging others to come forward with him.

The Pistole kids, John in red, always fascinated about something.

L to R, David, Carole, John, and Cindy.
John has climbed all his life.

The Pistole kids, L to R,
David, Carole, John, Cindy

Chapter 4

Model Kid?

Life would be infinitely happier if we could only be born at the age of eighty and gradually approach eighteen. —Mark Twain

The main condition for the achievement of love is the overcoming of one's narcissism in which one experiences as real only that which exists within oneself. —Erich Fromm

Spiritually speaking, John Pistole was "converted" to Christ in the summer between the sixth and seventh grades. It happened at Camp Challenge near Bedford, Indiana, at the end of an emotional service that called the young campers to such a daring life decision. His confession and commitment were undoubtedly sincere, although highly and maybe mostly emotional. Overly pressured altar calls easily do that to the young. Nonetheless, it was a real spiritual beginning.

Ahead was a dramatic experience of an almost tragic kind that would almost end his life. Actually, by God's grace, that accident would deepen the spiritual commitment of young John for a lifetime still to come. That story will be told in the next chapter. But first, some awkward teenage activity must be understood. Life isn't lived from eighty to eighteen. It always goes the other way. Some inner reality must be overcome before the maturity of adult love and faith becomes possible.

Random Scenes

John's Camp Challenge experience was much like his Pistole grandparents had warned would be the case with his father. If Hollis had been allowed to make a religious decision when too young to comprehend its full meaning, it would be more hurtful than helpful. John had surrendered his life to Christ at a young age, or so he thought.

He was a natural learner and willing to maintain family and church routines regardless of the limited understanding he had of his spiritual commitment. Or maybe it wasn't the level of understanding that was the continuing problem. Maybe it was his readiness to let that commitment actually shape his real life.

John was inquisitive, bright, and being reared in an educationally rich environment. His third grade teacher was Miss Martha Bronnenberg. She was kind and nurturing, but at least in her sixties, "ancient" thought John and the other kids. She was a descendent of Frederick Bronnenberg, Sr., an original European settler of the Anderson area. He and his family were on their way to Illinois in 1821 when the oxen pulling their wagon just couldn't go farther. He built a cabin near the present Mounds State Park on the edge of today's Anderson.[11] Frederick had no idea that one day, indirectly, he would be an educational blessing to one John Pistole, and to his sister Carole who was inspired to become a teacher by the same Miss Bronnenberg.

In the fourth grade John got his first—and maybe only—"D." He had been sloppy in writing a test. Shocked at the rare bad grade, he immediately got serious about the clarity of his writing. Once in high school, he avoided taking a class from his mother who taught Psychology. "That would have been awkward for both of us." What he did enjoy was the common judgment of his friends. "Your Mom's the best!"

In the fifth grade John delighted in a math classroom where a competitive game was sometimes played. The teacher would hold up flashcards with little math problems on them. The first to call out the correct answer was rewarded. John prided himself in a long series of firsts. "I would sometimes beat the whole class because I was quick and also loud."

Athletics was clearly a positive for young John. It started at home. The Pistole boys had a competitive relationship. David was eighteen months older than John, but by the seventh grade John suddenly had grown taller. Hardly warming David's ego, John thoroughly enjoyed the prideful symbolism of his growth spurt. He now looked more like their grandfather Pistole and David their smaller grandfather Price.

John was emerging as a lean, tall, muscular, handsome, young man who could attract all the female attention he wanted. At least that's what his friend Jerry Fox recalls. John just smiles at this observation. "Wish I'd known that at the time!" One thing was clear. He was a bright and good-looking kid who was much too preoccupied with himself.

Why not? He seemed to have it all. He was athletic and fun along with being a serious student. He watched a little television, enjoying diversions like *McHale's Navy*, *F-Troop*, *Bonanza*, and *Mission Impossible*. And he was beginning to wonder what actually was possible for him in life. When in the family driveway shooting baskets with friends and mother Elizabeth announced that it was homework time, or time for piano lessons, he would yield, usually without complaint. Whatever the mission ahead, disciplined learning likely would be necessary.

Being preoccupied with himself, however, he balked when his mother insisted that he get dressed up and attend the wedding of his sister Cindy. It was a grand occasion at Park Place Church, a first-rate celebration of the extended Pistole family and their many friends. It was 1967, Cindy was twenty-one and the apple of Carl Poikonen's eye. John was eleven and gazing mostly at himself as the best of apples. His reluctance to attend his own sister's wedding was finally overcome, in part by the announcement that there would be plenty of cake in the Fellowship Hall afterwards.

When young, John recalls seeing only one horror movie and deciding never again. It was bad enough when he saw *The Wizard of Oz* and was frightened—a tornado destroying a home, a man with no heart, and a menacing witch with a broomstick. He couldn't imagine that as a grown man it would his job to spend many days working on the forensics of a plane crash recovery off Rhode Island and having to access many body parts smaller than hands.

John's early preferences were books and basketball, maybe not in that order. He was active shooting baskets outside as much as possible and soon became quite good at it. By the sixth grade he was a leading player on the team of Park Place Elementary School. Jerry Fox was a neighbor friend and teammate who often watched John admiringly from the bench—they couldn't all be really good. When games and school were over, the two of them, and often several other neighbor boys, would gather in the Pistole driveway for more community hoops. John readily included

Jerry even though he was just learning the game. After all, education and kindness were in the Pistole DNA.

One day on that driveway there was an ugly scene that shocked John and Jerry. A rat had gotten into the Pistole's household, a rat, not a mouse. It probably had come from a neighboring house that was poorly kept and recently burned. Cindy first saw the creepy thing upstairs and screamed. It ran to the basement where brave father Hollis managed to trap it. With the girls still a bit terrified, he got pliers and carried the thing up the stairs and out to the driveway with it jerking all the way. Then with a hammer, and in front of the boys, he dispatched it to wherever nasty dead rats go. John's reaction? "My Dad, a leader in the peace fellowship, an exterminator!"

More typical of Hollis is a very different moment recalled by John's sisters Cindy and Carole. On a cold winter day when Hollis was leaving home for his work on the nearby campus, he routinely opened the usual door to depart. This time, however, he quietly closed it and left by a less convenient side door. Why? He explained to his girls in a near whisper that birds were outside on the snow trying to eat and he didn't want to disturb them. The rat hadn't been so lucky. Rats and birds aside, basketball continued to grow as a definite preoccupation of John.

Just as industry and work opportunity had drawn the Pistole and Smith families northward in the 1920s, so had come the Jenness family southward to Anderson from Wisconsin in the 1930s. Later their son Jeff encountered the Pistole's son John through basketball in junior high school, Jeff attending Northside and John Central. They would become friends, really good friends. In fact, John says, "This became a guy I've lived life with and loved deeply." They met on the basketball court as their schools competed, two Indiana boys passionately in love with basketball—Hoosier Hysteria.

John also ran track until he had a growth spurt, lost some speed, and decided to try tennis. With no coaching at first, just a racket, ball, and brick wall next to the parking lot of Warner Press near home, he practiced and practiced on his own until the high school tennis coach, Charles Newberry, selected him for the team, and eventually named him number one singles player. He was a natural athlete.

Anderson High School in the early 1970s had great basketball teams. John was good enough to make the team, but not the best by far on a team deep in talent. As a junior he contributed modestly as the team went 25-3 for the season and made it to the state semi-finals. His lifelong friend Jeff Jenness was a star on a team that also was blessed with Roy Taylor, named 1974's "Mr. Basketball" in Indiana. Center Tony Marshall was named All-State. Another Indiana player that year, Larry Bird, later an NBA all-star, also made All-State in Indiana, but not Mr. Basketball as Anderson's Roy did!

John was confident that he had a good shot at making the starting team his senior year when the pre-season rankings listed Anderson High School number one in the state. The whole City of Anderson was in a swirl of Hoosier Hysteria. As fate, or divine providence, would have it, John would be forced to miss that great year when his team managed to go 26-0 without him, just missing the state championship.

The coach, Ray Estes, was a strong disciplinarian and motivator, a really rough and tumble guy. He commented to John that maybe they could have won the state championship that year if John had been able to play. But something dramatic had intervened that made that impossible. That shocking circumstance will be explained in the next chapter.

A Double Life

The worlds of the academic classroom and the basketball court were mostly on the positive side of John's life well into high school. But there was a negative side. He was a complex young man, conflicted, often choosing to have a great time inappropriately while being hounded by the contrasting feeling of knowing his priorities should be otherwise. He was baptized into the life of Jesus Christ. He was a faithful ringer for Pastor David Coolidge in a junior high handbell choir at Park Place Church.[12] He also, on the side, pursued a life of quite a different kind.

John had returned from Camp Challenge to his home in Anderson bringing with him his "conversion" experience. At age twelve he was baptized in the family's home congregation, Park Place Church of God. It was all very real for him, but the reality was nonetheless shallow. Soon peer pressure and life's locally available excitements overwhelmed his tender soul. He really wanted to be "a good Christian," but began drinking with his friends and living "a double life."

Sister Cindy married when John was eleven, helping to clear the home a little and free the boys to begin some "wild" life experimenting. Most of it was outside the home and done when they could manage some safety away from parental surveillance. Bicycles were handy friends. John may have been a baptized young Christian, but in terms of spiritual maturity he had a long way to go. He began to do his "own thing," started "breaking bad," wanting to be "one of the party guys." Being loyal to Jesus, while very important to him, would have to take a back seat and wait for another day to blossom into a functioning reality.

Brothers David and John were both rivals and fellow mischief makers. David, likely to deny an accusation or two, does admit that "we weren't angels by any means." Sister Carole says her younger brothers both "could be a pain." Today John doesn't hide the wild oats he sowed liberally from grades seven through twelve. Fortunately, they didn't get so deeply rooted that they couldn't be dug up later, although the digging would require something very dramatic.

Being the youngest of the four Pistole kids, maybe John was allowed to get away with a little more than the older ones. His memory is that his brother David "pushed the envelope" first, and quite a bit, with John certainly not far behind, later calling this phase of his life a "double standard." I was "a model kid" until the "excitements of life's experiments kicked in."

At home and church John was a rule-follower and good Christian boy; beyond the home he did what he could to be a rule-breaker and increasingly rebellious. His first experience of being drunk was at age thirteen. It was at a friend's house not far from his own. John is reluctant to share that family's name—they had strong church ties. Another friend unrelated to the church had a mother, maybe an alcoholic, who bought beer, wine, whiskey, and vodka for "the gang" to consume while they played small-stakes poker in that home.

John still wasn't even aware of what words like "alcoholic" meant. Those weren't actions or topics of conversation in the Pistole home. Fortunately, much later when John was very different, he would be pleased to report that he apologized to his parents for the grief he had brought them when young. He readily reports that he was blessed to have been reared in such a godly family. It kept him grounded when he was trying to fly away.

His parents were good at turning negatives into positives, consciously from a Christian perspective. They created an environment ripe for learning. Once in a family meeting the kids were told that there was only enough money for a new TV, color no less, or joining the Dolphin Club in town where they could swim in the summertime. John was honored to be included in such a big decision. The Club was chosen and the following year they also managed to get the TV. Hollis and Elizabeth modeled what they tried to teach. John remembers them as people with integrity, generous servant leaders—the very core values that one day he would espouse at Anderson University as its President.

Hardly any spankings landed on John. When the parents became aware of bad behavior, typically they reacted constructively and redemptively. They were more teachers and nurtures than heavy-handed disciplinarians. Mom was firm and loving. Dad was a peaceful man who tended to see the best side of almost anything. The result? John admits, "I got away with quite a bit." Once, after a drinking party, a girl who had had too much sideswiped the Pistole's VW Bug that John was driving. Hollis saw the damaged side panel the next day and inquired of John, who admitted that he had been driving and this girl had hit him—only slightly. John carefully made no mention of alcohol. Hollis was understanding, made John pay for the repairs, but remained unaware of the alcohol truth.

That would hardly be the approach in House or Senate hearings later in Washington, D. C. Once when John was about to be grilled by a Senate committee about his qualifications and his past, he was asked in a pre-interview if there were anything that would be embarrassing about his early life if it appeared on the front page of the *Washington Post*. He admitted a few of the boyish oats he had sown when young. This question followed. "Were you ever arrested?" "No, nothing like that, though maybe a time or two I should have been." That was good enough. The hearing went well. In typical Washington terms, and as opposed to many others, John really had nothing of substance to hide.

When President of the campus near which he had stretched his young wings in awkward directions, he would be open with everyone about the stretching, thinking that his frankness would be a good witness to high school and college students who might be dealing with the same issues. In an Anderson University recruitment video in early 2020, he would be candid with current and prospective students about the downsides of his early life and how crucial this campus had been to him personally.

That report usually would include a frank recounting of a dramatic event that nearly took John's life, but instead added important dimensions to his spiritual life. It would be a life-altering wake-up call that jolted John's life into a much better direction.

A few members of Handbell Choir IV, Park Place Church of God, 1967, Rev. David Coolidge, Director. L. to R., Mike Jenkins, Doug Hall, John Pistole, Jim Newberry, and Mark Noffsinger.

Park Place Church of God, Anderson, Indiana.

The stained glass window, sanctuary of Park Place Church of God,
features the crucified and resurrected Jesus.
Young John Pistole was about to do the same with his own life.

Chapter 5

Wake-up Call!

I had a lot of growing up to do. A lot of times, I learned the hard way. —Allen Iverson

What the devil meant for harm God has worked for our good. —Charles Myricks at the presidential inauguration of John Pistole, referring to John's near-tragic car accident in high school.

Jesus said, "Anyone who intends to come with me has to let me lead. You're not in the driver's seat; I am." (Mark 8:34)

The double life of young John Pistole was about to be interrupted, in fact his life almost eliminated altogether. The interruption would be sudden, painful, costly, and maybe providential in the larger picture of things. No, it wasn't a near-death experience from a drug overdose or drunken spree, although it was an abrupt crashing of John's whole life.

The horrific event would bring front and center the comment of Jesus in Mark 8:34. Who should be in the driver's seat of life? It happened in a little car with John in the front passenger seat. It was nearly his last ride anywhere. It suddenly was time to allow Jesus to lead John into the future.

Before the crisis, and at about every opportunity, even after practicing with the beautiful boy's bell choir of Pastor David Coolidge at Park Place Church, John would slip away on his bike to a friend's house. The goal was whatever they wanted to do that day, often something not the best. These activities, beyond the parent's sight of course, often would involve drinking and partying with friends. Then, after some four years of this double life, and without any warning, John slipped off from the high school with friends for a relatively innocent lunch break. It was a near tragedy that turned out to be one of the greatest blessings of his life.

On Top of the World

"I was a kid who thought he was on top of the world," John now recalls. The boys, especially John and his basketball buddies, were living a dream, caught up in "Hoosier Hysteria." John, somewhat reserved in demeanor with lots going on inside, was not necessarily the easiest guy to really get to know. Even so, he was obviously gifted and liked by most everyone. It was a wonderful world for a young man, one suddenly about to come crashing down.

John had barely begun his senior year at Anderson High School. The months ahead were so full of promise. He likely would be a starter on the high school basketball team that had a pre-season ranking of number one in Indiana. The huge gymnasium in Anderson, the Wigwam built in 1961, said to be the second largest in the world, would seat 9,000 often delirious fans. It was jammed full for every home game.

The colorful school mascot, an Indian chief adorned in full headdress, would do his masterful dance at mid-court to fire the crowd. William Anderson had been chief of the local Delaware Indians. He'd settled his tribe along the White River, the spot white settlers soon were calling Anderson's Town. Chief Anderson refused to join the insurrection of Tecumseh, a Shawnee warrior and chief who tried to reclaim Indiana and Ohio for native peoples.

Now, many generations after Chief Anderson's original arrival in town, these young "Indian" athletes of Anderson High School were trained by Coach Ray Estes to go on the warpath whenever an enemy team dared come to town. Obviously, the cultural insensitivities so apparent now were hardly noticed in the 1970s.

Ray's boys were schooled to be menacing men who thought of themselves as almost invincible, ready to conquer on court every Indiana opponent. John Pistole was one of conquerors. He was respected for his emerging athletic prominence in both basketball and tennis. One telling day in John's junior year deserves remembering. Anderson High was in a tennis match against the vaunted Richmond High Red Devils. Since it was a clear mismatch, the Anderson tennis coach tried to pair players so that Anderson wouldn't be shut out entirely.

Anderson High School Indians,
1973, John Pistole back row, #52

As teammate Jeff Jenness recalls, John was chosen as "the sacrificial lamb" to play the top Red Devil, likely the best tennis player in the state. But this Richmond "phenom" didn't know what he was in for. John accepted the challenge, turned on his "can do" spirit, and forced the match of the season. In a few minutes word spread and a crowd gathered around that court to watch "the two titans duel."

While John finally lost "by a whisper," his opponent would never forget that difficult day. This tennis match, surprisingly competitive, was a dramatic instance of John's lifelong mantra—anything is possible! One should go all out for a worthy task, whatever the odds.

Everything now was in line for John's senior year, likely to be a highly successful athletic one, that is, until one lunchtime in September, 1973, when he nearly slipped out of this world. It would be the sudden blunt force of massive physical trauma leading, by God's grace, to a remarkable spiritual "wake-up call."

John Johnson remembers hearing it happen. He was sitting in a world history class on that warm day with high school's classroom windows wide open. He was jerked from hearing about some ancient event to a very present drama. He heard a crash that sent a gasp through the room. "What was that?!"

Then came the sickening sound of the sirens. In minutes word had spread that the vehicles involved in the crash included John Pistole, who already was being rushed to Community Hospital with his life hanging in the balance! For Johnson, two years younger and a great Pistole admirer, it was instant grief.

"Pistole had a magnetism about him. He was the guy with everything who now may have just lost it all!" In fact, if an EMT hadn't put a firm neck restraint on John before trying to get him out of the mangled car, death probably would have been certain from a severed spinal cord. As it turned out, the 5th and 6th vertebrae were broken and dislodged, one touching but mercifully not severing the spinal cord.

"Am I Going To Die?"

That day, September 12, 1973, had been ordinary enough. Groups of Anderson athletes had taken off in separate cars for a quick lunch away from the school. It was to a popular all-you-can-eat pasta place at Grandview Golf Course. The young guys filled up, finished late, and needed to hurry back to school. One vehicle was a VW "Bug" with Mark Mills, basketball team manager and one of John's drinking buddies, at the wheel. David Courtney tried to get in that car but there was no room left, so he got in another vehicle, a large sedan driven by basketball player Pat King. John was in the VW's fateful passenger seat with no safety belts or air bags.

On the rushed return trip, very near the high school, these two cars collided violently. The VW had run a stop sign, almost tragically. Courtney's head smashed into the sedan's windshield but with only minor injury. That large "boat of a car" had slammed into the VW broadside, causing the Bug to flip on its side. John was instantly trapped in the VW with three of his classmates also squeezed inside the little car. He was severely injured—or worse. It was just two weeks into his senior year. Courtney always would remember how close it came to being him in that fateful seat. But it was John whose life, if it remained, now would be forever changed.

When first responders got John out, still alive, they secured his neck and rushed him across town to intensive care. He had at least a broken neck and possibly much worse. Elizabeth Pistole was at the high school and Hollis at the seminary on the campus across town. Sister Carole was teaching at Greenbriar Elementary and got a frantic call from her mother. They all met at the hospital quickly, just before Rev. David Coolidge who was the first Park Place Church pastor to arrive.

On a later visit, Rev. Coolidge remembers vividly seeing John enclosed in a rotatable circular cage. He had been put in a Stryker bed that could be rotated twice daily to avoid bedsores and further injury by John having to make the turn himself. John wasn't only an outstanding basketball player. He also was the top-ranked singles tennis player on the high school team. Sister Carole remembers John's first words to her. "I don't think I'll be playing tennis this afternoon!" In fact, it wasn't yet clear if he would survive the first twenty-four hours.

Sister Cindy and husband Carl were teachers in the high school and middle school in Kendallville, Indiana, some two hours away. They rushed to Anderson that evening. Cindy recalls the hospital hallway crowded, mostly with high school students in various stages of shock. Carl had a brief chance to speak to John, whose wrenching question was, "Am I going to die?" Carl tried to be reassuring without actually knowing.

A most difficult memory was pondered through the long hours of that first night. Just one year earlier, a student athlete at Anderson High School had been working on a trampoline when something had gone terribly array. He landed improperly and was instantly paralyzed—and then died a week later! John kept thinking, "Is it now my turn?"

John would remain hospitalized for four weeks. He had numbness in one hand and at first feared that he might become completely paralyzed, but he never would be. His brother David takes some of the credit. "John looked like a skeleton. He preferred my massages best of all."

Paralysis, however, wasn't John's only fear. He fought sleep the first night because he was troubled with a double fear. One was waking up fully paralyzed. The other was not waking up at all and finding himself in the awful place of eternal judgment. "If I died I knew I would go straight to hell because I'd deliberately chosen life apart from God." He'd made wrong choices, knew it well, and now might die with them unresolved and unforgiven.

John's close friend Jeff Jenness, a former teammate and basketball star at the high school, already was a college student on the Anderson campus.

He had a part-time job at Community Hospital. After classes he would hurry there as a specialist in drawing blood. When someone was brought into the emergency room on his shift, he would be called to do the drawing, often testing the blood for levels of alcohol in some driver brought in by a policeman. On this particular day in September, something odd happened.

A doctor approached Jeff and told him he could go home early, no explanation, just go home. This doctor was a big basketball fan, as were most adults in the city, and knew both Jeff and John Pistole that way. He had become aware of John having just been brought into the emergency room badly hurt and wanted to shield Jeff from any personal involvement. Of course, Jeff soon learned what had happened. He quickly got in touch with several of their mutual friends and, as he later put it, "it was like an awful death watch."

John was in shock, afraid to sleep, but finally would, and he would wake up, not dead and definitely not in hell. The good news was that, despite the high level of neck trauma, the spinal cord had not been severely damaged. An EMT said that, had they not handled him so carefully in transport, it likely would have been. What John faced was a delicate surgery involving a spinal fusion, with bone grafted from his leg followed by the need to remain in a neck-body cast for twelve weeks.

His teachers rallied, helping him finish the semester and finally graduate with his class. Meanwhile, he had plenty of time to think—and now even to pray. Meanwhile, many visited John in the hospital with little awareness of what he had been and now was becoming. They included Dean Barry Callen of the School of Theology where Hollis Pistole taught. He was joined by Fredrick Shively who was being hosted at the seminary as a Minister-in-Residence and interviewing for a faculty position. Barry and Fred went to Community Hospital in Anderson to visit the son of a colleague, Hollis, having no idea that this badly injured young man one day would be the President of the campus!

Shively recalls that "when Barry and I entered the hospital room we saw John strapped in a special harness to keep him in the air and free of the bed. Even in his condition, John had come up with a positive and hopeful attitude. We didn't know then that his positive nature, now being enabled by God, would carry him through a lifetime of caring and responsible service." None knew all that was ahead, certainly not John. What he was learning was that the accident was his life's big wake-up call.

I Am the Lord's!

The badly injured young John Pistole was coming to know the real meaning of songs he had heard often as a child at Park Place Church of God. John had weeks of recovery during which to think and reflect deeply. He began to realize that he was not the one in control of life and death. God is, and God had spared his life and was giving him an undeserved second chance.

John realized that God had not caused the accident, not at all. His friend Mark had run a stop sign. As John began yielding gratefully to Someone greater than himself, a wonderful realization began to take hold. "God wanted to use me in ways I couldn't imagine." Ahead was "a chance to live a life truly transformed." Jeff Jenness came to a related realization about John over the following months. "I saw a life transformation that was truly amazing."[13]

Decades later, this near-tragic event would be brought up at John's inauguration as the new President of Anderson University—an occasion totally unimaginable while he was recovering in that hospital bed and hadn't yet managed to finish high school. Charles Myricks, a major leader of the Church of God Movement, sponsoring church of the Anderson campus, announced this. "What the devil had meant for harm God has worked out for our good!" Charles then joined other campus trustees in surrounding John, praying a blessing over him, and giving thanks for the amazing goodness of God.

Nor could John know in that hospital bed that one day his personal testimony would influence countless university students and even numerous world leaders. Included would be his high school basketball coach. The tough Ray Estes, as Jeff Jenness recalls, would never forget John and eventually would come to Christ himself. Would that be because of John's experience? Possibly, although John prefers to give credit to the witness of Jeff and the work of the Holy Spirit.

Two songs from John's church boyhood now were coming alive for him. They were "I Am the Lord's, I Know" and "Blessed Assurance, Jesus Is Mine." Their lyrics started filling John's mind and heart. His earlier conversion to Christ now was shining much more brightly. Of all the prayers offered for John in his weeks in that hospital room, including those of various ministers, the one John most remembers was offered by Bill Vetter, a very unpretentious layman from Park Place Church. "His prayer was heartfelt, yet so simple and authentic that I knew I was in God's presence, and when he left the room I knew that I really was going to get better."

Much spiritual growth was certainly still needed, but at least John now was encouraged and pointed in the right direction. That direction would take him into college, but not his first choice. He had hoped to earn a basketball or tennis scholarship at a Division II school. That now was off the table. His second chance at life as it should be then would take him into legal practice, soon not his preference either. No matter. John was beginning to learn that even at life's lowest points God is there with some big things in mind.

A future college classmate and fellow 1978 graduate of Anderson University would also be heading into the legal profession. Patricia Seasor (Bailey) was aware of John, of course, but they weren't particularly close in those years. That vague awareness would change big time one day.

Many years later, in 2015, Patricia would become Chair of Anderson University's Board of Trustees and John the university's President. How unlikely was that?! When now reflecting back on the car accident, she offers this judgment. "That crash and its aftermath form a paradigm for John's whole life. It's colored everything after. He's an overcomer. John's story is one of overcoming." While that is the case, John would rush to add, "overcoming only because I now have the blessed assurance that Jesus is mine!"

Chapter 6

HOMETOWN COLLEGE

The task of a university is the creation of the future, so far as rational thought and civilized modes of appreciation can affect the issue. —Alfred North Whitehead

Anderson University's history, published at its seventy fifth-anniversary, is titled *Guide of Soul and Mind.*[14] This school served student John Pistole well in both regards, spiritual and intellectual.

Anderson University ("College" at the time) was a very familiar place to John Pistole. He had grown up near the campus ever since his family moved to Anderson, Indiana, when he was still learning to walk. His sisters already had attended and graduated from there, Cindy in 1968, majoring in English and secondary education, and Carole in 1972, majoring in elementary education. His brother David would be a 1977 grad, one year before John. He would go on to a doctoral program that involved his becoming a specialist in some parasite that lives only in bats. The future is made up of many things.

Later, John would specialize in investigating various parasites of the more human and public-policy varieties. Whatever the diverse endeavors of its graduates, however, the mission of Anderson University always has been "the creation of the future," encouraging "rational thought" and inspiring "civilized modes of appreciation." This mission, informed especially by the wisdom of the Christian faith tradition, would be quite successful for John Pistole and his siblings.

Kathy Harp grew up in the Washington, D. C., area and had a relative living in Anderson. Her family would come to Indiana every summer to the big national Camp Meeting of the Church of God staged on the Anderson campus. Her father, Rev. H. Richard Harp, was a pastor in this church body, as was John's father Hollis who was an educator of the church's pastors at its seminary located in Anderson.

John would attend the Anderson campus and so would Kathy. While growing up worlds apart, one day they would become their own family world together. But nothing had been automatic. John had hoped to go elsewhere to college; hindsight would suggest that God wanted him in Anderson. Ironically, he would benefit greatly from missing the athletic "big-time" somewhere else and staying close to home.

The word "providential" became increasingly meaningful to John across his four years as an undergraduate. He didn't run across Alfred North Whitehead's view of the proper role of higher education, but he was about to experience it anyway. His four years on the Anderson campus would "sharpen his modes of appreciation" and definitely help in "the creation of the future."

A Big Come-Back

As previously noted, John Pistole thought he could be a starter his senior year on what promised to be a truly great Anderson High School basketball team. Naturally, it crossed his mind that maybe he could get an athletic scholarship to some university after graduation that had a national footprint athletically. He had excellent grades and considerable talent, and in his junior year in high school his team had several stars who had attracted college scouts to the Wigwam to see them play. Maybe John could ride that wonderful wave to some glorious shore. Beyond the athletics, he had graduated from Anderson High School *cum laude*.

But, of course, the car accident had robbed him of most of his senior year on the team and any real chance of being noticed by the recruiters. Near the season's end he actually was cleared to play again, amazingly, but was very rusty and the coach was hesitant to test his physical endurance. The team did make it to the state semi-finals. John dressed and warmed up with the team, proudly and thankfully, but then stayed on the bench as the team finally lost.

With the athletic scholarship option gone, the back-up school choice was obvious. It would be Anderson University, still called Anderson College in John's college years (1974-1978). This campus was right up the street from his home. His father, Dr. Hollis Pistole, was a prominent faculty member in the graduate School of Theology, and that faculty position made available to John a generous remitted tuition benefit. The family had limited funds to enable John to choose just anywhere and pay whatever price. They might be able to help some with a first year somewhere, but that would be it. So the local, familiar, convenient, and fully affordable campus was John's lot.

Anderson University, Anderson, Indiana,
John Pistole's undergraduate alma mater.

He had come back from near death, a broken neck, vertebrae fusion, and feared total paralysis to join the Anderson University basketball team his freshman year. Granted, he "played scared" at first, naturally being a bit tentative, fearing any new injury to his neck. Even so, his recovery defied all expectations and soon he would emerge an accomplished college athlete in tennis and basketball. His friend Jeff Jenness was an A. U. basketball teammate. He also was a skilled athlete and someone well aware of the earlier accident. He recalls amazement that John soon managed to be back on the court and even quicker than most of his teammates.

John was a shooter and sometimes could score points quickly. Barrett Bates, the basketball coach during John's sophomore, junior and senior years, was told of the terrible high-school accident but observed no lingering effects. John never mentioned it to him or to his teammates, including close friend and two-year roommate Stan Deal. An admitted "late bloomer," by his college senior year John was again playing at a high level. He scored a career high thirty-two points against arch-rival Taylor University. If ever an Anderson Raven were to soar, it should be against Taylor!

Since there was no three-point shot in those days, John was best at coming center court from the left side and hitting jump shots from fifteen to eighteen feet away. Coach Bates describes player Pistole as cordial, consistent, a natural kind of "glue" that holds a team together by the example he presents more than with the mouth he exercises. To use firearm terms for this Pistole, John was a good gun, a skilled straight shooter.

John claims that teammate Stan Deal, his roommate for two years, could sing with loud rock music blasting while jumping rope in the dorm hallway as many as a 1,000 times without a miss. Maybe that's why, at only 6'3", with John 6'4", Stan could easily out dunk him any day. The dorm director, of course, preferred far fewer jumps and the music turned way down.

These two friends had planned to be featured in a "Cheap Thrills" program singing and playing Ted Nugent's "Dog Eat Dog." They had practiced the wild bodily gyrations and electric guitar playing with their tennis rackets. Unfortunately, the event had to be cancelled for weather. The world is still waiting for Stan and John to let loose with their rendition of "It's a Dog Eat Dog World!"

John was unaware at the time, of course, that he would spend a large portion of his adult life investigating that very world, often at its most raw. Their well-practiced but aborted song performance would have announced,

> Sabotage on a downtown street, Police cars overturned, You can't do nothing to beat the heat, And if you don't, you'll get burned.

It wouldn't be long before John would himself be the FBI "heat" trying hard to "burn" the perpetrators of social injustice. But in his college years such a possibility never appeared on the radar screen.

John did manage to take this show on the road. Actually, it was just down the street to his boyhood home. It was an occasion meant only to involve popcorn and TV with his Mom and Dad and girlfriend Kathy. But suddenly there was more. The musical urge to perform hit him. He wanted to show everyone how a great rock star makes the dramatic stage appearance. This appearance, however, would go a bit wrong.

He had cranked up the mandatory dramatics, pretending to strum wildly on his invisible guitar. Then he came leaping through the doorway between the living room and kitchen where his "audience" was seated, only to crack his head on the upper door frame in the process, knocking himself nearly unconscious on the floor! John remembers seeing plenty of stars and hearing Kathy laughing. She probably shouldn't have, getting the "death stare" from his mother. Elizabeth's worried words were chilling as her son's face was still face-down on the carpet. "John, you could have broken your neck again!" This time he had escaped with only a little embarrassment. His brother likely would have judged, "You Knucklehead!"

Young Pistole, even if a bit weird at times, was on a physical comeback and a spiritual pilgrimage. His big spiritual "wake-up" call had come with the car accident early and fortunately hadn't been repeated in his boyhood home. By his own report, "Since I was about twenty years old I have been rather consistent in seeking God's face daily and determining to be obedient. I always ask how I can honor the Lord today regardless of circumstances." Note the timing of that reported growth. It means that, for at least the first two years of college, he was still rather "inconsistent" spiritually.

The need for his continuing growth was made clear one snowy day after basketball practice John's freshman year. He and three friends decided to enjoy the snow by going together in a car to the big parking lot behind Park Place Church. They let themselves and the car loose, spinning, doing "donuts," until the driver lost control and the car slid sideways into the curb. It slammed hard and tilted dangerously on its side. Just before turning over, the car caught its balance and bounced back down on all four tires.

The young men were quiet for a few seconds. John had hit his head on the door but not hard enough to be injured again. He was the first to speak. "That's enough. I want out!" Jeff Jenness recalls vividly John walking away in the snow, headed back to the dorm alone. As Jeff interprets it, John was "cementing his will not to blow the second chance at life that God had given him, physical and spiritual." His friend Stan Deal soon heard about this event and agreed. John was on an upward spiritual journey—with a long way to go.

In fact, the day came when John felt that, given his growing friendship with Kathy Harp, he needed to confess something to her. As a teenager he had nearly become an alcoholic. Her response, rather than being condemning, was most constructive. "Well, John, why do you drink?" "To get drunk, of course," he responded.

"Do you still drink?"

"I still want to."

"Do you think God might be calling you to something else?"

That last question impacted John deeply. People like Stan Deal were aware and appreciative that Kathy was having a good influence on an exceptional young man who was trying to find his way. Student Jerry Fox, a life-long friend and now colleague of John's at Anderson University, worked in the campus Natatorium as a lifeguard, as did Kathy. His view was that "she was perfect for John. She was more focused and disciplined and tended to bring these critical qualities out in him. She once said to John, 'Before we get serious, I need to know how serious you are about your faith'."

Jerry certainly knew all about John. He was the resident assistant in Dunn Hall who more than once had to stop John and Stan Deal from making so much noise with their blaring rock music. And the needed discipline would indeed come, even if slowly at first. Years later, Jerry would ask John how he could manage to handle terrorist plots against the American public during the day and then come home and manage to invest the little time available to play with his girls and even help them with their homework. John's reply was brief and simple. "Only by God's grace!"

Miss Strong's Old Testament Class

The Anderson campus is church related and exposure to Bible study is required for all students. This fact had set the scene for John and Kathy Harp to first meet as freshmen. Professor Marie Strong was a prominent instructor of biblical studies and found their names on her class roster in September, 1974. It was "Introduction to the Old Testament" that met at 8:00 a.m.

Kathy already knew a little about John from an earlier visit out East of John's sister Carole and her husband Tim Bagwell. Carole and Tim had met on the Anderson campus after his time as a Marine in Viet Nam and then an assignment in Washington, D.C. He was anxious to get out early and managed that by declaring that he was a conscientious objector. Probably because his grandfather had been a Church of God pastor, Tim found his way to Rev. H. Richard Harp, pastor of the National Memorial Church of God and Kathy's father. Tim was befriended and supported in his CO discharge request. Now Tim was anxious to introduce his new wife Carole to the Harp family that had become important to him.

John Pistole prior to his FBI years.

On this visit to Washington in the summer of 1973, Carole (Pistole) Bagwell mentioned to Kathy Harp that she had a younger brother, John, who was Kathy's same age and would be going to Anderson University shortly. Kathy told Carole that she had the same college intention and had been encouraged by the fact that Tom Harp, her father's youngest brother, was already a student on the Anderson campus.

Maybe Kathy and John soon would meet, and maybe she should be cautious. After all, the first Harp-Pistole contact hadn't gone all that well.

When Tom Harp was ten and Carole Pistole sixteen, Tom now admits to being "in love" with Carole. Unfortunately, he learned that apparently she was in love with some fifteen-year-old who was "way cooler than me." Worse yet, Carole's kid brother, John, somehow learned about Tom's wayward feelings toward his sister and supposedly warned Tom with, "Stay away from my sister or I'll grow up to be a cop and shoot you!" Tom did stay clear, John would grow up to be a cop, and fortunately would never shoot anyone. Nor would he remember this encounter ever happening.

Miss Strong was an excellent teacher, like John's mother in many ways. She exuded confidence in her subject and held high expectations of her students. Although naturally in a less mature way, such characteristics were similar to those of her student Kathy. She admits to being a "bossy boots" as a college student, always knowing the right way to do most everything. She was the oldest of five and grew up with a "big sister" mind-set. John, youngest of four, was on the strong-minded and somewhat pampered side himself.

The scene was set for John and Kathy to meet in Marie's class—and maybe learn something about the Bible while more interested in learning about each other. John admits to at least some Old Testament learning, particularly about the Song of Solomon. Divine revelation includes a little poetic material leaning toward the erotic side of young life. Kathy would become known among the college guys as "the mysterious beautiful girl from the East." Although a little hard to get to know, John was beginning to penetrate her mystery.

These Bible students began to spend some of their time studying each other in and out of class. They began meeting in the cafeteria, with John sometimes walking her to Morrison Hall and hanging out with her as they watched things like "McHale's Navy" and "F-Troop" on the lounge TV. There slowly evolved a real relationship of strong attraction, one mixed with fascination and some occasional mild friction.

This relationship development was watched carefully by Bob Coffman, later to be a lifelong friend and professional colleague of John's. Bob was dating Vivian Barrett who happened to be Kathy's roommate, so these the two "couples" began to get rather well acquainted. In fact, Kathy would be Vivian's maid of honor in her marriage to Bob in 1978, just before Kathy would marry John in 1979.

John struggled with a bit of jealously when seeing Kathy get almost daily letters from some guy back East—competition? Meanwhile, Jeff Jenness, John's good friend from high school, was dating a Debbie and soon the four of them became friends, and are to this day. Their marriages would be in the summer of 1979. Decades later they would travel the world together on trips celebrating their 30th, 35th, and 40th wedding anniversaries.

The most recent of these trips was an amazing sixteen days spent together in 2019 retracing the journeys of the Apostle Paul in Turkey and Greece. John loved to travel and would do all the detailed planning for the couples. By then John's work would have taken him to Rome and Jerusalem, but now it would be the locations of the letters of Paul coming alive. A walker/runner himself, John was impressed at how far St. Paul had to walk from city to city. The Jenness and Pistole couples were deepening their understanding of the Word of God. But that's getting way ahead of John's story.

A "Big Idea"

Kathy Harp had come to Anderson University to study Spanish, not having a clue about what she would do later with such a major. She was sure of two things, however. She didn't want to teach and after college wanted to go home to the Washington, D. C. area where there was family and a large Spanish-speaking population. She added to Spanish study becoming a lifeguard in the campus Natatorium, joined by a new friend Gwen Plough who later would marry John Pistole's boyhood acquaintance, John Johnson, and also become lifelong friends.

At first John Pistole also wasn't sure of his future intent. Even so, for him the timing was ideal for his eventual professional needs. A shift in curricular philosophy was in progress on campus. The previous decade of the 1960s had seen campus enrollments nearly double, requiring that most creative energy go into managing what such growth demanded. Now in the 1970s, led by Dean Robert Nicholson and his new Dean for Academic Development, Dr. Larry Osnes, big curricular questions were being asked and explored again by the faculty.

What is a "liberally educated" person? Creative voices were saying that surely that person must have had the privilege of "experiential learning," real-life exposures and experiences. Therefore, a "Big Idea" was taking hold on campus. There already was the TRI-S program (student summer service) sending many of the college's students around the world for brief periods of work and Christian witness. Faculty members often led such groups, including John's father, Hollis.[15]

In the summer of 1975, John and seven of his basketball buddies from the campus ventured to the West Indies on a TRI-S trip. These student athletes would island hop from Jamaica to Trinidad and Tobago. They'd touch base with churches, witness for Christ, do manual labor as needed, and play basketball with national teams and whoever wanted to play. Usually there was more Christian witnessing at each game halftime, with one possible exception.

The A. U. team racked up an overall 19-1 record on the trip, downed only on the little island of Tobago by a team that had a seven-footer playing center. There was no defense against that size when a perfect long shot by John Pistole was swatted out of the basket by the giant. It was a clear case of goal-tending, apparently allowed by local rules. Chuck Hise, Resident Director for Dunn Hall on the Anderson campus and a 6'6" earlier star at Anderson, was leading the trip and acting as player coach. He got so frustrated that he inserted himself into the game. He positioned both himself and Stan Deal under the opponent's basket to see that nothing of theirs went in again.

TRI-S was joined on the Anderson campus in 1973 by the Center for Public Service. This was an aggressive venture conceived by Dr. Larry Osnes and enabled by a large grant from the Lilly Endowment. New partnerships would be built quickly between the campus and business, industry, the local medical community, and the federal government.[16] Larry was from a Church of God family with a long history. He was a star football player, an A. U. graduate in 1963, and in 1969 a new faculty member in the field of history.

Osnes led the new CPS from its founding, assisted by an outstanding consultant provided by the Endowment, Robert Greenleaf. His 1975 book *Servant Leadership* formed the philosophic heart of the new campus endeavor.[17] The power-centered authoritarian leadership so prominent in the Western world wasn't working. Greenleaf advocated the opposite. Being a servant-leader means doing what's required to help others succeed. To lead well is to serve well, helping all involved to grow and perform at their best.

John Pistole would be a key beneficiary of the new Center. It selected as "Fellows" of the Center a small number of the top students on campus from a variety of disciplines. Bob Coffman, who had graduated in 1972, was a good friend of John's sister Carole and an assistant in the Center beginning in 1974. John, an American Studies (pre-law) major, became a Fellow and through the Center, and soon went with another, student Gale Hutchins, to Harvard University for direct experience with a Model United Nations event. While John was sitting in a history class, he realized that it was no better than classes back at Anderson, especially outstanding ones like Dr. Eppinga's "Diplomatic History of the United States" and any class taught by Dr. Larry Osnes or Dr. Doug Nelson.

As a CPS "Fellow," John also spent four weeks in the Indiana State Budget Office and six weeks one summer in the Washington office of Congressman Bud Hillis. There he got to ride the new Metro and become acquainted for the first time with a city he would come to know very well in later years. He was close enough to visit his girlfriend Kathy, three years later to be his wife. Beyond enabling this evolving romance, these outstanding experiences taught John to do critical thinking. "You can get facts anywhere," he explains, "but there's no substitute for critical thinking about those facts, processing, analyzing, and preparing to present."

The undergraduate experience also enabled John to do critical thinking about his Christian faith and what it might mean for his future personal and professional life. He would never forget a campus gathering one evening of the "Fellowship of Christian Athletes." The guys talked frankly about their faith lives. "I was on that journey, trying to figure out what full surrender means for all of life. A lightbulb came on for me. Doing life on my own and for myself wasn't how I wanted to live my life!" Dr. Osnes says that John was one of the select few students who really grasped the goal of the Center for Public service—preparing servant leaders to make a large public difference.

Immediately after graduation in 1978, John spent six weeks in Costa Rica and Colombia as part of "Sports Ambassadors." There he encountered marvelous young Christians "who were on fire for Jesus." This time away solidified for John an awareness of how God could use for good his near-tragic high school accident. He even tried some witnessing in Spanish, in part hoping this might impress Kathy, his Spanish-major love back in the United States.

This trip with Sports Ambassadors, and the previous extra-curricular experiences, were crucial in John's early spiritual and professional development. One problem with the Costa Rica and Colombia venture was its timing. The conclusion date was inflexible and made John three days late for beginning his law school education back in Indianapolis. Even so, when he did get home he was well positioned to excel. The experience was more than worth it.

Cager John Pistole, left, receives his "Outstanding Senior Athlete" plaque from Dr. Dick Young, director of intercollegiate athletics.

John Pistole Touring South America With Team Of Sports Ambassadors

The value derived for John was partly that he had met through Sports Ambassadors, and been greatly encouraged and instructed, by two men in particular—and with reference to more than basketball. John Jauchen was the player-coach who led the training camp in Texas and the time in Costa Rica, while Ric Escobar from Columbia led in the game playing and worship leading in that country. John now reports that these two men, in their mid-thirties at the time, were "on fire for Jesus and so solidly rooted in God's Word that they had a huge impact on me as I wrestled with how best to live out my faith." Further, "they provided good pre-marriage counseling that led me to 'propose' to Kathy several months later."

Providence Is Real

Like the Pistoles and Smiths migrating northward in the 1920s, John Pistole's attending Anderson University, in hindsight, was full of the providential grace of God. He now judges, "Anderson may not have been my first choice but it turned out to be a great choice." God had his hand on John all along. A quality education combined with undeserved Divine grace had positioned John for a coming career to be marked by *integrity* and *excellence* in all things.

These critical characteristics and goals had been previewed in John's very first class on the Anderson campus. Just weeks before his initial enrollment as a freshman, Richard Nixon had resigned from the presidency of the United States. That first class was about government, taught by Dr. Larry Osnes. He made the point that "we are living in historic days." That was timely and stimulating for young John who was just beginning his studies in the chosen areas of political science and American Studies. He was thinking of becoming a lawyer, maybe one day even serving the public in some significant way. Historic days were full of opportunity.

Who knew, certainly not young John, that eventually something very surprising would eventually become known. "Deep Throat," the whistleblower who eventually helped bring down President Nixon, was Mark Felt, second in command of the FBI. Who knew that John would often visit the Oval Office in Washington on official business with future presidents, himself then being the second in command of the FBI? Definitely not John himself when a pre-law freshman.

John had no idea that in 2006 he would be the honored commencement speaker back at his Anderson alma mater. On that occasion he would call the name of Mark Felt and urge graduates to think outside their comfort zones as they sought for whatever God might have for their unexpected futures. Whatever it would be, integrity and courage would be required.

It's unusual for a small church-related college to be blessed with a cluster of high-quality faculty members in the same area of study. But in John's years on the Anderson campus there were Drs. Larry Osnes, Douglas Nelson, and Dick Eppinga. He also was highly appreciative of Fred Milley in English and Marie Strong in Bible. While never his personal teacher on the campus, John would want the name of his father Hollis Pistole mentioned as well. The Center for Public Service was new on campus and laden with special opportunities for John to test his wings in the practicalities of various public spheres. It had a "learn by doing" philosophy like the TRI-S campus program that helped John begin to see and determine to serve the wider world.

Anderson University

Founded, 1917

Be it Known that
in recognition of distinguished attainments the Board of Trustees of Anderson University
with the commendation of the faculty has conferred upon

John S. Pistole

the honorary Degree of

Doctor of Laws

with all the rights and privileges pertaining to that degree.
Given at Anderson University in the City of Anderson and the State of Indiana
this sixth day of May, Two Thousand and Six.

President

Dean

The honorary Doctor of Laws degree was awarded to
John Pistole when he returned to his alma mater in 2006
as the celebrated Commencement speaker.

John would look back on his undergraduate education and make this judgment. "If I'd gone to some secular school and been an athletic jock on scholarship, I'd probably have continued my earlier partying and drinking, which would have been a disaster for my spiritual life and a ruining of my God-intended destiny." Anderson University had been his "back-up" choice of schools. It actually had been God's number one intention.

In the summer between John's freshman and sophomore years, he was working as a trashman in the large Warner Press facility adjacent to the campus. He regularly saw a little old building attached to where a truck was loaded with his collected trash. How could he not recall how all those broken windows in the building had gotten that way?

Years before, he and his older brother David had grown up just blocks away. They had been quite good at mock fighting with the neighbor's borrowed garbage-can lids employed as shields, and sometimes throwing stones at inviting glass targets behind Warner Press. Beyond being merely mischievous, John would develop a potentially dangerous personal habit, a teenage taste for alcohol.

Fortunately, things would change because of the car crash, especially during John's college years. He had enjoyed friendship with Mark Brewer, a great roommate in Dunn Hall for John's first two college years. Suddenly John's supervisor and father approached him one day while on his trash-collecting job. They had some awful news. Mark Brewer had just been killed in a car accident! He'd fallen asleep at the wheel. Stan Deal, another Brewer friend in Dunn Hall and basketball teammate of John, shared the shock. It "helped us all realize that we were not immortal after all."

Stan now became John's roommate, first still in Dunn Hall and then moving together to the new West Campus apartments their senior year. He was a pastor's son like John, a great guy, a star with John on the college basketball team. Coach Bates says Deal could jump clear out of the gym and "could dunk the ball every which way." He also could get in trouble by playing much too loudly the rock music that he and roommate John so loved.

After many years of maturing and being sobered by tragedies like Mark's death, and later by his own FBI investigating of human traffickers in Minneapolis and Mob bosses in New York City, John Pistole would be able to look back with greater understanding. With a twinkle in his eye, he now gratefully observes this about his own career path. "From juvenile delinquent to Deputy Director of the FBI to Administrator of the TSA to University President, God has been gracious indeed!" John, like a mother hen, now protects campus windows and lighting bills and the school's minimal endowment dollars. To whom much is given much is required.

Speaking of God's providence, there's that lovely young woman who had come to the Anderson campus from the eastern United States. Kathy Harp, a freshman at Anderson with John, soon would become an essential part of the rest of his life. That surely would be God's doing. So was a badly injured high school athlete who had lettered four straight years in both collegiate tennis and basketball, and had received Anderson University's

1978 "Outstanding Senior Athlete Award." Surprising doors had opened, with many more still to come.

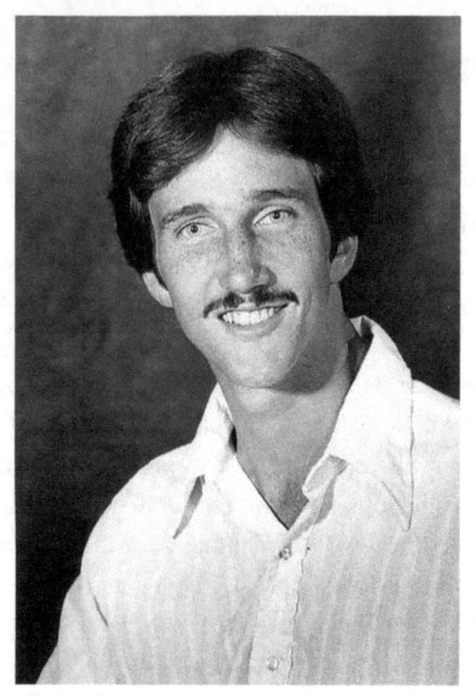

John Pistole, Anderson University undergraduate

Opening of the Anderson University Ravens 1975-76 season. Jeff Jenness (20), John Pistole (23), and Kurt Moreillon (24).

Chapter 7

LAWYER TO FIELD AGENT

You've got to go out on a limb sometimes because that's where the fruit is. —Will Rogers

It's easy in the world to live after the world's opinion; it's easy in solitude to live after your own. The great man is he who, in the midst of the crowd, keeps with perfect sweetness the independence of his own solitude. —Ralph Waldo Emerson

John Pistole, at least in Emerson's terms, was emerging as a "great man." In solitude he was becoming a man of prayer, a contemplative, a true Christian believer. In his public actions, he increasingly would be able to avoid being seduced into living after the world's opinion, even though surrounded with numerous temptations and dealing with some of the world's worst characters. That avoidance and noble ideal would be tested often, beginning right after college.

The greatness, especially in the public sphere, usually involves taking a chance. As Will Rogers puts it, "You've got to go out on a limb sometimes because that's where the fruit is." For John, leaving law practice early would be taking a calculated risk. It would be going out on a limb of apparent opportunity. He would take this risk and eventually find good fruit on the new and several extensions of the big FBI limb.

Leaving Anderson, Indiana, in 1983 at age twenty-seven definitely was a risk, a new adventure, an open door of seeming opportunity. At the same time, his brother was setting the course for his own professional future. David completed his doctorate in 1983 and, still single, accepted a tenure-track teaching position at Indiana University of Pennsylvania where he would be for his whole career.

John had a solid pre-law undergraduate preparation, a quality graduate education in the practice of law, and now some practical experience of functioning in a legal firm. With all of that, the time and chance had come for him to move on. His first professional attempt hadn't work out all that well. It was time to try again in a very different arena.

As opposed to the professional stability of brother David, a series of roles and locations were ahead for the younger John. By divine grace and the persistent obedience of God's young servant, over the years John would keep that "sweet independence" of his own solitude with his Lord. It would be the stabilizing factor in his life, private and public.

Lead-in to the Law

John's recollection of home life when he was young doesn't include hearing discussions of legal or political matters. He just knew that both his parents were "pro-life" before that was a well-known phrase. Later, he personally would be inclined in a similar direction, although "with some nuances since some exceptions are important to consider, including pregnancies resulting from incest and rape."

Hollis and Elizabeth Pistole were conservative parents. That was true religiously and politically. Apparently they were Republicans since John's sisters, Cindy and Carole, remember a bit of shock in the household when their parents realized something about Robert H. Reardon, longtime President of Anderson University. He was a Democrat![18] The parents had been openly uncomfortable with the possibility of John F. Kennedy being elected the nation's President and then likely allowing a powerful man living in far-away Rome to quietly run the United States.

The youngest Pistole son, John, wanted to get a job in the Anderson City Parks Department when he was sixteen. He was asked by the city's hiring official if he were a registered Democrat. John said he wasn't even old enough to vote. "Of course not," came the reply, "but you can still register and you must be sure it's Democrat. It's kind of a pledge of loyalty in this city." So John did.

As an adult, John would switch his registration to Republican. Over the coming years he would move from a simple job in the Anderson parks to being a longtime federal executive serving under Presidents of both political parties. He would try to function in as non-political a manner as possible.

Father Hollis was a committed pacifist. So far as John remembers, his father rarely discussed such issues at home or tried to ensure duplicate attitudes in his children. Still, Hollis certainly had strong personal convictions that weren't easily missed. Some of these are reported in his autobiography. For instance:

> I love our nation, despite its shortcomings. I lament any emphasis on its supposed role as the greatest nation on earth. I have supported limitations on political contributions, fiscal responsibility, environmental protection, gun control, and limited abortion rights for women. I hold for the common good as guided by our Lord. I puzzle about homosexuality and same-sex relationships. I belonged to *Amnesty International* and while in Maryland served on the Prisoners' Aid Association. Having once observed a government hanging in Baltimore—certainly a horrific and hardly flawless process—I since then have strongly opposed the death penalty.[19]

Since all that wasn't in print until near the end of Hollis's life in 2004, the Pistole boys would have only a vague awareness of their father's strong views. Neither David nor John would experience military service themselves, more for timing and educational pursuits than for reasons of personal conviction. John was too young to be drafted for Viet Nam. When he turned eighteen in 1974, that terrible conflict that so divided the nation finally had subsided and active military drafting was mercifully over.

So many young men John's age had vigorously opposed U. S. involvement in Viet Nam, even to the point of openly burning their draft cards. John wasn't even close to any such person. While on the nightly news he certainly saw the wrenching pictures of body bags and the latest numbers of deaths and national protests, he was quite preoccupied otherwise. The overriding truth for John as an early teenager was anything but international politics. It was his intense self-preoccupation.

John's youthful rebellion was free of anti-government political overtones. The first person he knew who had served in Viet Nam was Tim Bagwell who had come from California, married his sister Carole in 1973, and knew Kathy Harp out East before John did.

John and Tim weren't very close, with Carole and Tim divorcing after ten years of marriage "because of his bouncing from job to job, their moving from city to city, and Tim always looking for life's answers and never finding them." Later it was assumed that he suffered from Post Traumatic Stress Disorder, a burden brought home from Viet Nam.

John's political views weren't influenced by Tim or the Viet Nam war, as were so many of his contemporaries. He was too self-occupied in those years to pay much attention to the bigger world outside. That would change dramatically in later years when he would both be aware of and an active influencer of many such affairs.

The idea of being a lawyer likely had first been planted in John's head by his mother. It was sometime during high school when many of John's actions were, let's say, outside the prevailing family and church standards. Mother Elizabeth once had a frank "greening" conversation with son John, trying to point him forward, hoping for good out of some things clearly less so at the time.

"Son, you are so good at arguing that maybe you should be a lawyer." That stuck in John's head and key elements of his coming college experience would be deliberately directed that way. The reasoning was simple enough. If good at it, why not pursue it as a way to make a living?

Elizabeth's constant honesty with her students at the high school would be tested when her son John later would become professionally involved with the FBI. One day an FBI agent would come to the Pistole home to interview the candidate's parents as part of his initial security check. Jan Callen remembers Elizabeth later sharing this with a women's group at Anderson University. She admitted to them having been quite nervous at that interview. She had hoped not to "mess things up for John." One only-half-serious question came from these university women.

"Elizabeth, were you or Hollis harboring some big secret about John?"

"No," she responded, "not that I know of, but if we had been, I'd probably have blurted it right out!"

Eventually John would be granted a Top Secret/Sensitive Compartmented Information clearance, and eventually oversee the granting of clearances to others. But first, how did the FBI ever appear on John's radar in the first place? There first would be several years of graduate study and legal practice.

It's McKinney for Me

Graduation from Anderson University was fast approaching in 1978 for both John and Kathy Harp. What next? She would go back East where her family lived and find a job in an insurance office. He would be off to law school in Indianapolis. But what of them as a couple together? They stayed in touch by phone and kept processing that critical question.

Even though there was some friction times, Kathy had come to think of John as a man with "an incredibly compassionate heart" who was unusually wise without ever being arrogant about it. Not a "typical romantic," she admits, "he never did propose marriage, not as such. They simply talked things through, mostly from a distance, and decided over time that their futures should merge. They could and should make things work. Being mutual encouragers, they determined that they would be better together than apart, whatever the coming challenges—which would be considerable.

John spent his first year out of college as a graduate student at Indiana University's School of Law in Indianapolis, later named the McKinney School of Law, the largest law school in Indiana and a place where other Anderson University graduates had and would attend. At first he lived in a near Eastside Indianapolis duplex with his college friend and basketball teammate Stan Deal who was beginning an accounting and sales career in the city.

Meanwhile, another 1978 graduate of Anderson University, Patricia Seasor (Bailey), was also a new student at the I. U. School of Law. Neither she nor John could possibly have imagined in late 1970s that in the second decade of the following century John would be the President and she the Chair of the Board of Trustees of their beloved Anderson alma mater. That was completely unthinkable.

On the 28th of July, 1979, John and Kathy were married at the National Memorial Church of God in Washington, D. C. Their two fathers co-officiated, with John's brother David the best man and the groomsmen two college friends and Kathy's brother, Stuart Harp. Friend Jeff Jenness would marry the following month and Stan Deal one month after that.

John and Kathy were both independent-minded and gifted young adults. She admits that their marriage has always been "a work in progress," but progress consistently in the right direction. As most couples need to do, "we've learned to adjust and make things work." Kathy kept the Harp name, not adding "Pistole" to hers, something unusual in the 1970s but a personal preference of hers. Her family name was central to her identity and she wasn't prepared to give it up. John was accepting of this. It was part of his making things work for them. That left these two a bit separate in names while increasingly very much together in love and life.

Kathy returned to Anderson, Indiana, to be with John who soon moved back to Anderson to be a law clerk while continuing his graduate education. She served for three years as the university's Assistant Director of Admissions. Meanwhile, for the first two years of marriage John was heavily absorbed in his studies to be a lawyer at the Indianapolis school that one day would honor him with an Outstanding Alumni Award. Kathy was the main breadwinner. Various matters pressed on the new couple, making their first years of marriage "rocky" enough that they had fleeting thoughts of maybe having made a mistake. These hesitations were only temporary. Big life decisions lay just ahead.

One pressure on their home was limited dollars. Another was having to be apart much of the time. Still another was the path to parenthood that wouldn't be problem free. They would wait a few years to have children, and the first would miscarry. That would bring a pain hard to describe. But they would manage to move on, later having two beloved daughters, Lauren to be born in New Jersey 1990 and Jennifer in Maryland in 1992.

These births would be back East in Kathy's home territory, but that's jumping ahead of the story. John's particular career path was completing law school and then practicing law in his hometown of Anderson. That would be short-lived. In only two years it would lead him to an unexpected destination, the Federal Bureau of Investigation.

John and Kathy's wedding.

John's parents, Hollis
and Elizabeth Pistole

Kathy's parents, Clella
and H. Richard Harp

Struggling as a Lawyer

Beginning in his college years, John Pistole had gravitated toward the law as a profession rather than the family standard of education. He would deal one day with Mob bosses in New York City and networks of terrorists around the world, but that was hardly where his motivation or life work started. In fact, after his excellent education at Anderson University, he went on to graduate with his Doctor of Jurisprudence from Indiana University's School of Law in Indianapolis. At first he had in mind several of the routines of legal practice, especially tax and estate planning, but also tort and liability issues, but not criminal law. His vision was more local than national.

John would begin as a lawyer in his hometown of Anderson but practice for a mere two years. He handled relatively few court cases. None involved big-city mob bosses nor were any particularly satisfying experiences. He wasn't challenged by what he found himself doing most of the time. John was a new lawyer in the small firm of Teague, Cole, and Hamer, and for a short time himself a junior partner. All the firm's principals had Anderson University connections. These were the very difficult economic times in the early 1980s. Anderson, Indiana, was suffering an unemployment rate above twenty percent, one of the highest in the nation.

There came across John's desk a constant flow of wills to be written and divorces to be executed, all with their seemingly unending legal paperwork. There was no shortage of clients for the legal firm, but so many clients failed to pay their legal fees on time, if at all. One of John's first clients was a woman who soon declared bankruptcy. She had written John a check, but it bounced. This and other such circumstances caused John to begin pondering a question.

"Why am I in this kind of practice?" The bills at home were coming regularly, but not the needed income or personal fulfillment. Further, John was watching some colleagues in the firm come and go. Two left for real estate adventures in Colorado, one later winding up in jail. Another young colleague, Bob Coffman, quickly tired of spending all day "dealing with negative energy." Most clients were coming for legal help because something bad had happened.

Bob just wasn't wired to continue in such a setting and went back to work for many years of satisfying service to Anderson University, his beloved alma mater and that of John. With at least a bit of nostalgia and even curiosity, John watched Bob's moving on. "Maybe," John began to think, "I'm making a mistake staying here. Is there an alternative for me out there somewhere?"

John had married Kathy after his first year of graduate school and began commuting from Anderson to McKinney in Indianapolis. They lived in a home rented from John's parents, then in an apartment, and finally in a purchased home. Meanwhile, after his initial experiences of legal practice and the related financial strain, John began reaching the limit of his patience. On what limb should he climb out to find the needed fruit?

The reasons for reaching out were multiple. He was disturbed by the undependable finances, the nature of much of the work, and even the ethics of a partner or two who soon would leave the practice of law altogether. Kathy hoped for an eventual location other than a small Mid-West city, preferably back East where her family was located. John also began to realize that what he was doing was not easily transportable. Legal practice is based on a developed local clientele. So, wasn't there some better alternative, perhaps something in the Washington, D. C. area?

The young couple could dream but at this point hardly imagine that what actually did lay ahead for them would involve more than three decades of federal service, a significant portion in the Washington area, and then, of all things, an eventual move back to Anderson, Indiana. Life certainly would come to have its odd twists and turns. God would be depended on to guide through them all.

It would take John's sister Cindy nearly a quarter of a century to decide that it was time for her to retire from her professorship at Anderson University. She loved her work, getting to sit daily in her lovely Decker Hall office gazing out at the stately steeple of Park Place Church. By 2011, however, she had tired of grading all those papers. In fact, that same year John's other sister, Carole, also would retire from a satisfying career of teaching. For her it was in the Anderson public schools. Brother David would enjoy many years in one Pennsylvania university before his retirement.

Readiness for a professional change came rather quickly in John's career and, as of now, his retirement still lies somewhere in the future. He began exploring possibilities of change and learned of two individuals active in the FBI who were willing to talk to him casually about that work arena. One was a brother of Tom Hamer, legal colleague of John in Anderson, and the other a friend of his sister Cindy and her husband Carl who then were located in a small town in the vicinity of Fort Wayne, Indiana. Contacts with these two FBI men were encouraging. The FBI's main role at the time was investigation of crime. It was looking for young persons with quality training in the law and skills in accounting.

That was John. He was well-trained in the law, had some practical legal experience, and was still young. If he wanted a change with some exciting possibilities and a regular paycheck, even if modest, the FBI appeared to be well worth a look. So he decided to proceed and soon applied. He envisioned a better future, more variety, increased excitement, even adventure, and with the comfort of more stable support of the routine financial needs of Kathy and himself.

John's legal colleague Tom Hamer recalls John coming into the firm one day and announcing his coming departure. Tom now admits that he thought to himself, just a bit selfishly, "Good for you, John, and now maybe there will be enough money coming in at least for me!" For John, the looming new work would be far less routine in nature and much farther away from home. Little else was known at first.

Merely *Hakuna Matata*?

In John's more romantic and somewhat naïve moments, he now was being tempted to envision a more fulfilling career in the Federal Bureau of Investigation. Hopefully it would be something like that famous Swahili song of the animals in Disney's *The Lion King*.

> Hakuna Matata! What a wonderful phrase,
> Hakuna Matata! Ain't no passing craze.
> It means no worries for the rest of our days.
> It's our problem-free philosophy,
> Hakuna Matata!

The FBI recruiter had encouraged him, painting a rosy picture of the possibilities. All would be well, at least John hoped.

It appeared that John had everything it would take to make a fine FBI field agent, and it was time to act. Having been assured he would report to Quantico in 30 days, John and Kathy put their home in Anderson, Indiana, on the market, and it sold in one day! That surely was a sign of better things to come, *Hakuna Matata*! Then the sky surprisingly darkened. John learned that there was a snag that threatened to keep him out of the FBI altogether.

With the home sold, John's application was turned down because the examining doctor hadn't checked the box saying that he was capable of strenuous physical activity. John countered that, yes, he had experienced a serious car accident in high school, as he had detailed in his employment application months before, but since then he'd functioned well as a college athlete in basketball and tennis. A second application chance and physical exam were granted and got that required box checked.

Now, presumably cleared to train as a new FBI agent, another unexpected problem surfaced. It was noticed this time by some FBI admissions operative that Clella Harp, the mother of John's wife Kathy, had been born in the 1930s to a Bill and Vada Fleenor when they were in Egypt. This obscure fact was judged by someone at FBI Headquarters to be a possible security concern. Wouldn't that Egyptian connection, distant as it was, make the whole family somehow a potential threat to the current security of the United States?

John countered again. He admits that this was his first private thought when forced to explain why Clella was born in Egypt—a thought reflecting the kid still in him. "Why had Clella been born in Egypt? Because she preferred to be close to her mother when she was born!" Fortunately, he thought but never said that out loud. Instead, he explained to the recruiter that Kathy's grandparents had been U. S. citizens serving as Christian missionaries when their daughter Clella, Kathy's mother, had been born. There had been no relationship with the politics of Egypt back then, and certainly none at the time of John's application for employment.

This explanation was noted, the bureaucracy churned again, and the paperwork cleared once more. How fortunate that the recruiter hadn't come into possession of a secret video of John as a rock music fan "performing" in Dunn Hall on the Anderson campus. It might have captured him gyrating wildly, with a tennis racket substituting for an electric guitar, and singing at the top of his voice Ted Nugent's song "Dog Eat Dog." That might be followed by an outburst of John's skilled renditions of Curly, one of the Three Stooges comedy team. If that had appeared, likely the box "Emotional Stability" wouldn't have gotten checked.

John much later would report the lesson he had learned through the pains of this application process. "Be patient but be persistent!" That lesson would be needed almost immediately. John finally was approved and soon on his way to his initial FBI training. His "Entry on Duty" date was September 18, 1983. In Indianapolis he was sworn in as a new FBI Special Agent, flown to Washington, and bussed to the FBI Academy in Quantico, Virginia.

During his training, Kathy at first stayed with relatives in Indianapolis. Lou Gerig is a cousin of hers who had worked in public relations support of Indiana's beloved Senator Richard Lugar and then in the White House in support of President Ronald Reagan.

Once at Quantico, it wouldn't take John long to appreciate the judgment of boxing champion Muhammad Ali—"I hated every minute of training, but I said, 'Don't quit. Suffer now and live the rest of your life as a champion'." Actually, John didn't hate every minute of his training, not at all. He thoroughly enjoyed his time at Quantico overall. However, there certainly were negatives. John was determined to survive them, be patient and persist as necessary, and keep moving on.

His first days in Quantico caused him to almost wish he could be back in Indiana or elsewhere practicing law again, even with its challenges. He had temporarily abandoned for sixteen weeks the pleasure of living with Kathy in exchange for rooming with an alcoholic ex-cop from Chicago in a setting that struck him initially as "animal house!" His roommate threw up in their room the first night after an alcoholic binge. No matter. John would survive, no, actually excel in both the academic and physical dimensions of the training.

One positive was another trainee in the room next to John. Christopher Favo was a Notre Dame graduate, a well-conditioned athlete soon to be John's good friend. John recalls all this with gratitude, saying, "Praise God, no problem with the physical fitness aspects of Quantico. I maxed out the physical tests, one of only three in the class to do so, Chris being another. I wanted to prove myself to that FBI recruiter back home. My awful neck injury was truly healed." John indeed would be an FBI man, one finally ready to live the rest of his life as a champion of justice. One of the training days, however, was quite the beginning. Here's Chris's memory.

The day was set aside for a practical exercise in FBI investigation. It was announced that the bank had been robbed at Hogan's Alley, the mock-up town at Quantico. The recruits must identify and catch the culprits. They were divided into teams. A good thing was that John and Chris would be together. A bad thing was that their team leader was a guy nicknamed "Zeus" since he acted like he was the god of gods, and for some reason didn't happen to like John. John, Chris, and another trainee were assigned by Zeus to spend the morning on command-post security, likely a meaningless and boring task with all the interesting action elsewhere. It had snowed and the three on dead-end duty were to march silently back and forth in the snow all morning, sadly away from the real action of the recruits who likely would capture the bad guys and get the glory.

Frustration grew. Suddenly, Chris was hit in the back of the head with a snowball! John had nailed him although, when Chris whirled around, he was gazing innocently at the sky. An all-out rain of snowballs followed. They were spotted and punished after a lunch that Zeus cut short just for them. He relocated the trio for the afternoon to an even poorer task, waiting things out by securing an old bungalow on the edge of the sprawling grounds where a forest began and a dirt road led off the property to a dead-end in some clay hills just out of sight. No robbers would ever flee to that hopeless location. So, after putting some logs across the dirt road just around a bend, the bored three were sunning themselves on a little hilltop. Then it all happened!

The pretend robbers had been hiding in the bungalow of all places and decided to escape down the dirt road, a plan causing the recruits to fail in their task and learn to plan better for the unexpected in the future. As it turned out, the robbers were two exercise leaders and a top official of the FBI. The trio accidentally positioned by Zeus in the obscurity of a supposed nowhere were alerted that the robbers were coming right at them. Their car came around the curve in the dirt road and lodged awkwardly in the logs. It was the personal car of the FBI official. Two men jumped out and ran, with John's two colleagues after them, hollering, "John, you get the boss man!" John was left to deal alone with the prominent FBI "robber" official, facing the music since the man likely was surprised, embarrassed, and angry about his damaged car.

No matter. John successfully "arrested" the lead robber as he should. It wasn't the best of days for the training planners or for Zeus. It was the accidental success of John's first investigative assignment as an FBI man. Chris now recounts this dramatic training incident to show that over the coming years John sometimes would face other unfair and even dangerous circumstances. Reports Favo, "John consistently would do the right thing regardless, and not get discouraged in the process, whatever the outcome."

Who could have imagined that one day John, the successful dirt-road recruit, would be at FBI headquarters in Washington as second in command of the entire Bureau? Certainly not John or even his admirer friend Chris. Despite Zeus, John had begun crawling out on the right limb of a fruitful future. There is a "god" higher even than Zeus and a fruitful tree only divinely made.

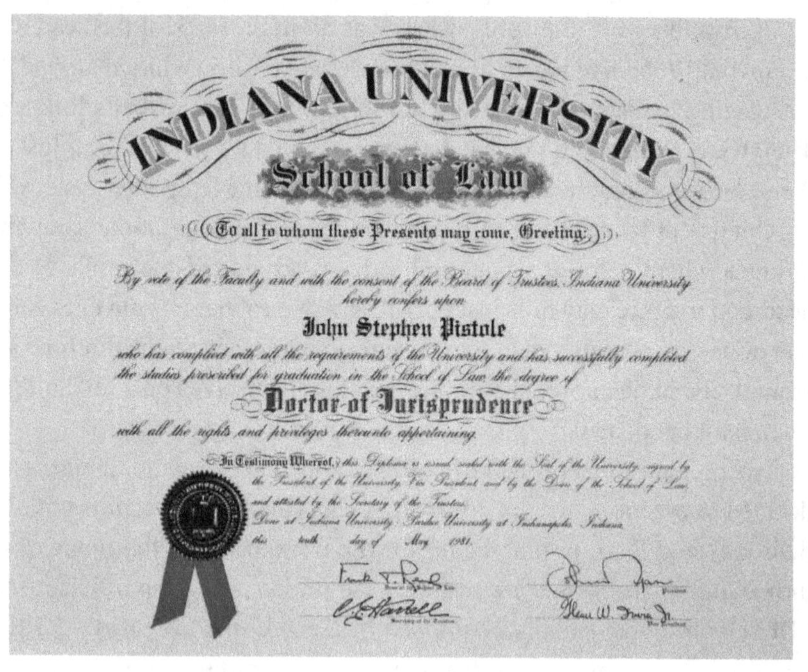

INDIANA UNIVERSITY
School of Law
To all to whom these Presents may come, Greeting:
By vote of the Faculty and with the consent of the Board of Trustees, Indiana University
hereby confers upon
John Stephen Pistole
who has complied with all the requirements of the University and has successfully completed
the studies prescribed for graduation in the School of Law the degree of
Doctor of Jurisprudence
with all the rights and privileges thereunto appertaining.
In Testimony Whereof, this Diploma is issued, sealed with the Seal of the University, signed by
the President of the University, Vice President and by the Dean of the School of Law,
and attested by the Secretary of the Trustees.
Done at Indiana University - Purdue University at Indianapolis, Indiana
this tenth day of May 1981.

The Degree, Dr. of Jurisprudence, 1981.

Chapter 8

LOCAL STREETS TO NATIONAL HEADQUARTERS

God has shown you, O mortal, what is good. And what does the Lord require of you? To act justly and to love mercy and to walk humbly with your God. (Micah 6:8)

All the things I once thought were so important are gone from my life. Compared to the high privilege of knowing Christ Jesus as my Master, firsthand, everything I once thought I had going for me is insignificant. I've dumped it all so that I could embrace Christ and be embraced by him. (Philippians 3:8)

John Pistole, a new FBI agent, and his wife Kathy Harp, soon to be a teacher of the hearing impaired, both had heard and were heeding Micah's report of God's requirements. This Old Testament prophet made clear what is required of God's faithful. John and Kathy would seek throughout their coming lives to be faithful to this divine requirement. The high goal is to implement justice with mercy and do it in an attitude of humility before the One who finally is the Judge of all.

There are multiple facets to the public service of John Pistole on behalf of justice. Only a collection of highlights is possible in a single-volume biography. Part of the impossibility of comprehensive recounting more goes beyond sheer volume. National security concerns still keep some things in the shadows away from public view. Justice is a complex, delicate, and often secretive business.

Occasionally, while conducting the many interviews for this biography, John and I would tease that, if he told me more, he'd have to kill me! Of course, our long friendship, his gentle nature, and his training on how to be a guarded witness under congressional pressure combined to avoid the possibility of such an outrageous outcome for the biographer. On a rare occasion he would say, "I could go into that a little more deeply if you'll turn off the recorder." To which I always replied, "No thanks. That which I can't report I don't want to know."[20]

What has become known is considerable and will suffice. Since John is sharp in memory, unusually open, frank, and vulnerable, much that is allowable for public knowledge has come to light. The resulting story will be presented in several parts. The first will cover in chronological sequence the several phases of John's FBI domestic career. Then will come the numerous phases of that career from an international perspective.

That wrap-up of the FBI years will be followed by the nearly five TSA years, a domestic behind the scenes glance, and then a look at John's new world of Anderson University. The final two chapters draw numerous loose ends together and move toward life's concluding issues.

Career Path and Sample Events

John Pistole would serve a total of two years as a practicing lawyer, nearly twenty-seven years with the FBI, four and one-half years as head of the Transportation Security Administration, and six years to date as President of Anderson University. We begin with the domestic portion of the FBI years.

Minneapolis

John's initial FBI assignment was as a field agent in Minneapolis, Minnesota, beginning in January, 1984. He and Kathy encountered there three cold winters and life among "the frozen chosen." In this cold but culturally rich environment along the upper Mississippi River, Kathy would pursue her graduate education while John's investigative emphasis was on human trafficking, drug trafficking, and public corruption.

He was on the streets for the first time as a man with a badge and gun, learning what it means to be an agent and how things get done in the FBI. He learned that much is based on one's reputation, so "I worked hard, tried to excel, and it finally helped me get a transfer to a plumb assignment elsewhere (New York City)."

Some of the learning, unfortunately, wasn't pleasant. John found himself forced to grow spiritually. There was plenty of opportunity, he reports, to "break bad." He saw several agents making very poor personal choices. He had to ask himself seriously, "What am I going to do with this new profession of mine?" He determined to stay clean and excel, learning that the keys to the future are a quality reputation and who you know.

Good fortune smiled on John in the persons of two outstanding individuals, Dag Sohlberg and Sue Rose. Dag was John's supervisor, and a really good one who came to respect and encourage John. Sue was Kathy's faculty advisor at the University of Minnesota who hired her as a graduate assistant, helping greatly with the cost of the masters degree. Sue eventually would give Kathy a great and well-deserved reference when John would be reassigned from Minneapolis to his second position in New York City.

John worked on a range of cases in Minneapolis related to problem groups, including the Hells Angels motorcycle club often accused of violent acts. One case involved a young woman who claimed that she had been forced to star in a porn movie then playing in a local theater. John's supervisor asked him to attend the theater, view the movie, and report if her claim was accurate. Here was an awkward test case of building a good reputation while also staying true to his own values.

Chosen by John was the road less traveled. He hesitated at this request and did what few new agents would do, ask respectfully to be relieved of an assignment for personal reasons. The private reason was that viewing such a movie was morally reprehensible to him. Fortunately, the supervisor appreciated his concern, wouldn't hold it against him, and said he'd have no problem getting volunteers for the assignment.

There existed in Minneapolis at the time a world of prostitution and great need for compassionate ministry. By police estimates, some 1,500 prostitutes were active in the Twin Cities, with many eighteen or younger. It was the Mid-West's largest recruiting and training ground for this ancient "profession." John's inaugural work would include investigations of this dark world of human trafficking.

On one key occasion in January, 1986, John located and had compassion on a 13-year-old girl, already a hardened prostitute. Despite his tall and imposing stature, and dressed in a neat suit with his FBI badge visible and his firearm close at hand, John gently gained her trust. She became willing to tell her story of abuse, first at home and now at the hands of heartless pimps. She dared to testify in court, resulting in her pimps confessing guilt and being convicted without trial.

Such a heartwarming story, such Christian "ministry," would have no satisfying ending, as so often is true in this imperfect world. Shortly after this incident, John would be transferred to New York City for his second assignment and never know what happened to this young teenager. "I hope I had helped change her life, but in fact I never knew if she went back to the streets. At least she was gotten out of the business for a short time and maybe had a choice about the future."

The frightening possibility is that later she might have been transported to "work" on the stretch of New York's Eighth Avenue near Times Square nicknamed "the Minnesota strip." Many of the "successful" prostitutes from Minneapolis eventually were brought there because the money was better. This young and much-abused teenager may have been in the Big Apple at the same time as John, with ministry still needed and justice never fully served. Child advocates sometimes label teen prostitution the twenty-first century's "slavery." John came to know it quite well.

Agent Pistole would get some "ministry" satisfaction years later in 2008. Then, serving not as a young field agent but as the FBI's Deputy Director, he would oversee the completion of "Operation Cross Country II" involving twenty-nine cities and featuring the arrest of seventy-three pimps. He would counter human trafficking and other forms of public corruption as he was able over the years, and consciously do so as a representative of the FBI, then the TSA and, he would add, always a servant of the kingdom of God.

New York City

John's second assignment was as an FBI field agent in New York City, 1986-1990. He was helped by the advance good word of his Minneapolis FBI supervisor. Dag Sohlberg had contacted a friend in the NY front office, saying, "Pistole's a good guy. Get him on a good squad." John and Kathy soon moved to the new assignment where he was assigned to a Joint Organized Crime Task Force composed of FBI agents and members of the New York Police Department. Its focus was investigating and prosecuting select leaders of La Cosa Nostra, the Italian Mafia.

The change of culture involved with this move was dramatic. John again would have to try to figure out the ropes of how things worked in this very new setting. There were over 1,000 FBI agents in New York, with nine different squads working on organized crime. It was a "target-rich" setting that would prove very fulfilling professionally for the young agent Pistole. But there were personal challenges right from the beginning, quite apart from the long daily commute to work each way, an hour "on a good day."

John and Kathy located in a little home in Plainfield, New Jersey, causing the long daily commute into Manhattan. That's the best they could do financially. They were satisfied with what was possible. Soon John met other agents living in Plainfield. One proceeded to do him a "favor," showing him how to fill out a fraudulent expense form. "Everybody does it and we'll look bad if you don't too." John refused and said to himself, "This is the FBI? I thought we were the good guys!"

The same financial strain was being felt deeply by Earl Pitts. He and John both had joined the FBI in 1983, sometimes sat next to each other for the sixteen-week training at Quantico, and now both had come to New York under similar circumstances. However, John absorbed and managed the strain while Earl did not. Both were from families of modest means, Earl from a farm family in Missouri and John from an educator family in Indiana. They had been transferred from their first FBI assignments into the same high-cost-of-living situation. Their low salaries matched closely. John recalls the annual figure as $28,000, with no raise from Minneapolis.

John stayed straight, making do; Earl did not. He became frustrated and then inwardly angry about the painful budget demands. He was humiliated when having to seek a loan from his father. Earl soon discovered a way to get out of the money jam—self-recruit as a spy for the Russian KGB, gaining over $200,000 across seven years. While John went on to flourish in the FBI work in New York, Earl eventually got caught in a sting and was sentenced to twenty-seven years in prison, only the second agent to be convicted of Cold-War espionage. Earl and John now would be sitting in very different places.

Quite the contrast from Earl and some others, John continued working hard, attempting to excel as he had done in Minneapolis. His good friend from Quantico training, Chris Favo, was now also in New York, working hard and doing well. Not so everyone in John's immediate squad. A few agents were observed just putting in their time and waiting for a transfer. Sharp supervisors soon sorted out who was who.

John's very first move was on the positive side of things. Not even moved into their little home yet, his supervisor called, desperate for someone to help with the surveillance of a Russian mob guy. Other agents were already committed. John, in the area hardly a week, said he was willing and available to do whatever was needed and whenever. After all, he had done some of that kind of surveillance work in Minneapolis and was anxious to build a reputation of being willing to be available and always doing good work. Fortunately for John, in this instance he was able to gather some valuable evidence in this mob case and, in the process, make a very good impression as a newcomer with a future. These years in New York would be very stretching and fulfilling for agent Pistole.

Toward the end of the four-year assignment in New York, John and Kathy would have Lauren, their first child. It was just before a very public incident in John's FBI work. Usually his assignment involved investigations of lieutenants in organized crime. Some agents were undercover. John was active more above cover in conducting interviews and wire-tapping, work he found satisfying, even fascinating. He was involved over two years in successful investigations leading to the convictions of several members of the Colombo mob family.[21]

John's assignment focus then switched to the Genovese family. On one occasion the result of an investigation suddenly demanded newspaper headlines nationwide. FBI agents other than John had completed an extensive investigation of suspected labor racketeering by a prominent mob boss, Vincent "The Chin" Gigante, who turned out to be the top boss of the powerful Genovese family. Vincent's odd nickname came from having once been a boxer able to take a good punch.

More recently, however, Vincent had come to fear an FBI punch tougher than his chin could absorb. Wanting to build an insanity defense in advance of any coming arrest, for years he had been checking himself annually into a mental hospital for a brief stay. If he thought he was being followed, he would wear a purple bathrobe and wander New York streets babbling incoherently. A favorite spot was just south of New York University where there were many college students and tourists.

When an inditement finally was at hand, the dramatic moment came. John Pistole led the arrest team since Gigante had been spending much time with his mother in John's area of New York. After the dramatic arrest, John spent hours with Vincent getting fingerprints, photos, and statements. He began wondering if "The Chin" really were a mentally sick man, although he recalled surveillance that had watched Vincent and a girlfriend counting huge piles of cash, filling in a detailed ledger, and appearing quite sane, if very criminal, in the doing. Given the personal uncertainty, John was glad he didn't have testify in the following trial.

While with John, Vincent asked permission to call his brother, a priest in the Bronx, who proceeded to rail at the agents for daring to arrest such a sick man. John recalls this man of the cloth using "colorful language" that he didn't recall being in the Bible! Stories of this arrest soon appeared in *Newsweek* and other major magazines. One referred to Vincent as the

"Oddfather" instead of a Godfather. *The New York Times* called him "the last great Mafioso of the century." In 2003 Vincent's son Andrew was convicted of racketeering and extortion, the same year his father finally admitted that his long insanity claim was a ruse. Vincent then died in a Missouri federal prison in 2007 at age 77.[22]

On the dramatic day of the big arrest, did John finally go home and tell Kathy all about this national drama that he had led at the last stage? No, she actually learned about it days later from all the newspaper reports. He did come home that day, exhausted, as often he did, sharing little about the details of his day's work. Some things couldn't be shared for security reasons, some weren't shared to avoid her unnecessarily worrying, and the energy sometimes just wasn't there for sleep-deprive parents with a colicky infant now in the home.

John Pistole on the left, the dramatic arrest of the "Oddfather"

Washington

John's third FBI assignment was based in the Bureau's headquarters in the nation's capital. From 1990 until 1994 he was assigned to the organized crime section. It was here first that he became involved in organized crime investigations internationally. John encountered and resisted a "siloed approach" to information sharing between the FBI and select intelligence agencies worldwide. Organized crime is international and must be encountered as such. The increasingly large international dimension of agent Pistole's constantly expanding work is summarized in chapter nine.

John was given new responsibilities and increased pay, gaining a leadership role beyond that of a street agent. He had become a "case agent" and managed to put together several solid criminal cases for prosecution. Using his legal background to good advantage, John demonstrated that he could prepare quality wire-tap legal documents. This built his reputation as a competent man who gets things done. This growing reputation was key in bringing him to FBI headquarters. So was the desire to be closer to Kathy's parents, especially now that there was a young daughter who needed more regular contact with grandparents.

While located in FBI headquarters in Washington working in the organized crime section, John journeyed occasionally to the FBI Academy at Quantico, Virginia, to teach a ten-hour block on organized crime, domestic and international, for classes of new agents. His previous work in New York had involved considerable learning about the Italian Mafia and his current work in Washington was increasing his awareness of the crime syndicates in Asia, the Middle East, and elsewhere. Such experience and knowledge qualified him to be an ideal instructor. His educator parents were proud, and also hoped for more family contact.

Indianapolis

John's fourth FBI assignment was back in his home state of Indiana with the focus of responsibility shifting to the newly evolving problem of cyber-crimes. These Indiana years, 1994-1999, were pleasant for the Pistole family and enriching for its coming future. From the beginning, the assignment in Washington had been understood as short-term, a career development move. Eventually John necessarily would move on, and he really had wanted to return to New York City, scene of many positive experiences. He had waited for an opening there, but it hadn't come.

Finally thinking that more time in New York apparently wasn't in God's plan for him, John had become open to a supervisor's position in the FBI structure. One of these had opened in Indianapolis. Even though it would focus on white-collar crime, something he had little experience with, John judged that such diversification of roles would be good for his long-term career. He was right, and Indiana it would be.

In addition to this professional thinking, there also was the family front to consider. John and Kathy now had two daughters, Lauren and Jennifer, and an Indianapolis location would bring the family into close touch with the Pistole grandparents and two aunts in nearby Anderson. As John gratefully puts this, "two moves at government expense to be close to grandparents!"

In general, the Indianapolis work was not as demanding as John had experienced previously. This allowed for more significant family time and soon deep involvement with St. Marks United Methodist Church in Carmel. Kathy and John went through an extensive discipleship series there, first as students and then leaders. The saying is, "happy wife, happy life." Kathy in particular came to love this congregation, their new friends, and actually the whole central Indiana scene.

John wasn't far behind. He had at least one assignment in his hometown of Anderson. There were allegations of corruption and voter fraud in Madison County and John had occasion to converse with local judge Dennis Carroll about this. Dennis had been a college student with John's sister Cindy and had first taken the bench when John was a practicing lawyer in Anderson. They worked well together. Much later, Dennis would be vice-chair of the Anderson University Board of Trustees when John would be called to the school's presidency in 2014. But much of John's life story would have to transpire before that would be the unexpected reality.

The Indianapolis supervisory role was enjoyed by John for the most part. One challenging task was guiding and motivating other FBI agents. He had to deal with two agents who "had checked out and were retired in place." One he demoted, stimulating a retirement, and the other he successfully redeployed and newly motivated. John, in his mid-thirties, was having to deal with the issues of "old-timers."

One related frustration bothered John. It was the relative hesitation of local officials to go ahead with some prosecutions for which John's agents had prepared excellent cases. Back in New York there had been numerous prosecutors anxious to take cases and launch their careers. But the attitude on the U. S. Attorney's office in Indianapolis was a little different, more cautious. More satisfying for John were the occasional international experiences now coming his way—detailed below.

So far as the FBI was concerned, there was no time-limit expectation for the Indianapolis assignment, but there would be if John moved elsewhere and to the next level of career development. Further, that next level would mean that John likely would be moved here and there over the coming years as the Bureau chose for him. Kathy, happily settled, wondered when they could stop moving and stay in a good place for the family, like central Indiana.

John was conflicted. He wanted to move up the FBI career ladder, but became willing to make that professional sacrifice for the family's sake. Then Kathy had a change of mind after a serious talk with their pastor's wife. She would be open to whatever was best for John long-term.[23] So, he began looking for a good next career step, making several applications, one successful. It would bring future family moves and some dramatic changes to John's range and level of professional responsibilities.

Boston

John's fifth assignment, 1999-2002, would be based in the Boston area but extend throughout much of New England and then across the whole nation. He now was ASAC, Assistant Special in Charge, one of three in the large Boston field office. Likely this would be, at most, a three-year assignment and then probably he would go back to the Washington FBI headquarters. Initially John was placed in charge of supervising white collar, civil rights, and cyber-crime investigations in the New England area.

John would move forward quickly in this new setting. By the summer of 2001 he would be promoted to the level of "Senior Executive Service," one of fewer than three hundred among the 35,000 or so agents in the FBI. With the SES status came the role of "Inspector," which meant a move into the highest tier of pay and benefits. While now John could have relocated to headquarters in Washington, he elected to remain in their home in the Boston area. That was best for the family and, as an Inspector of field offices, he could travel the nation from the Boston base.

On the negative side, the circumstance couldn't have been much worse when John had first arrived at his Boston assignment in 1999. He encountered a large FBI staff in serious disarray. To be frank, there had been outright corruption. He found himself with, as he puts it, "the opportunity to set a different tone." One part of the problem was most prominent.

The Irish mob boss James "Whitey" Bulger had been under investigation for racketeering, murders, and more. When finally about to be apprehended, he had fled successfully for a time, having been tipped off by John Conolly, an FBI agent. Both eventually would be convicted, with Bulger's defense team insisting that the FBI was infected with widespread corruption and should be held accountable equally. This claim, unfortunately, had some merit.

John had begun with the Boston office reeling with all this turmoil, and soon it would be rocked even more. When the September 11, 2001, terrorist attacks happened, killing about 3,000 Americans and causing at least $10 billion in infrastructure and property damage, it was learned that some of the hijackers had flown undetected from Boston's Logan Airport. By then John was active in office inspections around the country, but in this national emergency he was switched to a heavy emphasis on investigations of counter-terrorism.

For about ninety days, John now joined with others in serving for long shifts going around the clock. This disastrous terrorist attack had created the greatest time of crisis in the entire history of the FBI. Terrorism was now much more than an annoying reality in distant lands. America's homeland was under attack!

FBI Director Robert Mueller briefed President George W. Bush, assuring him that those responsible for this horrific attack would be found and prosecuted to the full extent of the law. The President is reported to have responded, "Fine, but I care more that you guys see to it that it doesn't happen again!" Counter-terrorism now must be a very high priority, and John Pistole was thrust into a leading role of such urgent efforts.

There actually were two fronts of dramatic pressure now on the FBI. First was the tremendous push to stop another 9/11 terrorist attack, forcing an entire shift of the Bureau's past way of working. The shift was from a reactive body, investigating a crime after the fact, to a proactive one, preventing the crime from happening in the first place. John Pistole now was a major player in this huge new anti-terrorism effort. It was widely assumed that another horrendous attack surely was coming. Every meeting was tense and every one of the thousands of leads that kept filtering in had to be pursued around the clock.

This extraordinary pressure was compounded by "a wall." According to the Attorney General, "The single greatest structural cause for September 11 was the wall that segregated criminal investigators and intelligence agents. Government erected this wall. Government buttressed this wall. And before September 11, government was blinded by this wall."[24] There was a push by many to split the Bureau into two independent bodies, one domestic and one international, like the pattern in the United Kingdom. Since the intelligence community had failed to anticipate and stop 9/11, shouldn't it be reorganized to function more effectively in the equally dangerous future?

As the FBI's Deputy Director beginning in 2004, John Pistole would oppose this move to divide that was being pushed especially by some Congressional leaders. He saw it as a threat to the integrity of the FBI and its crucial work. Director Robert Mueller, to whom John would report as Deputy Director, fully agreed, as did Deputy Attorney General Paul McNulty. Eliza Manningham-Buller from the United Kingdom came to Washington more than once to testify on the matter, urging no break-up of the FBI.

The perspective of Robert, John, Paul, and others prevailed. The FBI was most effective when all its functions are under one roof, being coordinated as closely as possible. John received a humorous note from Eliza Manningham-Buller announcing a key lesson of how governments tend to work in times of crisis. If not sure what else to do, *reorganize*! She included a quote to that effect, noting that its source was a government leader from over two thousand years ago. Some things never change!

What was now changing fast was the level of John Pistole's responsibilities. The best of leadership was needed by the FBI, and quickly. John's work ethic, integrity, and wide experience in the Bureau were well known. They were really needed now.

Washington

John's final FBI assignment was back at FBI headquarters in the nation's capital from 2002 to 2010. Things were happening quickly, including John's career. He and Kathy moved from Boston to Virginia "in a very challenging and demanding new world." He served first as Deputy Assistant Director in charge of the greatly expanded Counter-terrorism Division that had been established quickly after the 9/11 attacks. He questioned this assignment at first, reporting that he had little actual counter-terrorism experience. He had specialized in white-collar and cyber-crimes, along with public corruption and civil right violations, but not counter-terrorism.

That didn't matter. Urgent times require unusual actions. If one must risk relative inexperience in the necessary rush forward, so be it. The decision was made that risking on John was likely the best option available. A reputation for high growth potential and a high level of integrity really counts when the pressure is on.

Soon John was promoted to Executive Assistant Director for National Security, overseeing counter-intelligence matters and contributing to the formation of the counter-terrorism policies in the administration of President George W. Bush. In 2004 John was named Deputy Director of the FBI under the highly respected directorship of Robert Mueller. From rookie street agent in Minneapolis, John now had risen about as high as one could go. He was the number two man in the entire Bureau!

Soon Lisa Monaco joined the FBI as Special Counsel assigned to Director Mueller's office and then became Chief of Staff. She was part of the executive team that often met for daily briefings as early at 6:30 in the morning, John having already managed his long commute to work. Lis recalls sitting at the Director's immediate left with John at his right hand. "John clearly was Bob's valued partner and most trusted advisor."

Reasons for Climbing the Leadership Ladder

The terrible 9/11 terrorist attacks against the United States was a pivotal event that certainly grabbed Washington's full attention and that of the whole world. John Pistole was pushed forward rapidly in the sudden rush to counter additional terrorist attacks. Why John in particular? The recollection of Lisa Monaco seems to be the common judgment.

"My three years in the FBI brought me into daily contact with John. He's a man guided by faith who has a strong sense of duty and service. I often had to lay thorny problems on his desk. Rather than lamenting the problems, he was that rare leader who knew that his job was to manage his team in the direction of some good conclusion. He told me about his terrible car accident in high school and I could see that it gave him a sense of perspective and responsibility and the ability to stay calm in a crisis. I watched him deal with all manner of problems and never lose focus, never deviate from the mission. He knew how to step back and not take himself too seriously."

In the 190th podcast of retired FBI agent Jerri Williams, John reports on these years, shifting the spotlight away from himself. He expresses gratitude for the marvelous men and women who made the FBI the wonderful organization it is. He was given great opportunities and was richly rewarded. "I often was just at the right place at the right time. I was the warm body who kept showing up." In addition to such a gracious assessment on John's part, of course, there were contributing circumstances. At one point in the FBI ranks, for instance, there were five people positioned between John and the Director. Various things happened to the others and suddenly John was next in line.

Here's John's explanation. "They kept retiring and I wasn't old enough to do that, so finally I was given the great gift of becoming Deputy Director." In a sense, advancement was a gift, but clearly one well earned. In the same circumstances, such rapid upward movement wouldn't have happened for a lot of other people. Ask John to respond to that observation and he probably would hesitate. He's always more self-critical than judgmental of others.

Part of the reason for the rise was John's quiet and patient collaboration skill that had been on display in his work with the Italian authorities when on temporary assignment there. That skill was joined by an equally effective communication skill. For instance, the 9/11 Commission and various committees of Congress would seek to hear from John on dozens of occasions. He would be featured in public hearings in April, June, and August of 2004, becoming the Deputy Director of the FBI in October, 2004.

The overriding concern of these hearings was the prevention of future terrorist attacks. John discussed the threat levels from Al-Qaeda and the changes being made in the FBI to help ensure a safer future. Questions tossed at John from some congressional leaders sometimes were sharp and critical since there was a perception that failure of the FBI and CIA to communicate with each other had been a key reason why 9/11 had happened in the first place.

John's FBI colleague Michael Mason, despite the sweet spirit that he has, confesses that sometimes it was good that John instead of him was the one being fired at with sharp and unfair questions and comments. "I probably would have shot back in an unhelpful way, but not John." John's answers were typically straightforward, informed, and not defensive. Whether the Commission and congressional committees always liked what they heard, at least they learned to trust the integrity of the witness sitting before them.

Mike saw this integrity on display one day when only he, John, and an instructor were alone at the FBI firing range. Once finished, Mike carefully racked his weapon and then it accidentally went off! No one was hurt, but the embarrassment level was high and he knew he "had messed up." With no less than the Deputy Director present, the instructor rushed to cover it up as a freak accident, maybe his own fault. John, however, knew differently.

So did Mike, an FBI veteran very familiar with firearms. He had been deeply involved in solving the 2002 Washington Sniper case where ten people had been randomly killed. He had been a swat-team sniper and knew that now John should report this as a negative in Mike's personnel file. Despite their close friendship, he also knew that John would do what should be done. So Mike quickly acted. He "rescued John" by making clear that he would self-report. He did.

There are reasons why John Pistole became the longest-serving person in the roles of Deputy Director of the FBI and later Administrator of the Transportation Security Administration. There always were surrounding circumstances, of course, but they don't account for everything. Few persons serve long in such roles without an accumulation of controversies and increasing numbers of insiders hoping for leadership change. In John's case, his eventual departures from the FBI and then the TSA would be lamented by most. Why? The answers include his competency, transparency, integrity, and modesty despite the power possessed and the temptations to use it selfishly.

John was known to be decisive without being impulsive in the face of the fresh and frightening demands confronting the nation. Especially as the FBI's Deputy Director from 2004 to 2010, he was pivotally involved with both the George W. Bush and Barack Obama presidential administrations. The pressure forced on the FBI to succeed in preventing further terrorism was extreme and the White House wanted to be kept closely informed.

One thing became common knowledge about John in government circles. He was a model leader possessing the three essentials, one who knows, shows, and goes the right way. Robert Mueller had become Director of the FBI just before 9/11 and needed a key leader for the rapidly-expanding counter-terrorism effort. He didn't know John personally but did know his reputation for integrity. He wanted John on his leadership team. Hesitantly, John agreed—"how do you turn down your Director?"—and he would rise rapidly to being the FBI's Deputy Director responsible for overseeing all of the Bureau's daily operations.

While John would raise a questioning eyebrow about any comparison of him and President Lincoln, he is in fact a little "Lincolnesque." Both Abraham and John had modest beginnings, were Midwest lawyers before going to Washington, and were tall and lanky young men. Abe's national leadership was forged in the terror of the Civil War. John's was forged in the 9/11 terrorist attacks, rated by many equally impactful on the nation's psyche as was the Civil War or the Japanese attack on Pearl Harbor. During the 9/11 attacks, near panic forced President George Bush to quickly board Air Force One and spend much of that fateful day circling over the Gulf of Mexico in case he personally was a target. Unfortunately, President Lincoln did become the target of a successful assassin.

Why had Director Robert Mueller called on John in 2004 to be his second in command, the FBI's Deputy Director? Let's use Mueller's own words shared with the students of Anderson University when later he would be a special campus guest of then President Pistole. "You're successful in your career when people believe you have integrity. That's at the root of everything. You can be smart, astute, and funny, but if you lack integrity people know it. A true leader is a servant honestly serving the people."

In 2004, the people of the United States needed served with the highest of skill and integrity. Mueller, a model servant himself, knew a good leader when he saw one. He chose Pistole as his Deputy, the chief operations officer of the best investigative organization in the world. Part of what Mueller saw in John is what John's Anderson University basketball coach had seen in him many years before. Coach Bates describes player Pistole as "cordial, consistent, a natural kind of glue that holds a team together by the example he presents more than with the mouth he exercises." Mueller said this about why he named John the FBI's Deputy Director in 2004. "John had a remarkable career as an FBI veteran, had the universal respect of others, and possessed wisdom, experience, and most importantly the judgment necessary to serve in this high role."

Senator Dan Coats, a fellow Hoosier, recently added this. "A servant leader is just John's personal style. It's based on his Christian faith. He lives his faith every day in every way. People are drawn to him because of his integrity and how he deals with people. He took the values of his faith, his father, and his Anderson University education with him to Washington, a very challenging setting indeed. If I were looking for an example of how to believe and live and serve, it would be John."

John is a Christian "minister" and the FBI people around him were his "congregation." Take colleague Michael Mason. By 2005 he had risen to Executive Assistant Director responsible for the entire criminal branch of the FBI, one of the highest ranking African-Americans in the Bureau's history. But Mike had been searching since a boy for God's meaning in his life. He knew of John's "deep and abiding faith" and began talking to him privately. John gave him a published plan of Bible study. Mike absorbed it gladly—not quite finishing because his dog chewed up part of the Book of Revelation. "John never pushed anything, letting me drive the conversation. When we talk these many years later, with me now a senior Vice-President of Verizon, he always asks where I am on my spiritual journey. I gratefully report."

John conducts his personal life with an eye on the long haul. Whatever the schedule and pressures, he always keeps his body lean and muscular.

One way he has managed to keep a cool head and healthy body is his personal habit of daily running and occasionally distance bike riding.

When headquartered in Washington, he often would rise at 4:15, have devotions, drive to Washington and, prior to morning prep run to the Lincoln Memorial, run up the steps, pay his respects to the great man of yesterday, and stride back to the tough work of the day.

Two small incidents illustrate well the respect given to John. On the occasion of one of the State of the Union addresses of President George W. Bush to a joint session of Congress, one Cabinet chair was empty by design. Attorney General John Ashcroft was that year's one chosen to be out of town on the occasion just in case something horrific happened to the bulk of Washington's leadership during the high-profile event. Presumably thinking that it wouldn't be a bad idea to have a senior FBI official and trusted friend with him, Ashcroft had Pistole called at the last minute and asked to join him in leaving Washington for that evening—no details could be given on the phone, he was just to show up at the plane at an appointed hour.

John did, curious but trusting. They flew to the area of Yale University, Ashcroft's alma mater, where his wife's twin sister lived. They had dinner together, watched the President's address in the private area of a restaurant, and soon were on their way back to Washington. Why pick John to be with the designated survivor? Here's Ashcroft's answer. "He's one of the most comfortable persons to be around. He can fit in anywhere. He always would pull his weight without throwing his weight around. There's a constancy and reliability about John. He's very capable but not slick, cares more about substance than appearance. What you see is what you get, and I like that."

On another occasion Ashcroft was leaving on one of his many trips to Europe on business for the Justice Department. He again asked John to accompany him. Again, why John? In part it was because these two serious Christian believers had much in common. Ashcroft had government business in Paris, but not on the plane ride "across the Pond." Soon these Johns found themselves alone near the front of the aircraft while the security detail was relaxing with little to do except prepare for the demanding work ahead. It was a chance for a brief break from all the serious terrorism business.

The former Attorney General now reports that, if ever accused of being a Christian, "I sure hope there's enough evidence to convict me!" Some of the needed evidence was on this plane and would have been known if any of the security detail had bothered to notice. Ashcroft pulled out of his carry-ons a baritone ukulele and invited John to join him in singing familiar songs of Bill and Gloria Gaither, Charles Wesley, and others. "We are what we sing," Ashcroft judges. "I'm a Christian who loves to sing." John Pistole joined in with pleasure, reporting later, "We hit it off as fellow Christ followers." John Pistole's Church of God heritage is Wesleyan in orientation, filled with music, and two of its leading contemporary composers, Bill and Gloria Gaither, are well known to him personally.[25]

Ashcroft came from a parallel Christian tradition in Missouri and the two prominent government officials quickly realized that they knew by heart the lyrics of many of the same Christian songs. First a chosen partner to be with the designated survivor in case of tragedy coming to the Washington's top leadership, now again John had been chosen to be on a musical adventure of the spirit.

Hard Issues, Wise Decisions

Things in the FBI office of John Pistole were rarely relaxing. Hard decisions came constantly. John has a fun-loving and spiritually rich heart, had a pacifist father, and faced issues of violence regularly. He had never fired a gun before his FBI training, but carried lethal force on his person throughout his decades of federal service. He originally had hesitated to apply for the FBI since he knew he might have to use a firearm and might freeze instead of fire if a critical moment ever came.

Fortunately, in his thirty-one years of federal service, John never had to fire his weapon at another person. Even so, he came to accept the concept of a "just war" and the potential use of violence when absolutely necessary in service of the greater good. Capital punishment? John recalls vividly the story of his Dad attending a hanging. Hollis always after that had strongly opposed capital punishment in any circumstance. John deeply appreciates his Dad's position, although it's now not quite his own.

John explains his position this way. We live in a society of law where wrongdoing has consequences. Occasionally, when beyond any reasonable doubt terrible things have been done to innocent people, capital punishment may be justified. "My one hesitation is the fact that there are instances when an individual is wrongly convicted, and capital punishment can't be reversed!" Once back to Anderson University as its President in 2015, he would support visibly-armed campus police. There "must be teeth in enforcement." The hope is that the presence of a visible weapon will help deter wrongdoing.

Because of tense arrest situations, living in areas of high crime, and constant long commutes in large cities, John came to a point of comfort about being prepared for almost anything. Lethal force was to be used only in extreme situations of self-defense or the defense of colleagues or innocent bystanders. One day was almost one of those extreme situations.

John encountered a tense incident of road rage when driving through the Holland Tunnel from New Jersey into Manhattan on his daily commute to work. A man jumped out of one vehicle to encounter another. They were angry about something and had drawn their available weapons, a tire iron and a ball bat. John could have pulled out of the jammed traffic snarl, drawn his own weapon, and tried to control the situation however necessary. But he didn't. Anxious to get to work and not anxious to get delayed further or involved in something "not in my jurisdiction," he got clear of it and went on.

Some things, however, couldn't be avoided when he got to work, first in the FBI and then in the Transportation Security Administration. Attorney General John Ashcroft became a good friend of John's, liked to call him *Juan Pistolé,* and teased that finally the FBI "had gotten itself a real pistol!" Ashcroft used the *Juan Pistolé* because it "seemed more adventuresome and signaled a personal and not just professional relationship." *Juan* became known and respected as a straight shooter. He, however, has always been less an instrument of lethal force and more a man of integrity and a source of hope.

For instance, John insisted on limits to allowable force within FBI ranks. He approved and sent a memo making the limits clear. No such policy had existed before but new circumstances now made one necessary, partly because FBI agents were embedded overseas with various CIA operations and occasionally participated in or at least witnessed the interrogation of terrorist captives.

Valerie Caproni was General Counsel of the FBI and principal policy writer. It directed representatives of the FBI not to participate in any coercive interrogation of captives taken during the post-9/11 "war on terror." Nor were they allowed to sit in on or benefit from any intelligence obtained from any interrogations conducted by third parties that had used "advanced techniques." If such coercive interrogations were suspected, the concern was to be passed up through the FBI chain of command.

Some in the U. S. government and intelligence community believed that the terrorist stakes were high enough that virtually any method of gaining desired intelligence was justified. John disagreed.

Glancing Ahead

As Deputy Director of the FBI beginning in 2004, John would be the Bureau's chief operating officer, overseeing an annual budget of about $7 billion and some 35,000 employees. This chapter has highlighted the domestic side of his FBI functioning before and after 2004. The next will give attention to the other side of his FBI service, the international. John's responsibilities would take him all over the globe as an agent of justice.

An unusual "photo" created by a TSA officer and comprised of "bricks" (photos) of TSA officers from around the country.

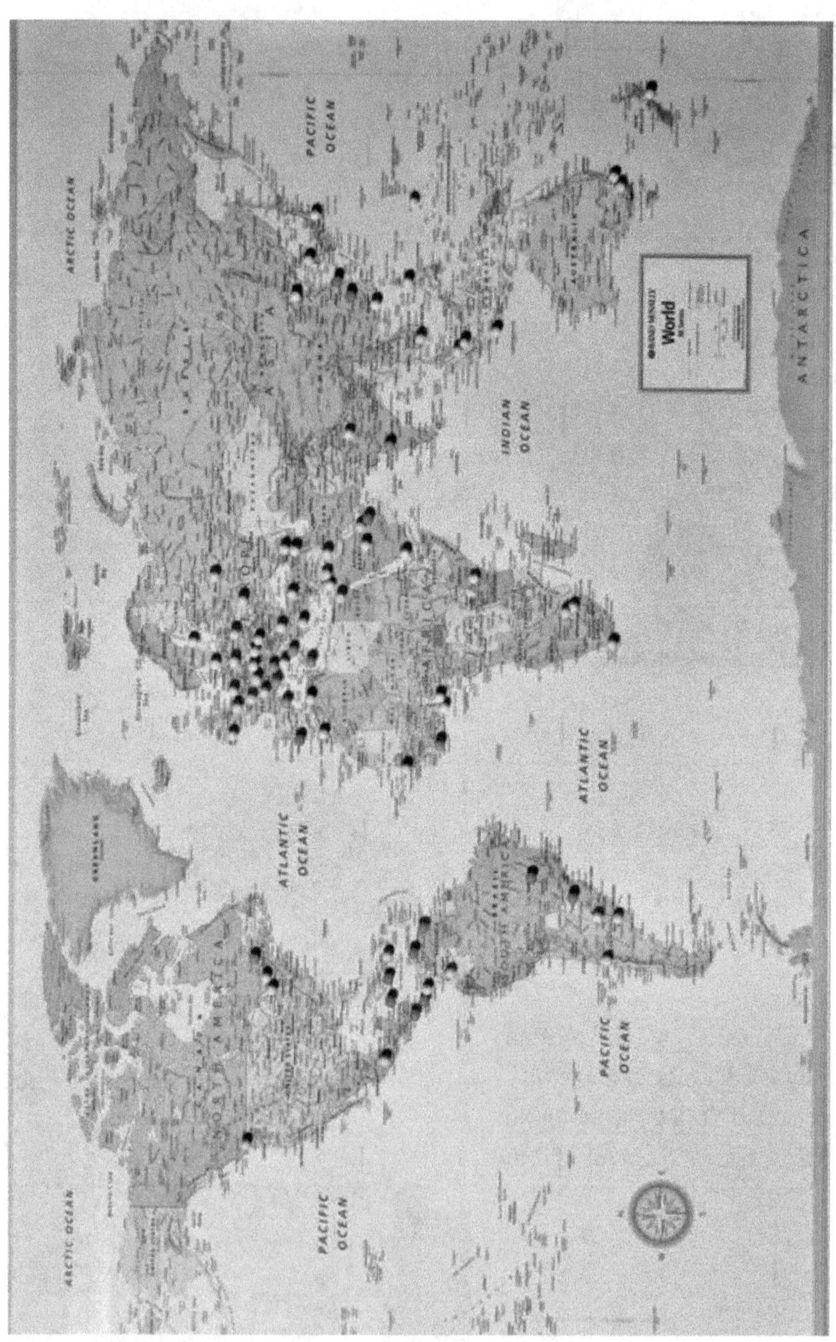

John S. Pistole was trusted and privileged to represent the United States literally across the globe.

Chapter 9

SERVING THE WHOLE WORLD

Live as if you were to die tomorrow.
Learn as if you were to live forever. —Mahatma Gandhi

John Pistole had learned that the security of Americans is now very much dependent on the security alliances of the United States around the world.
—Janet Napolitano

The Church of God Movement from which John Pistole emerged tended to sing more than theorize its theology. Some of the songs spoke of the glorious universality of the gospel of Christ. John finally was finding it possible to travel internationally as part of his FBI work. He was carrying in his heart, and sometimes sharing globally with his lips, the faith he had inherited and increasingly embraced. Whatever the country or culture, whatever his particular assignment, the Jesus John knows was the very Someone others needed to know.

The love of travel had been instilled in John by his parents. They had taken advantage of the wonderful Anderson University TRI-S program to lead student groups to Australia, Brazil, Egypt, Japan, Kenya, and New Zealand between 1974 and 1985. Son John, quite unexpectedly, would find it possible to do even more travel, much more over the years as part of his federal responsibilities.

As a young and unfulfilled lawyer in Anderson, Indiana in the early 1980s, John Pistole had longed for more. He had begun looking for something that would bring increased personal fulfillment, a dependable income, more Christian witness, even world travel and adventure if possible.

He had found his way into the FBI as a promising route to all of this. By the 1990s and into the early years of the new century he was finding what he longed for—to put it mildly!

John had begun traveling the nation inspecting FBI offices. Increasingly he was being drawn into cyber-crimes and forensics work that would have no geographic boundaries. Then came international terror that often is multi-national in character. Soon John was to be found conducting serious government business in multiple nations. The monster of international terror had numerous interconnected expressions that covered the globe. John would encounter personally and help alleviate significantly many of these unsavory connections.

For instance, the hijackers of the disastrous 9/11 attack on the United States received their financing from the Middle East, trained in Afghanistan, did their planning in Germany and flight training in the United States, and finally had fine-tuned their operation at a meeting in Kuala Lumpur, Malaysia. Consequently, international cooperation and educational activity necessarily became specific goals of the Justice Department's fight to prevail over future terror. One of the people implementing this cooperation would be John Pistole of America's FBI.

Far from Washington, D. C.

The global reach of John Pistole's service began barely a decade into his FBI career. The Italians were in need of forensics assistance from the FBI because of a double assignation of two anti-Mafia Italian leaders. FBI Director Louis Freeh had strong personal contacts in the Italian law enforcement intelligence communities, allowing John Pistole to be sent there to help. This 1992 collaboration process was expanding and fulfilling for John. So much was this the case that in 1998, near the end of his FBI tenure in Indianapolis, John focused his hope for a new career step on a possible position abroad. He applied for two FBI Assistant Legal Attaché roles, first in the American Embassy in Rome, Italy, and then the one in Tel Aviv, Israel.

He and Kathy talked through these mind-stretching possibilities. Kathy reports that John was always "beyond considerate in involving me in such decisions." They agreed that such possible moves, dramatic as either would be, held considerable potential for family enrichment, such as their daughters learning a new language and being exposed to a new culture.

Overall, Kathy judged these "fabulous opportunities." Both roles, however, while enticing, were not to be.

John failed to receive the Italian role because of not speaking Italian well enough. He also did not gain the role in Israel, but not because he didn't speak Hebrew. While his application was pending in August, 1998, and he and Kathy both were viewing Israel as a truly exciting possibility for the family, more overcoming of disappointment became necessary. During that very month, Al-Qaeda terrorists attacked American embassies in East Africa and threatened more worldwide. John feared that this was the possible beginning of targeting other U. S. embassies, including in the Middle East. The FBI's legal office in Tel Aviv was housed in the U. S. embassy, so John and Kathy reluctantly decided that they shouldn't risk putting their two daughters and themselves in that much harm's way. He withdrew his application.

How disappointing. Who knows how different would have been the lives of John, Kathy, and their daughters had things gone as they had hoped at first? Instead, a favorite saying of John's came into play. "A new crisis is another opportunity to succeed." In fact, a few years later John would be sitting in the Washington chair of the Deputy Director of the FBI instead of strolling the streets of Rome or Tel Aviv as an attaché. How different that would be from the expected! Nor might it ever have happened had John been stationed abroad for several years and not at the Bureau's headquarters busily building reputation and key relationships.

More than all this had developed during his Indianapolis years, 1994-1999. In 1995, right after the Oklahoma City bombing, John received a surprising and rewarding assignment. The FBI agent scheduled to teach at the newly opened International Law Enforcement Academy had been diverted to the bombing site and John was named to replace him. He traveled to Budapest, Hungary, to teach for three weeks at the ILEA, funded by the United States State Department.

On behalf of students from Russia and various countries of Eastern Europe, John used curricula designed to provide regional criminal justice training to improve legislation, law enforcement, and democratic institutions in participant countries. Some of this curricula was instruction he had developed previously for the FBI's New Agent Training. He would repeat this critical educational task by functioning similarly in locations like Bulgaria and India.

In all of this, and with much more to come, John would be quick to say that God was graciously active in his life, overruling, guiding, resourcing, keeping doors open and spirits strong, regardless of the negatives. At times he was quite frank about this with his colleagues, although never in a way that offended anyone. Quite apart from his faith witness, John's expertise now was frequently needed abroad. He loved to travel internationally and the FBI leadership had come to trust his diplomatic and relational skills. On occasion, Director Bob Mueller of the FBI, either unable or preferring not to make a particular trip himself, didn't hesitate to send John in his place.

An important stance had come to define John. He saw himself as an "equal opportunity investigator" when examining politicians of either or no political party. When functioning internationally, he avoided judgments about the rightness or wrongness of the actions of the United States. If American special forces raided an enemy compound and discovered computers, phones, documents, anything that could assist American commanders with troop safety, positioning, or initiatives, the FBI was there to examine them carefully and share the results frankly and without political bias. When American citizens with any possible ties to the enemy were identified, they were to be interviewed and evaluated. It all was to be done as objectively as possible.

Dangerous and Enriching Ventures and Friendships

None can deny that danger always was potentially lurking nearby, waiting for a government official investigating the Mob and aggressively trying to foil terrorist plots. Long-distance travel into the unknow always has its risks. For instance, Abraham Lincoln was the Illinois lawyer of the man who organized the ill-fated Donner Party that left from Springfield in 1846. Half of them would not survive the ordeal. Abraham had expressed his strong desire to go with this expedition westward but his wife was pregnant and the Lincolns already had a toddler in the home. Had he not been convinced to stay home, American history might have been quite different.

John Pistole loves travel and on occasion his FBI responsibilities took him on assignments that easily could have been ill-fated. Having two daughters at home didn't abort these international forays, many heading far to the east instead of the Donner's westward travel. Two ventures abroad in the 2003-2004 period were very important and particularly dangerous for John Pistole.

The first came because of the bombings in housing compounds in Riyadh, Saudi Arabia's capital. Twelve Americans were killed as well as many non-Americans killed or seriously wounded. The significant presence of the U. S. military in this conservative Muslim kingdom had been cited by Osama bin Laden as a main reason for the September 11, 2001 attacks on the World Trade Center and the Pentagon in the United States.

The White House in Washington worked out an arrangement with the King and Crown Prince to send a large American group to assist the Saudis with the needed investigation. John Pistole, then the FBI's Deputy Assistant Director for Counter-Terrorism, volunteered to lead the team. The Americans mainly helped with forensics rather than with direct interviews since many, including John, did not speak Arabic.

Another high-risk trip and assignment was to Iraq during active warfare. John went this time with Robert Mueller, Director of the FBI, to visit its agents embedded with American and Iraqi forces. John has vivid memories of this heart-pounding venture to Baghdad, a city of some eight million, the second largest in the Arab world. Transport was needed for the American leaders from the international airport near the city to the relatively safe "Green Zone."

The conveyance was a Blackhawk military helicopter. They flew as low as three-hundred feet over the city with no lights on and side doors open where gunners were ready should someone on the ground try to launch a rocket their way. John was carefully harnessed in, of course, but that hardly relieved his anxiety. "The harness wouldn't help if we get shot down!" They didn't, completed their task, and readied to leave in an aircraft that could take off upward in a corkscrew pattern that defied ground attack.

While generally less high risk, but always enriching and productive, John made professional trips on government business to India, Australia, New Zealand, Japan, South Korea, China, Singapore, South Africa, and several other countries in Asia, Africa, and Latin America, a total of fifty some countries. Usually there was a primary goal, like signing a Mutual Legal Assistance Treaty prepared by the Department of Justice or final- izing some other bilateral treaty. John always would work in coordination with the U. S. Embassy country team and Chief of Mission, the U. S. Ambassador. Occasionally he would meet with a country's president, such as in Argentina and Colombia.

Alvaro Uribe was Harvard educated and President of Columbia from 2002-2010. John Pistole met him in his Bogota office on a day that was particularly memorable. The President was in the midst of peace negotiations with FARC (Revolutionary Armed Forces of Columbia). On the very day of the meeting with John, a female FARC leader turned herself in under an amnesty program. It turned out that she had been personally responsible for killing Uribe's father years earlier!

Perhaps most "impressive" for John was a meeting in Yemen involving John, Bob Mueller, and President Ali Abdullah Saleh. John's strong impression of this encounter was mostly for negative reasons. They met in Saleh's presidential palace. John recalls thinking that the President was a little "high" on some mild narcotic as he pointed rather erratically a laser pointer on the ceiling and walls and talked about things that didn't quite make sense to John and Bob. A few years later Saleh's government was overthrown by rebels, with his 2017 death listed as from "ballistic trauma."

Sometimes John would become better informed about organized crime bodies in various countries that did "business" in the United States. One example is his visit to the tri-border area of Brazil, Argentina, and Uruguay where there was considerable activity of Hezbollah, a Shia Islamist militant group based in Lebanon. This group was also present in the Detroit and several other large metro areas of the U. S. where there are large Middle Eastern populations.

An occasional crisis prompted other kinds of international activity. One assignment of John Pistole's was situated just off American shores. EgyptAir flight 990 had crashed into international waters off the East Coast. Since Egypt didn't have the resources to salvage the aircraft, it requested the United States to lead the investigation, naturally coming to involve the FBI since there was much speculation of a criminal act being the crash cause.

John Pistole joined several national Directors, including George Tenet, Director of the Central Intelligence Agency (left), and Mike Hayden, Director of the National Security Agency (right), in celebrating the opening of the National Media Exploitation Center.

John spent many days working on the forensics of what could manage to be recovered off Rhode Island. Sometimes he had to deal with located body parts smaller than hands. There now is a monument to Flight 990 in Island Cemetery in Newport, Rhode Island. Even more vivid than a stone monument are the images lodged in John's memory.

Then there was the awful 2005 bombing of multiple sites in the underground rail system in London, England, with John supporting from Washington the British authorities in identifying those responsible. The G8 world leaders had been meeting in nearby Scotland and Prime Minister Tony Blair called "barbaric" this largest attack on Great Britain since World War II. Fifty-six were dead and hundreds wounded. Blair was appreciative of U. S. assistance in the subsequent investigation.

In 2006 there came another major terrorist plot organized in London. Lisa Monaco recalls vividly John Pistole's "steady hand" as the tense investigation proceeded day after day. He was in regular contact with his British counterparts, finally leading to a take-down by the British of numerous bomb builders and potential suicide bombers. They were planning to transport the liquid explosives disguised as soft drinks aboard multiple planes headed for the United States and Canada. This led immediately to passengers being allowed to carry aboard aircraft only a very small amount of any liquid.

John became even more directly involved in an intense investigation in the U. S. when a 2009 plot was uncovered by the FBI intending an attack in New York City similar to the 2005 ones in the London Underground. In this case, however, John as Deputy Director and his FBI colleagues, along with various state police agencies, successfully tracked the gathering killers and managed an arrest and prosecution with no loss of life.

In all of the above assignments, John readily admits that "doors opened for me that I didn't expect or deserve. I lean on the wisdom of James 1:5, namely, 'If you don't know what you're doing, pray to the Father. He loves to help. You'll get his help and won't be condescended to when you ask for it'." Some of that divine help and encouragement would come from two unexpected new friendships abroad. These friendships were with two Andrews, each the head of a law enforcement/intelligence agency, one in the United Kingdom and one in Australia.

These Andrews became not only colleagues but personal friends and even soul-mates of John. Andrew Parker was Deputy Director General of the British Security Service when John was Deputy Director of the FBI. Andrew Scipione was Australia's New South Wales Police Commissioner. John had "deep conversations" with each about living out their common Christian faith—along with plenty of talk about counter-terrorism, of course.

These two men, John gladly recalls, "lived out their Christ-centeredness every day." Andrew Scipione is a good friend of Darlene Zschech, inspiring Australian song writer and recording artist who sometimes is called the pioneer of the modern worship movement. She has joined the two Andrews in impacting John Pistole's spiritual and worship life significantly.

Behind the Scenes

Let's glance behind the scenes of all this international travel for the United States government. John Pistole would do his own personal packing. He wore business suits when abroad, as he always did on the job at home for thirty-one years. He usually was careful to include his running and swimming gear, wanting to be ready for every opportunity to keep himself in top physical condition.

There were standard government protocols for all the actual travel arrangements and usually an advance team landing in the destination country days before John's arrival. Typical travel was aboard a Gulfstream 5 or G5 aircraft reserved for use by the Attorney General or Director of the FBI or their designee. On board with John usually would be five or six armed security agents and whoever else was needed to prepare him with classified briefings and a detailed itinerary. High-level activity such as John's was hardly simple to execute.

There was a time when John visited five countries in six days, each with its own unique circumstances. The required logistics were handled by as many advance teams and other specialists as necessary, including someone to teach John a few courtesy words in the language of the coming hosts. Typically the Americans were greeted most graciously since the FBI tended to be held in high regard globally.

John recalls one occasion when he was hosted lavishly in New Delhi, India. His personal quarters was a presidential suite on the third and fourth floors of a top hotel. It had gorgeous grounds that included gardens and a wonderful outdoor swimming pool. He was in that pool alone early his first morning there, happily swimming laps. Suddenly a lone man appeared. This was a secure inner area of the facility so there was no safety concern. The man watched him swimming and finally called out with a simple observation.

"Sir, you seem to have something wrong with your right arm."

John gladly responded with an explanation. "It's because of an old neck injury when I was young. No problem. Thanks."

Once back on the balcony of his quarters, John gazed down at the lovely view where he had just been and then out just beyond the hotel grounds. There he saw clusters of little shanties leaning against a wall along the sidewalk. Very poor people were slipping in and out of them, barely surviving wretched daily lives. The contrast of wealth and poverty right against each other was stunning, unforgettable. Such circumstances there and elsewhere, he knew well, were obvious breeding grounds for injustice. He would do whatever possible to counter such human misery.

Honored as a Distinguished Executive
by President George W. Bush.

Flag of Honor flown on the retirement of John Pistole
when leaving the FBI in 2010.

Two Lows, One High, and the Eye

Having now reviewed highlights of the domestic and international dimensions of John Pistole's FBI service, we soon will consider his next two major responsibilities, Administrator of the Transportation Security Administration and President of Anderson University. Beginning in 2010 he would be responsible for supervising over sixty thousand federal employees who in turn were charged with protecting all aspects of the sprawling transportation system within as well as to and from the United States.

Often, as with the FBI roles, particular crises soon to be faced would involve cargo or passengers arriving in U. S. airports or ports from cities worldwide. The demands would be complex and sometimes the dangers highly emotional and usually urgent. Before all that is considered, however, it's important to understand something of who John Pistole had become from his years as a rookie street agent to his sitting as the trusted Deputy Director of the Federal Bureau of Investigation.

What would John bring with him to his next major assignments? Why would he be trusted with such multiple great responsibilities? There are at least four pervasive characteristics of the man to be considered. What of John's way of thinking and acting made the difference? I suggest that two lows, one high, and a calming eye had come together to characterize John's very person. They now framed his growing reputation at home and abroad.

Low #1

The first low is John's consistently keeping a low public profile. John never has been a man driven by ego in search of the spotlight. What then has characterized his public profile in the midst of the highly charged political partisanship that often nearly paralyzes Washington? People had come to know that John could be firm and decisive, but never would he do so in a caustic manner that downgrades others, even those with whom he sharply disagrees. Pushing himself forward at the expense of others was never John.

For the most part, John chose to keep his head down and his personal opinions to himself. Typical would be his keynote speech to a 2017 technical cybersecurity symposium in San Antonio, Texas. Even when baited, he would not express highly-charged judgments against the current presidential administration. What he did say was reflective of his keen awareness of the importance of international cooperation, especially through alliances that allow nations to share with each other sensitive intelligence about terrorists.

John offered one critical point at that symposium, although even that in a low-key manner. "The unconventional approach to diplomacy and national security of the current administration has caused a lot of our international partners to question just what is their relationship with the U. S., and it has left many countries wondering how they can work with a partner in such an unpredictable environment. We'll leave it at that."

Low #2

The second low is the level of John's personal needs that necessarily must be met in order for him to feel successful and properly respected. The fact is John Pistole's long career, before and after his outstanding decades of federal service, has hardly been a smooth upward journey. There have been bumps, frustrations, second choices, reverses, limiting circumstances, failing associates, and other obstacles to be overcome. The first, of course, was the car crash in high school that nearly ended his life journey entirely. Next came the two hitches in his application acceptance that almost kept him out of the FBI in the first place. John learned early that one "must be patient and persist!"

Anderson University was John's back-up choice for college, although it turned out to be a superb one. He "played scared" on the college basketball team his freshman year, not sure how injury-prone his neck really was after the big car crash. The law school attended, while excellent, was not John's first choice. Pepperdine in California was more appealing to him but quite beyond his financial resources. He practiced law for a brief time in Anderson, Indiana, but the financial circumstances of the time and his sense of personal and professional fulfillment weren't there. These tensions stressed his new marriage, but that was managed well over time by the power of love.

By nature, John is a "fixer." When faced with a crisis, he tends to confront the situation with an inner optimism that manages to see the threat as an opportunity in disguise, a chance to negotiate the trouble into a new success. Put poetically by Emily Dickinson, "Hope is the thing with feathers that perches in the soul." John Pistole has such a perching deep within. So does his wife Kathy.

The thing with feathers showed itself in John's senior year of high school. After suffering the awful car accident in September of 1973, he was forced off a championship basketball team. Amazingly, by early March, 1974, with that team in the state semi-finals, John was in uniform and on the court warming up with his teammates. Coach Estes was so pleased to have him back but unlikely to put him into a high-pressure game. John was too rusty and it was physically risky. Still, John was there, proudly there, determined to be ready if called upon.

John began training for FBI service in September of 1983 in Quantico, Virginia. His wife Kathy stayed with Lou and Bev Gerig in Indianapolis for part of the time and with her parents in the D. C. area the rest. By the second week John had managed to adjust to the awkwardness of an alcoholic roommate. He then "maxed out" the rigorous test of physical capabilities to do strenuous work (only one of three in his class to do this).[26] There was strong motivation to show the FBI that his initial application refusal because of the high school the car crash and neck surgery had been a mistake. "See, I can do this!" He surely could.

Once solidly in the FBI ranks, John often expressed an unusual combination of the drive to excel and the low need for the extras that colleagues in high positions of leadership typically expect, even demand. He showed himself to be a man needing/requiring relatively low maintenance, even while being a man carrying very high levels of responsibility.

Years later, in 2020, a group of retired FBI agents shared this memory among themselves. They recalled a time when John had flown to Colorado for a large gathering where he would be featured. A local FBI agent did the typical thing for the arrival of the Deputy Director. He arranged for a security detail and special very secure transportation from the airport to the hotel. What actually happened was that John's flight arrived, he gathered his things, hailed a taxi, and arrived at the hotel like any regular person. He didn't think the extra fuss and cost were necessary.

The High

With these two lows tended to come a pervasive high. One point made consistently in the many interviews done for this biography was about John's high level of personal *integrity*. It came in several forms, like genuine, transparent, ethical, consistent, and a straight shooter. This high level of integrity is a key reason why John was tapped for leadership in the most difficult and complex of circumstances. Here is a man who had come to be known as one who will seek the truth, speak the truth, and can be trusted to act properly in light of the truth.

Something critical in the Washington culture is personal integrity. Can people trust and rely on you? On dozens of occasions it was John Pistole's responsibility to brief Presidents Bush and Obama in the Oval Office or Situation Room. His style of communication was simple enough. If John was not prepared to answer in a well-informed way, both Presidents learned that John wouldn't speculate or bluff, only respond that he would follow-up soon with the answer. John's integrity became respected in FBI, congressional, and presidential circles.

This respect brought John the high honor of receiving the "Presidential Rank Award for Distinguished Executive" in 2005. This was followed in 2007 with the Edward H. Levi Award for Outstanding Professionalism and Exemplary Integrity." Senator Dan Coats of Indiana would be named Director of National Intelligence by President Donald Trump in 2017. Coats would move quickly to form a Advisory Group to support him. He sought out the very best public servants with extensive experience in national security issues and with voices that would speak up frankly and could be trusted. He says that one of the first persons he thought of was John Pistole, who would agree to serve.

John's alma mater, Anderson University, chose this outstanding graduate to be its 2006 commencement speaker, as would Indiana University's McKinney, his law school, in 2009. Two related details show the integrity of this honored speaker. One woman was graduating in both classes that John addressed. When learning this, he sought her out and personally apologized for her having to endure him twice.

Aware of the length of the commencement occasion at Anderson, with so many graduates being recognized individually, John would make a promise. Different from speakers who relish their time in the spotlight as the featured guest, he would keep his remarks to fifteen minutes. Reviewing the recorded video now, John is pleased that his address lasted only fourteen minutes. He was hardly a man who would insist on inordinate personal attention. His comment? "Isn't brevity next to godliness?" Maybe. Integrity certainly is.

Something else close to godliness, at least as judged by many millions of the Christian faithful worldwide, would be a personal audience with the Pope of Rome. John Pistole once received this high honor, and with a humorous touch rarely received by a Protestant, non-clergy American. Pope Benedict of the Roman Catholic Church was visiting the United States in 2008. He granted an audience in the Vatican Consulate in Washington to the FBI's Bob Mueller, John Pistole, and a very few others.

These honored American leaders were granted more than a papal audience. They also received a special honor only the Pope has the right to give as sovereign of the Vatican City State. It was an honorific membership in the Knighthood Order of Saint Sylvester. With it came an unusual privilege, official authorization to enter any church on horseback, including Saint Peters' Basilica in Rome! Laments John now, "I doubt I'll ever get a chance to use that privilege." To this day John is seen regularly in Park Place Church of God in Anderson, Indiana, but never yet on horseback.

In 2008 John Pistole greets Pope Benedict of the Roman Catholic Church in the Vatican Consulate in Washington.

Eye of the Hurricane

Added to these two lows and one high is something else about John that was key to his past success and future potential. Many colleagues and friends comment on John Pistole's amazing rise through the ranks of the FBI over the years. They reach for reasons, noting his hard work, consistent integrity of performance, occasional fortunate circumstances, and his reliance on the enabling and guiding hand of God. John is clear that "I never had the ambition to be the head of everything. I was never a 'blue flamer,' FBI shorthand for someone determined to move up quickly through the ranks at almost any cost."

By contrast, as former Attorney General John Ashcroft puts it, cream rises to the top on merit. To this John Pistole would quickly add, "bolstered by hard work and a strong faith in God's enabling." A constant prayer of John's over the years has been the Renovaré Covenant prayer that reflects anything but raw personal ambition.[27] Its stress on "utter dependence" on Jesus Christ fosters a distinctive leadership style that brings us to the "eye of the hurricane" characteristic of the man.

Rev. Dr. Rod Stafford is a graduate of Anderson University's School of Theology and the pastor in Fairfax, Virginia where John and Kathy attended for several years. Now he also is a trustee of Anderson University where John later would serve as President. Rod's doctoral work in Anderson focused on the dynamics of how churches do and should make their decisions. He now speaks of John's leadership style as near the ideal. "He is so collaborative. Everyone has a voice. He listens respectfully but also is decisive, an unusual combination."

That was a judgment made in the Washington arena. Once John would be in leadership back in Anderson and being viewed from a trustee's perspective, Rod would say that "the Anderson campus is dedicated to raising up leaders to impact every channel of culture and it's great to have a man at the point, President Pistole, who has lived out that to which we aspire. John's honest, humble, vulnerable, and that takes strength of character. He looks trouble straight in the face and remains consistently optimistic."

Such an assessment is echoed by John's close FBI colleague, Michael Mason. Mike admits to being accused of wearing rose-colored glasses. "If I do, they get scratched up many times. When they do, I reach for my rose-colored paint and quickly spray the scratches. And that's John Pistole.

He treats everybody with an abundance of respect, never as servants of a bloated ego, and never with a hidden agenda. When he speaks, you listen because you know he is well-informed, thoughtful, and not just wanting to hear the sound of his own voice. He never assumes that he's the smartest person in the room, although he usually is."

Mike often was in the room observing Director Mueller and Deputy Pistole jointly handling a tough issue. He saw John as Bob's perfect balance. Bob was a hard-driving boss who would be in your face if something didn't meet his high standards—Mike and Bob both had been Marine officers. "John would soften the scene, be the eye of the hurricane. Always the gentleman, John would win you over through a collaborative process. He was the calm one never given to panic or anger. He has passion but not unrestrained emotion. He could be forceful without being coldly authoritarian. If someone deserved a reprimand, it would be done in private. He prefers to win hearts and minds rather than arguments."

John Pistole meets people easily, casually, and respectfully—not usual for persons in power who too easily look down on and sometimes use others for their own gain. As Chuck Rosenberg puts it, "John has an unusual decency, a kindness and civility that insists on treating all people respectfully as equals." Never has John hungered for attention or viewed himself as "above" others despite his impressive titles and significant gifts. John presents an important lesson in leadership. Casual encounters are important.

John is likely to forget something thoughtful and kind he did naturally for someone, while for them it was an outstanding and unforgettable experience. Rather than defensive and evasive, he's honest and up-front. Rather than fueling the hurtful emotion in some hurricane-like circumstance, he's more likely to function as its calming eye. He's a Proverbs 15 man, knowing that "a gentle response defuses anger; kind words heal and help; cutting words wound and maim."

Prepared for a New Arena of Challenge

These two lows and one pervasive high, when coupled with the ability to be the eye of a hurricane, make up the composite character that John Pistole demonstrated in his FBI years and now would bring to a new arena, the huge mission and workforce of the Transportation Security Administration. He had learned that the Earth is now one interconnected globe. Chaos anywhere can mean chaos everywhere.

For instance, complicating the timing of John's arrival at the TSA in 2010 was the recent attempt to bomb a portion of Times Square in New York City by a man who had nearly gotten away on a plane to Dubai. Prominent in everyone's mind in 2010 was the highly-publicized "Underwear Bomber" flying on a Northwest flight from Amsterdam to Detroit on Christmas day, 2009. After this frightening incident, John initiated new and more stringent security measures, including the use of full-body scanners and aggressive pat-downs to avoid such a near tragedy in the future.

Soon after John had been sworn in as TSA's Administrator, the same master bomb builder, located in the Arabian Peninsula and associated with Al-Qaedia, completed the preparation of a mixture of composition explosive similar to that carried by the Underwear Bomber. This time the explosive was hidden in printer toner cartridges and mailed from Yemen in two packages placed on different planes and addressed to synagogues in Chicago, Illinois. Fortunately, Saudi Arabia had an intelligence source that provided the tracking numbers of these two cargo bombs. The explosive packages were on planes at stop-overs in Dubai and England on their separate ways to the United States. John Pistole quickly would order an end to all cargo into the U. S. from Yemen.

Globalization and rapid technological advance were stark realities at the opening of the second decade of the twenty-first century. John had come to know these well and was ready to employ this knowledge in a new arena of federal service.

John Pistole honored by Director Robert Mueller
on leaving the FBI in 2010.

John Pistole's colleagues in the Department of Justice
of the United States honored him in 2007 for "Exemplary Integrity," a
characteristic defining his life in general.

Chapter 10

NUMBER TWO TO NUMBER ONE

The only true wisdom is in knowing you know nothing. —Socrates

Your living is determined not so much by what life brings to you as by the attitude you bring to life, not so much by what happens to you as by the way your mind looks at what happens. —Kahlil Gibran

Succeeding as number one is a difficult task. It involves understanding the limits of one's own wisdom and having an attitude that profits from that wisdom. Life at the top tends to bring many unwanted things. The focus of one's mind can make all the difference. It's more than what happens. It's how things are seen and approached. John Pistole was highly skilled and experienced. He also knew himself and the God he was serving. He now would be an organizational number one without losing the servant's heart.

John had sought to remain respectfully a-political throughout his decades of federal service. His loyalty in the FBI had been two-fold, faithfulness to the rule of the nation's law and to the ultimate law-giver, God. His quest for justice always had been without regard for who was occupying the White House. He often briefed Presidents of both political parties. He served proudly under FBI Director Robert Mueller, a valued mentor in public service. John reports that "Bob Mueller doesn't have a political bone in his body. His was a non-political approach to doing what's right for the country while serving an outstanding twelve years as Director."

The administration of justice, of course, should be a-political. Chuck Rosenberg, veteran of the U. S. Department of Justice, observed this about himself and John Pistole. "We grew up where the rule of law is paramount. We're not political people. We just try to stand for what's right regardless of who's in the White House." When asked his view of J. Edgar Hoover, the famed first Director of the FBI, John was careful to express mixed evaluations. "I appreciate this man for the many outstanding things he did to make the FBI what it is. But I wouldn't want to be identified with many of the ways he operated. He was a great builder and organizer, and also a bundle of contradictions."

The current concern about political trends in Washington has been explored extensively by a prize-winning journalist. He asks if the FBI and CIA are now enemies or protectors of America's democracy. The answer given is protector despite the claim often heard that they are seeking to undermine the executive powers of the presidency.[28] John, carefully avoiding direct criticism of any presidential administration, says merely that critical comments about the FBI and the larger intelligence community, especially with no supporting evidence, are less than productive. Large organizations always have their failures, no matter how good they are.

John's one political appointment would be as Administrator of the Transportation Security Administration (TSA) in 2010. This responsibility would have a demanding beginning that would make necessary John using to best advantage his wide experience of how Washington works. When he was approached about moving from the FBI to the TSA, he felt a little like how Socrates defines wisdom. Granted, John was well acquainted with terrorist plotting, including against aviation, but he knew virtually nothing about the young, sprawling, and chaotic TSA organization—except that it was in turmoil and little respected in Washington circles.

At least John knew what he didn't know, and what he did know about the TSA wasn't altogether encouraging. No matter. He isn't a man to shy away from a challenge if he thinks the calling of God is involved. It isn't what comes at you, as Gibran observes, but how it is perceived and approached. The thankless task of heading the TSA certainly wasn't anyone's dream position, but it came to John, had to be done, and would be done well.

Coming to the TSA would be somewhat like still another professional move detailed here in later chapters. A call would come in 2014 for John to be the President of his own alma mater back in his hometown. It would be to a much smaller and older organization than the TSA, but it also would be one with significant challenges from day one. Again, it would be a role for which John would feel quite unprepared. But also again, for John as a man of faith, the reality now and then would be, *nevertheless* . . . .

Yes, I'll Serve If Called

Congress authorized the formation of the TSA immediately after the 9/11 terrorist tragedy. It has been called the largest public mobilization since World War II—tens of thousands of employees marshalled quickly and trained as possible in a context of such urgency. One of TSA's original executives was Gale Rossides who had served as co-chair of the Blue Ribbon panel charged with overhauling the Bureau of Alcohol, Tobacco, and Firearms in the wake of the chaotic and tragic 1993 Branch Davidian event in Waco, Texas. Gale was put in charge of all TSA training and culture. She was skilled, although the task was somewhat beyond anyone's skills.

In the months before the appointment of John Pistole to leadership of the TSA, Gale was acting Administrator. When he arrived, it was to her great pleasure. "I was thrilled for the TSA. John was a widely-respected man who really understood how government works, especially the symbiotic relationship between Congress and the agencies, and he was a man who had access into the intelligence community that the TSA needed and was just broaching."

In May, 2010, on the recommendation of the Secretary of Homeland Security, Janet Napolitano, President Barack Obama sought John's willingness to assume the directorship of the Transportation Security Administration. Obama's first two nominees withdrew after revelations surfaced of issues from the past that would complicate Senate confirmation. Sixteen months had gone by without a confirmed appointee. It was a delicate time for a young but massive organization trying to ensure the safety of millions of daily travelers to and from 450 U. S. airports and the country's numerous trains, roadways, bridges, and ports, all potentially threatened by imminent terrorist attack.

Secretary Napolitano had the task of choosing someone to head the TSA, a big and troubled organization within her broad Homeland Security jurisdiction. She had worked with the FBI on various security matters and thus knew John's management skills and superb reputation. She thought such a leader would be good for TSA's sagging morale. So she had checked with FBI Director, Robert Mueller, to be sure it would be appropriate to speak with John about this TSA possibility.

With Mueller's reluctant agreement, she had "pitched" the possibility to John, and "somehow I convinced him." Here was part of her strategy. To help make-up for the organizational mess he would face, she had emphasized the positive. "John, you have done your service as a 'number two' in Washington. Now is the chance to be a 'number one'." That ego stroke didn't fall on completely deaf ears. John admits to being interested in the opportunity to run his own national agency, even if it had to involve the challenge of heading a troubled one. Then had come the presidential interview.

John Pistole, in his typical soft-spoken and self-deprecating style, recalls that everybody in the ornate room wondered if he really wanted this job. After all, they likely were aware that back in 2005 John had received the Presidential Rank Award for Distinguished Executive, authorized by the President of the United States and presented jointly by the Attorney General and Director of the FBI. Even more, in 2007 he had been chosen for the Edward H. Levi Award for Outstanding Professionalism and Exemplary Integrity. Would such an man, now deserving the most comfortable of seats, willingly take on such a sprawling and thorny assignment? The answer was obvious even if somewhat surprising. He was agreeing to accept this difficult new role. Therefore, he was gladly nominated and shortly ratified by the Senate without a dissenting vote.

John didn't hide his judgment about this new role. Coming to the TSA seemed to him to be a "God thing." His role as a Christian is to be obedient rather than getting to pick what he prefers. Was this a new opportunity to succeed where the nation desperately needed a win? In his mind and heart, that seemed to be the case.

In John's modest and almost teasing style, he recalls some young lawyers from the White House personnel office vetting him before President Obama actually nominated him. "They took my pulse and told me, 'Congratulations, you'll probably be the next the Administrator of TSA!'" Observes John with a little smile, "It shows how desperate they were to get somebody in." Secretary Napolitano and President Obama certainly were grateful that someone like John was actually available and willing. It soon was a done deal.

A close friend of John's, Bob Coffman, joined many quietly wondering why John had been willing to leave his superb leadership position in the FBI for what appeared to Bob to be "a thankless and nearly impossible TSA job." He could only think that it was John's sense of public service and his willingness to follow any apparent call from God. As Kahlil Gibran puts it, it's "not so much what happens to you as the way your mind looks at what happens."

Not Arriving Unaware

While John Pistole was suddenly walking into the TSA's complex and troubled inner world, he didn't arrive at this difficult challenge unaware of the threats of terrorism that often focused on the transportation systems of the world. After all, he recently had been drawn into a series of such things as Deputy Director of the FBI.

As Janet Napolitano of Homeland Security observes, "John Pistole knew very well that the security of Americans is now very much dependent on the security alliances of the United States around the world." He had learned this through many of his FBI roles and experiences, and certainly now was having it underlined in his leadership of the TSA under Napolitano's direction. Terrorism is a global phenomenon and intelligence sharing is key to mutual survival.

Beyond previous hands-on awareness of the threats, and his considerable knowledge of the international systems in place for gaining and employing intelligence for quick intervention, John had valuable experience in managing a large workforce and dealing with the budget procedures and networks of government protocols required to get things done. The challenge for the new TSA leader was considerable, indeed, but so were the experiences and skills brought to its table by the new Administrator Pistole. The TSA was still being built, retooling as it went, needing to keep adjusting to changing circumstances and requiring a leader who could think "outside the box." That was John.

Once appointed by President Barack Obama and confirmed by the Senate as the new Administrator, John proceeded to employ his counterterrorism expertise in all phases of the nation's transportation system. He was privileged to report to and work closely with the Secretary of Homeland Security, Janet Napolitano, who had come to her leadership position just the year before and soon would make this judgment about working with John. "Everybody who meets him likes him. He keeps himself well-informed and you can trust whatever he says."

John also was privileged to serve with another woman, Gale Rossides. She was acting Administrator in 2010 when John arrived, and she was nearing retirement and assuming that John would bring with him a new executive team. They met, she offered to resign so that John would be free to select a new Deputy, and he refused her offer. He asked for time so that he could transition well with the assistance of her considerable experience. She gave him a valuable two years plus. During that time, in her words, "we had a tremendous working relationship. Neither of us sought the limelight. It was all about the mission. He reeked of integrity. He was a dignified leader who had impact in a very humble kind of way. His very reputation brought immediate credibility to the agency."

Such leadership soon won John high respect among TSA's thousands of officers and he became the longest-serving Administrator in TSA's history. That was no small accomplishment. Secretary Janet Napolitano observes that the public hears nothing about the massive work of the TSA unless something goes wrong. Senate Commerce Committee Chair Jay Rockefeller from West Virginia noted that this agency's work is often thankless. Despite this, Jay judged that under John Pistole "shifting the TSA from a one-size-fits-all approach to risk-based security has empowered the agency to provide the most effective security in the most efficient ways."

John would invest nearly five years of his federal career seeking to enhance the working effectiveness of the TSA. There was so much to do. The TSA's founding after 9/11 had been in emergency circumstances. Congress basically had said to the original executives, including Gale Rossides, forget old rulebooks, build this new thing from scratch, and do it fast! Gale had a strong management background.

Even with her strong management, however, the task had been overwhelming. Constant innovation was invited and necessary. There were frequent audits of TSA's operations since many of them were not following old standards and procedures. This unsettling organizational environment had greeted John on the first day of his arrival. The whole culture had to be managed and in many ways transformed. Fortunately, he had Gale as a managing partner.

Shifting to a Risk-Based Focus

By June, 2012, John was sitting before the House Committee on Homeland Security detailing the significant changes being made to maintain a first-rate TSA workforce. He spoke of the innovative procedures and technologies being used and how security was being ensured, partly by how airport passenger and cargo screening was now conducted. Success was difficult and never could be guaranteed, but it was proceeding rather well nonetheless. Security had been tightened with no tolerance for racial, ethnic, or other profiling. Increased partnering in detection practices had been established with Canada, the United Kingdom, the European Civil Aviation Conference, and others.

Particularly in the airports, John had addressed head-on the difficult tension between the screening of passengers, now seeming to be very necessary for safety, and the reasonable privacy protections of those passengers. He immediately went to work transforming the TSA into a risk-based, intelligence-driven, counter-terrorism agency. It surely wouldn't be easy. As opposed to Israel with a handful of international airports and the possibility of spending all the time judged necessary in screening every passenger, the TSA had to handle some 450 airports and their huge flow of American passengers not accustomed to a high level of personal invasiveness of their time and persons.

The U. S. public was nervous, critical, and rarely patient with new inconveniences at airports. When more invasive pat-down procedures were being introduced, John Pistole and other TSA and Homeland Security leaders met privately with Secretary Napolitano for a demonstration. John stepped forward and volunteered to be patted down personally. He wanted to know what this would really be like. There was the expected public outcry of increased invasiveness and difficult hearings before Congress. Members were hearing complaints from back home. In the week before Thanksgiving, 2010, John was interviewed forty-five times, usually live, by every national news outlet, to explain these new procedures and answer the question, "Why?" These interviews were usually aired with background photos or video of travelers being patted down and, according to some, "abused." John calmly held his ground and made necessary explanations to politically nervous Congressional leaders.

Later, John tried to roll back the prohibition of small pocketknives aboard flights—some twelve hundred were being confiscated daily at airports across the country, none from any terrorists, just from forgetful passengers. But the resulting outcry of again allowing knives was great enough that this proposed policy relaxation was never implemented. John says, "a reasonable policy that just wasn't politically palatable." What's proper isn't always practical.

John often had to be both patient and confident
when testifying before Congress on controversial issues.

The new risk-based approach would take TSA staff time and effort away from careful screening all passengers equally. John, working with a highly innovative and dedicated senior executive staff, conceived of and quickly implemented the popular "Pre-Check" program at airports. People who completed a process of government pre-travel qualifications and registration could pass through security more quickly. With that, however, also was introduced new full-body scans for higher risk and random travelers. While also controversial, these scans were effective in detecting non-metallic explosive devices such as used by the Underwear Bomber on Christmas Day, 2009.

Technical and procedural adjustments were soon made and the scanning became more accepted by the flying public. Such scanning of passengers and cargo is where John Sanders entered the life of TSA, and then that of John Pistole personally both at the TSA and even later with John would be President of Anderson University. Sanders was with a start-up company that had invented a CT screening device for cargo and luggage that soon was in widespread TSA use.

Sanders first met John when both joined the TSA staff in 2010, Pistole as Administrator and Sanders as Deputy Chief Technology Officer. They soon would be close colleagues, personal friends, and fellow Christian believers. Sanders had understood that you weren't to talk about your personal faith in government circles, but he quickly observed that John Pistole spoke freely of his and lived such faith openly. A core portion of that faith involved respecting all people and finding ways to dignify them in the workplace.

Empowering the TSA Workforce

John Pistole empowered the people around him. He made clear where he wanted to go, made assignments, provided the needed resources, and allowed trusted people freedom in how best to get the job done. John Sanders recalls, "I never saw him lose his temper or shout at anyone. He was never condescending, even to people briefing him on matters he knew more about than they did." Leading the TSA was a fresh opportunity for John to practice the philosophy he had learned back in his undergraduate days in the Center for Public Service at Anderson University—servant leadership in the public arena.

By his side initially was Gale Rossides who shared his servant leadership model and joined John in being very accessible to the frontline workers. She says, "I had a high level of trust in John, never fearing to tell him the worst of what we faced, and I always found him to be fair, upfront, and transparent. I knew he had my back and I had his."

One thing that Gale told John was that better training of TSA officers was essential. They had been trained in whatever rented facilities were available around the country. Congress had been deaf to pleas for financial help to improve this make-shift situation. These tens of thousands of TSA public servants were being called to serve the safety of the public in dramatic new circumstances despite their own relative inexperience, low morale, and limited training.

To succeed as a leader, John would have to find ways to help this workforce buy into the huge and largely thankless task at hand. They had to be prepared more adequately and motivated to succeed in their demanding and dangerous work. The new "Pre-Check" system that relieved some of the pressure at airports was a pleasing beginning. In fact, John had done a survey of the opinions of the officers doing this work. What about this new idea? He even had asked for their suggestions about its eventual name. That was only a beginning of enhancing the dignity of the workforce.

Here's one example of favorable progress obviously having come in staff readiness to serve and in the associated higher morale that would allow that service to be effective and more satisfying to the frontline workers. Bob Coffman, John's close friend from Anderson University, would be traveling with John on one occasion. Afterwards, he offered this observation: "Traveling through an airport with John is like traveling with a rock star! TSA agents recognize and respect him."

How did this big change of attitude toward the work happen for the typical TSA officer? Major reasons include John's initiatives in forming a TSA training academy and his openness to a unionizing interest of the workforce. He was determined to professionalize the whole operation and thus increase its dignity and effectiveness.

Gale Rossides had hoped for a training center for the TSA prior to John's coming but no funding had come from Congress. John had considerable experience with the FBI Academy and immediately saw the TSA's need for something similar. There already existed the Federal Law Enforcement Training Center in Georgia, but there was no TSA presence. So John began advocating for help from Congress concerning this need. Because of his reputation and credibility built up across his FBI years, John was well heard. Money came and John, Gale, and the entire TSA workforce were thrilled. Soon there was in Georgia a TSA training facility complete with a mock airline terminal and similar facilities for trucks and trains. Now TSA employees could receive quality hands-on training in facilities designed for their particular needs.

The TSA had been established as a non-union shop, with the Administrator having wide latitude to decide on all such matters. Pressure had grown over the years for a union, with a workforce of that size very attractive to several potential unions. John inherited this pressure and the freedom to pursue it as he judged best. He found so many inconsistencies in work and discipline rules that he thought a union might at least bring more consistency and fairness.

The new Administrator allowed the workforce to engage in a year-long process of discussing the matter and then voting on whether to unionize, and which union would be preferred. They said they wanted one and he allowed it, clarifying only that it must function without limiting his absolute authority to determine what constitutes a national security threat--and no workforce action would ever be allowed that, in his judgment, would increase that threat for the traveling public. For instance, there could be no strikes. That limitation angered some classic union organizers, but it was within the Administrator's authority and became understood and accepted by the workforce generally.

John was both a collaborative and decisive leader. He held townhalls with TSA staff members in about one hundred different airports. He usually would ask in his informal style, "What are your ideas, concerns, and personal experiences on the job? What advice do you have for me as Administrator?" He would sit with them almost as an equal who had come to really listen to the grassroots of this huge workforce.

Although an agent of the federal government on government business, he always was pleased to respond candidly when someone would ask about his life motivations and personal faith. "God constantly gave me platforms to share my Christian faith." He was so humble about this that no one was offended by his witness, in fact often quite the opposite. The same occasionally would happen in his personal relationships with members of his executive team.

One man, John Sanders, TSA's former Deputy Chief Technology Officer, would stay in active touch with his TSA boss after their years of federal service together. He explains that he didn't want to lose John's significant spiritual impact on his life. In 2020, when the Covid-19 pandemic would be raging and causing a school like Anderson University to struggle serving students face-to-face, John Sanders would be a helpful presence.

Then an executive of Daon and an also Anderson University Trustee, John Sanders would gladly assist President Pistole in making possible a high-tech safety software system for monitoring and tracking the health of campus personnel. It was a new form of the older "Pre-Check" system that Pistole had instituted in the nation's airports. Work experience and deep personal friendships would have ongoing importance.

On the Lighter Side

Real life, even in the midst of difficult and dangerous government work, is bound to have its lighter side. John Pistole certainly has a silly side himself. When asked to recommend a title for this biography, John's brother David teasingly suggested "Knucklehead!" Fun things sometimes did happen around this otherwise serious man.

John Ashcroft, when Attorney General of the United States, worked closely with John and his FBI colleagues in those difficult years following 9/11. Later, when John Pistole was TSA Administrator overseeing airport security, Ashcroft boarded a flight in Missouri to fly to an important appointment and photo opportunity with the President of the United States and the Prime Minister of Great Britain. He tore his pants badly on the seat handle when squeezing in. While changing planes in Chicago, with no chance for new clothes, he hurried to the TSA office and asked for help. He was given a strip of the yellow TSA tape used to stick on suitcases once checked in transit.

In a bathroom stall the drama deepened. Ashcroft took off his pants, taped the long rip from the inside, and made his appointment and the photo op with no one noticing. Once home, he took a picture of the inside of his hastily repaired pants, with the "TSA" strip very visible, and sent it to John Pistole with a note. "John, aren't your agents going a little too far, even inspecting the inside of my trousers?" TSA to the rescue.

There was in Washington the Combined Federal Campaign that annually raises funds from the agencies for charity. Each year that John was TSA Administrator, he personally helped his agency do well competitively. Being a previous basketball star still in excellent physical condition, and ever the competitor, John would urge giving among his immediate colleagues by challenging them to a game of "HORSE" against him. The winner would contribute liberally to the Fund.

John Sanders recalls it as quite a sight, "our honored leader who always wears a tie out there in shorts!" Sanders once arranged for a "ringer," a guy known for his basketball experience. No matter. John "whopped him." The chief of technology now had to be a chief contributor to charity. He was glad to do it.

It didn't work quite that way, however, on another occasion when the honored TSA leader faced the challenge of a young female attorney now on the TSA team. She had played college basketball and wasn't intimated by the tall and revered leader in shorts. She went into action and, as John himself puts it, "she smoked me!" It was all in good humor and certainly for a good cause.

There were other occasions designed just for fun, like the day John was chosen to throw out the first pitch at a Washington Nationals baseball game. The setting wasn't a basketball or tennis court, places so familiar to John. Even so, his athletic skills seemed to transfer quite well. With John that proud day were about 400 TSA employees. It was fun for all.

While likely not intended to slow down John's athletic prowess, there was a quiet competition among the women in the administrative suite where John's office was located. The break room was nothing but a tiny kitchen where a few people could lounge and snack. Women secretly got into the habit of bringing their favorite sweet dessert, hoping that John would come in and announce that today's temptation was the best yet. And he often did come in, relax a bit, and enjoy the available sweets, never aware of the conspiracy for temptation dominance. His FBI investigative skills, great as they were, failed him in this temptation room.

When Senator Dan Coats was leaving his last role in Washington in 2019, Director of National Intelligence under President Donald Trump, he routinely lost his TSA Pre-Check status granted to government leaders. So he approached the proper TSA office to regain it as a private citizen. Questions came in a flurry. Have you traveled to any other countries in the last ten years and, if so, why and who did you meet? Dan was honest. In his government roles he'd been to about forty-five countries and usually met with top political leaders.

The TSA official was properly careful, slowing the Coats process, raising an eyebrow at this maze of possible international intrigue, making it difficult for Dan to get his clearance. Dan now admits to wishing that his friend John Pistole had still been the Administrator. That way "I would have been tempted to call and ask for his intervention." However, Dan makes clear that he shares "Indiana values" with John and wouldn't have done so, although not above a little temptation.

John Pistole and his wife Kathy were fortunate in having good friends like Joe and Betsy Bush. In 2010 these two couples went together one day in Sky Meadows State Park in Virginia. They saw about a dozen red-headed woodpeckers and shared a giant puffball mushroom that Joe had found. He recalls that "the day was magical, even though John, as TSA head, occasionally was on his government Blackberry calmly dealing with some dangerous incident in an airport. He's the least paranoid person I know, part of the solidity of his Christian faith." Woodpeckers and mushrooms notwithstanding, the nation's security had to be maintained.

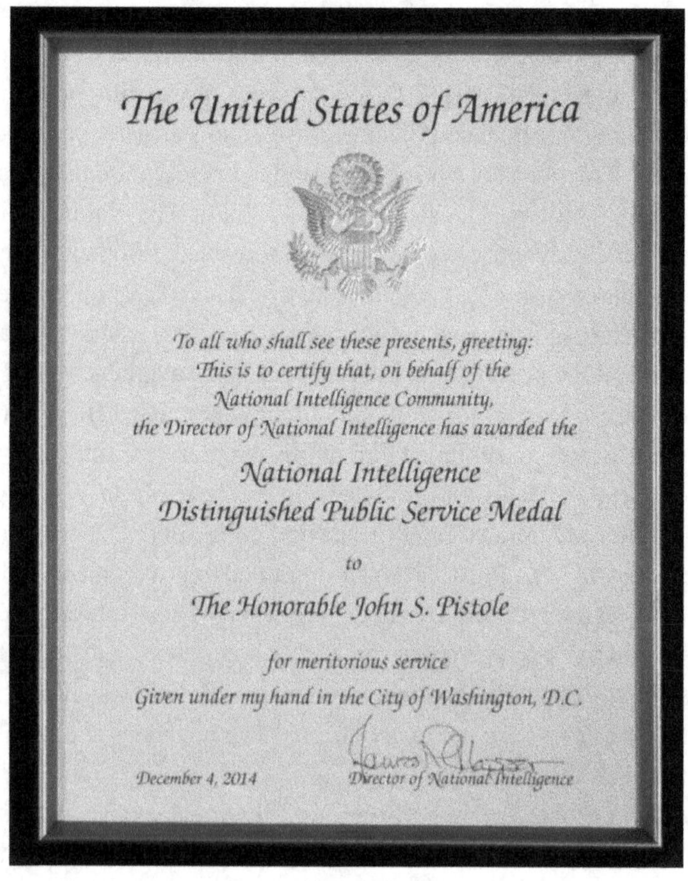

The United States of America

To all who shall see these presents, greeting:
This is to certify that, on behalf of the
National Intelligence Community,
the Director of National Intelligence has awarded the

National Intelligence
Distinguished Public Service Medal

to

The Honorable John S. Pistole

for meritorious service
Given under my hand in the City of Washington, D.C.

December 4, 2014 — Director of National Intelligence

On leaving the TSA in 2014, John Pistole was honored with a Distinguished Public Service Medal by the National Intelligence Community of the United States.

Threads of an Emerging Tapestry

By 2019, in the judgment of Senator Dan Coats, John Pistole had "straightened out" the TSA, was a valued and highly admired personal friend, and had made a great decision to come home to Indiana to be the President of Anderson University. Coats understood Christian higher education, having graduated himself from Wheaton College and his sister from Taylor University.

Paul McNulty of the Department of Justice had done a similar thing in moving to the presidency of Grove City College in western Pennsylvania. Michael Mason of the FBI was now a Trustee of Illinois Wesleyan University in Illinois and Janet Napolitano of Homeland Security the President of the University of California. They would understand and appreciate John Pistole's big decision in 2014 to leave his latest prestigious leadership position in Washington to return home as President his alma mater, Anderson University.

That phase of John's story is told in chapters 14-17. Before that, however, we must recognize that, from his years as a lawyer in the early 1980s to his resignation in 2014 as Administrator of the TSA, a lovely tapestry had emerged in the life and service of John Pistole. It consisted of the many threads of personal relationships, family commitments, a faith foundation, the two lows, and the one pervasive high, being the calm eye of numerous hurricanes, all detailed above.

This personal life tapestry would be critical for the coming future. Before considering the next major assignment to be accepted by John Pistole, attention must first be given to family commitments. Here's a glimpse behind the public scene so critical to what had and yet would happen in John's personal life and ongoing career. He was happily married, loved his two daughters, and drew strength from his wife Kathy, while encouraging her to flourish in her own right.

At the 2012 retirement of Robert Mueller, in the Great Hall of the Department of Justice. L. to R., Dave Margolis, John Pistole, Eric Holder, Robert Mueller, George Tenet, and James Cole.

Chapter 11

Never Leaving Kathy Behind

Most adults today have or will live in various houses, apartments, or trailers. Which is to be thought of as "home"? John and Kathy have moved many times during his complex career. They learned that home is where the other is.

Let the wife make the husband glad to come home, and let him make her sorry to see him leave. —Martin Luther

What has transpired in the various government roles of John Pistole are best understood by more than reading the above chapters, public headlines, and testimony transcripts. It's worth also being aware of John's home life throughout those publicity-packed thirty-one years. In many ways the home has been foundational for him, just usually out of sight. John avoided the pitfalls that have destroyed so many lives of prominent public leaders.

Why has he had this ability? His deep spiritual life is key, of course. The other answer is his wife Kathy. While out of the bright lights most of the time, she always has been there for John with her love, strength, financial sacrifice, quiet wisdom, and willingness to move several times. His observation about this? "She has learned the discipline of perseverance and fortitude."

The first two or three years of marriage were "a bit rocky," as Kathy frankly puts it. John agrees. "We had different paradigms but we survived." They had to work things out, do it together, and find ways forward in their faith, marital relationship, and professional lives.

The twin life goals, as Martin Luther puts it, are finding the gladness of coming home and creating the sadness of having to leave. The complex and demanding worlds of John's lawyer training and then high-profile FBI and TSA roles provided many challenges and opportunities in the Pistole home. Kathy was always sad to see John leave, but comforted in knowing that his tasks were truly important, and that he knew his true home was wherever she was.

Beginning a Family

One opportunity for Kathy Harp emerged quickly during John's first FBI field assignment in Minneapolis, Minnesota. This setting was plagued with enough public corruption and human trafficking to keep John plenty busy. But it also featured a rich array of cultural and educational institutions, and Kathy was ready to be stretched educationally and professionally. Both members of this young couple soon were on the move in different although equally productive directions.

John describes his wife with the words "loving," "engaging," "contemplative," "deep thinker," "very caring." The caring part would be quite evident both inside and outside their home. Kathy returned to school in Minneapolis, enrolling in the University of Minnesota. While John was an FBI field agent learning the ropes and dealing with human tragedy, often in the form of rampant human trafficking, Kathy began developing the skills needed to serve the hearing impaired. She earned a Master of Education degree in Special Education with a focus in deaf education and an initial learning of American Sign Language.

When John was reassigned to New York City, Kathy wasn't quite finished with the course work. John managed to get a three-month extension to accommodate her need. Then they took up life together in New Jersey. Why that far away from John's new work in Manhattan? It was a matter of money. Young field agents weren't paid very well and there was no raise in salary offered from Minnesota to this East Coast location with its higher cost of living.

Kathy and John managed to buy a modest home in New Jersey, helped with a loan for the downpayment coming from John's parents. It had two bedrooms, one bath, and not quite 1,000 square feet of floor space. Fortunately, Kathy found a job in a real estate office. Then, thanks to a contact arranged by her Minnesota degree advisor, she secured a teaching position in the best school for the deaf in the state.

Both faced long daily commutes, a necessary evil for years to come. She taught in a middle school for three years in the fields of math, social studies, and communication arts. After the first two years, while on a vacation, there came the personal trauma of a miscarriage. Kathy managed the emotional pain, returning to the third year of teaching.

Unfortunately, the stress level now increased considerably for Kathy and a decision had to be made. They wanted to start a family and were willing to risk another pregnancy, so the couple agreed that they could manage on John's income. What Kathy needed to do was leave teaching and begin caring for herself. In 1990 daughter Lauren was born while they were still living in New Jersey. Later that year John's role shifted to FBI headquarters in Washington.

They bought a home in nearby Maryland with room for a second daughter, Jennifer, who was born in 1992. Part of the motivation for this professional move was to be nearer to Kathy's parents so the girls could develop relationships with their Harp grandparents. These girls became a loved treasure in the lives of parents and grandparents. Each daughter now is a single adult, one a librarian in Boston and the other a customer service representative for a company in Virginia.

John, despite his many professional moves over the years, and the related family relocations, determined to be a real father and attentive husband despite the unusual demands. Kathy would be the home anchor and John supportive in all ways possible.

Levels of Danger and Distraction

How were things experienced by Kathy in John Pistole's home life, especially during the many FBI and TSA years? Kathy has been questioned about this and her answers aren't always the expected ones. Naturally, John couldn't tell her much about many of the things he was doing over the years. She admits that "I'd probably be proud of them if I knew what they were!" Typically, John would be up early most days for his long daily commute, and then arrive home rather late. Despite such stressful demands, Kathy would be especially proud of one thing about him. He was determined when he could be home to have energy left to be a real husband and father to their two girls.

Of course, John had to miss many of the usual daytime school events of their daughters Lauren, born 1990, and Jennifer, born 1992. Still, somehow he managed to let them know that he really loved them. It wasn't unusual for John to help with their homework despite his phone constantly ringing. He read to them the Nancy Drew mystery books, even after long days at work dealing with mysteries bigger than any in those books! Although traveling much, often out of the country, he was intentional about home, something very important to him. He reports, "I spent at home what personal time there was. No golf for me. That would have made things much worse."

Kathy might be expected to say that much of the time she lived in fear for John's safety. Despite all the necessary secrecy, she obviously knew that he dealt daily with dangerous people and circumstances. But that anxiety was lessened a bit by his telling her that organized crime bosses tend to respect the police and FBI agents. These shady characters tend to see themselves as respectable businessmen "doing their jobs," and they assume that people like John are just doing theirs.

What they hate, and are quick to "take care of," are the double-crossers and undercover infiltrators. Such people tend to have shortened lives. John assured Kathy that he was never an undercover man. Still, after 9/11, John was dealing with terrorist plots and people who have little respect for anyone they think of as enemies of the Muslim world. Even then, however, John was typically in investigation and administration as opposed to direct confrontation with the "bad guys."

Kathy admits to fearing her husband's long daily commute. There was that day when John got stranded in a traffic jam near the Holland Tunnel. Men jumped out of two vehicles ready for battle, one with a tire iron and the other a baseball bat. How could Kathy help her husband in such a crisis on the city roadways? Worrying and praying helped some, and there were other situations that also put occasional pressure on Kathy's emotions.

Shortly after the birth of their first daughter, Lauren in May of 1990, there came a fateful day in John's career. Mom was absorbed with the new demands of an infant in the home and Dad was spending long days away doing things from which she had to be shielded. On this day, John led the FBI arrest team for Mob boss Vincent "The Chin" Gigante. Finally home that day, physically and emotionally exhausted, John didn't mention the arrest to her. His priority agenda wasn't reporting but loving and hopefully sleeping. After all, by early morning he'd have to be off to something else unknown but likely not dull.

Not much home secrecy was needed in the case of "The Chin's" arrest. The big event was quickly pasted all over the New York media. There was an action photo featuring John and a handful of other FBI agents escorting the Mob boss from the U. S. Attorney's office and courts. Kathy was comforted at least in knowing what was going on. She also was naturally concerned for the safety of her husband. Little Lauren needed her Daddy.

While he would do all he could, some circumstances limited John's home abilities considerably, and certainly did little to lower anxiety levels at home. Eventually, especially after the 9/11 terrorist attacks on the United States, John would make many trips abroad, some particularly tense, like to Iraq and Saudi Arabia. Kathy always knew that he was going into difficult circumstances without being aware of the details. At least he was a true professional, well prepared, and accompanied by a skilled security detail.

At least Kathy wasn't left alone very often. "He was calm prior to going," she says, "and I was concerned for his safety, sure, but I was confident that whatever happened, it would be OK. And I did have a good support system with both of my sisters in the area and good friends at church and as neighbors."

Kathy's modest about her accomplishments in anchoring the home. She handled the "basic custodial roles" and cared for the girls in ways John couldn't. She admits to struggling with some occasional depression, and at such times "I only did the minimal to get along." While he needed to lean on her for many things, she readily admits, "I leaned on John a lot, the amazing husband that he is."

This leaning did go both ways. Marie Morris, current Provost of Anderson University, says she loves to see John and Kathy together, partly because Kathy's role is so interesting. When John gets excessively enthusiastic about something, and he does have the tendency "to get carried away a little," Kathy "just rolls her eyes in the cutest of ways." John smiles at this observation and says about his wife, "Yes, she's good at keeping me in my place."

One aspect of Kathy's place in John's life has been the provision of careful judgment. At key times in his public career, with a critical judgment needed, John would turn to her for perspective, and always has taken seriously her wisdom. Back in their college days, he had confessed to her his enjoyment of drinking as a teenager. Part of why he stopped drinking was her probing response. She stimulated deep reflection on his part by questioning his underlying motives for such a destructive practice.

The same would be true later in his public career in government. By 2013 John had begun wondering about his life after the federal government. He was being courted for a major position in the private sector that involved much international travel and a very large compensation increase. After a series of positive interviews, and a likely coming offer, he approached Kathy about it. He admitted to being intrigued and tempted on both the travel and compensation fronts.

But Kathy thought there was a possible problem. She quizzed John again about his motives. "The travel fine, that interests me too, but is your openness to this possibility also a lot about the big money?" He faced that question head-on, realized that any such attraction was in conflict with their Christian values, and soon said "No" to the looming big offer before the company had opportunity to make it.

Problems also came their way over the years because of several crises in John's extended family. There was the gambling problem of John's brother David and the heartbreaking death of their infant son, the divorce of his sister Carole, the death of sister Cindy's husband Carl, and of course the deaths of John's beloved mother in 2005 and father in 2006. Kathy reports simply that "we as a family responded to all of these issues with grief and compassion, processing each in stride over time."

Particularly difficult was the time of David's double problem of an addiction and the death of a very young child. While his need for money was known to John and Kathy, requests were resisted since the need was tied to the addiction and any co-dependency had to be avoided. John, of course, was very aware of the work of loan sharks and had to protect his own family while determining how best to lovingly support his brother. Fortunately, David could not draw down his Pennsylvania retirement fund and so now is enjoying a reasonable retirement after the crisis had been resolved. John fully agrees with Kathy's overall assessment. They responded to each family crisis as a Christian family should, with compassion as each circumstance required and permitted.

Church Involvement Always Important

What helped John and Kathy handle dangers and crises over the years was their determination to be faithful to regular church attendance and involvement to every degree possible. Their attempted congregational relationships from place to place included more than one Church of God congregation. This was natural given their backgrounds in this particular Christian tradition. Unfortunately, these experiences weren't always the best, with the exception of Fairfax, Virginia.

Sometimes a congregation, like in Minneapolis, turned out to be an older group of people with whom busy young professionals couldn't connect easily. At one church there was a minister who preached "fire and brimstone," quite unlike the nurturing home congregations of John and Kathy's growing-up years. Because John's parents were well known across the Church of God, he wasn't overly fond of hearing things like, "Oh, are you Hollis and Elizabeth's boy?"

They, Kathy particularly, needed some separation from the past and room to be herself. She loved her parents dearly, as John did his, but she "needed to become my own person." While located in New Jersey with John commuting to Manhattan, they developed a friendship with Jim and Betty York, he an orthopedic surgeon and tennis player—a great recreational outlet for John. Kathy's aunt was Elizabeth York.[29] Jim and John occasionally played doubles together.

After John's work took the family to the Washington, D.C., area, within driving distance of the church pastored by Kathy's father, she explained to her parents that she and John needed to attend church elsewhere. Richard and Clella Harp are very understanding people. They knew that Kathy and John both loved their parents deeply and they were very proud of what John and Kathy were doing with their lives.

As an alternative, they became active in the Union Village United Methodist Church congregation in New Jersey. There they met and became lifelong friends with Joe and Betsy Bush. On an Easter Sunday morning the two couples happened to sit near each other in church. They introduced themselves and learned that they all lived in Plainfield. Joe announced that he and Betsy had no particular plans for Easter dinner that day except going home and fixing pancakes. So the four ate pancakes together for Easter and became fast friends. As Joe puts it, "it was the simplicity of celebration and the celebration of simplicity."

Joe holds a Ph.D. from Drew University and had taught in a seminary in the Twin Cities where John first had functioned as a street agent. He had become a prominent professor and director of the practice of Christian ministry at Wesley Seminary in Washington. Soon after their initial meeting, a weekly Bible study was formed at the church. John attended faithfully despite his long commutes to New York City. Joe recalls that he "would bring his NIV Study Bible and contribute to the conversation by pointing out the footnotes and his own reflections." This was "a strong, supportive, and prayerful fellowship," recalls Joe.

Years later, while United Methodist members, a good place of part-time and supplemental church involvement for John and Kathy was the large Fairfax Community Church in Virginia. This congregation, affiliated with the Church of God Movement of John and Kathy's roots, was pastored by Rev. Rod Stafford. He had completed his seminary education through the doctoral level on the Anderson, Indiana, campus and his brother Gilbert was the theology professor there, a colleague of John's father. Rod had been welcomed into the ministry there in Virginia in 1986 by Kathy's father, Rev. Dick Harp, whom Rod came to respect highly. John and Kathy attended Fairfax a couple of Saturday evenings a month for several years while maintaining their membership in the Centreville United Methodist Church.

The Fairfax congregation, located just outside the Washington Beltway, included numerous members well connected at various levels in the Washington establishment. It held an annual multi-day conference on faith and vocation. It was called the "Blue Conference" because the sanctuary's seats are blue and it's assumed that the people sitting in those seats are best positioned to influence all sectors of Washington life. Explains Pastor Stafford, "That's how the Kingdom gets advanced, by believers fulfilling their vocations through the lens of their Christian faith. That's why we brought John Pistole one year as a featured speaker to tell his story. He's the perfect embodiment of 'Blue'."[30]

That embodiment was recognized elsewhere. A good friend of John's in Washington was Paul McNulty, Deputy Attorney General who now serves as President of Grove City College in western Pennsylvania. John and Paul once were invited to be joint plenary speakers at an annual convention in Washington of the Council for Christian Colleges and Universities, a prominent body dedicated to the life-changing work of Christian higher education.

This was another "Blue" conference. The idea was to feature two highly-placed and successful government officials who could address the issue of how their own experiences in Christian institutions of higher education had served them well in taking their faith commitments into the public sphere. At the time, of course, neither John nor Paul knew that in a few years both would return to their home campuses as presidents.

John and Kathy would affiliate with other United Methodist congregations over the years. Of special significance was the one back in Indiana in the years 1994-1999. John was then assigned to the Indianapolis FBI office and he and Kathy lived in nearby Fishers. They became very involved in St. Marks United Methodist Church in Carmel. This involvement was so significant that Kathy felt that "for the first time a congregation had become so like home."

They shared in a Bible study and discipleship training. Kathy was coordinator of parish care meals and sang in the chancel choir. John provided "a huge gift" to her by coming home from work early on her choir rehearsal days, caring for the girls then and also while she sang on Sundays. In this setting they were continuing to learn the richness of the Wesleyan Christian tradition, tied closely with the Church of God tradition of both of their originating families. In fact, when later John would become President of Anderson University, one of his early contacts was with the President's Fellowship of the Wesleyan Holiness Connection in which Barry Callen, Vice-President emeritus of Anderson University, had been a part since the WHC's beginning.[31]

For the most part John enjoyed being a supervisor in the Indianapolis FBI office. After five years, however, enthusiasm for his work there had dwindled. A promotion upward and elsewhere was a growing interest, but would mean becoming available to the FBI wherever needed, probably requiring more travel and multiple family moves ahead. Kathy understandably hesitated, telling John, "I can't leave here, this now is home."

John admitted that he had gotten "bored" with his work, but still responded with, "OK, then I'll stick with my present work in Indianapolis and turn down the new challenge available to me."[32] Kathy was appreciative of John's willingness to remain where they were, but she struggled with the rightness of her own feelings. Was she being selfish and unfair to John?

Kathy went to Karen Davis, wife of her pastor, to get advice. A move now threatened the comfortable home and school settings of the girls in Fishers. Further, there was the wonderful St. Marks congregation in nearby Carmel and the Pistole grandparents and two aunts of the girls only a short drive away in Anderson. Wasn't that too much to leave behind?

What she was expecting to hear was, "Stick to your guns, girl. You are home, so stay." Instead, Kathy was confronted with this question. "What did you promise John when you married him?" It was then that Kathy began to realize what should happen next. They would move again, probably more than once. They and the girls somehow would manage and to do it all together. Kathy's "change of heart" freed John to begin looking and applying elsewhere. Soon he would be the second man in the Boston FBI office, have opportunity to oversee FBI work in much of the New England area, and then be promoted to the broader role of inspecting FBI offices nationally from the Boston base (and still later much more after that!).

The family moved from Fishers, Indiana, to Shrewsbury, a commute from west of Boston that would require long daily drives for John, nearly forty miles each way. At least John would be provided with an FBI car. They settled that far out for reasons of affordability and the presence of a reasonable neighborhood and its educational opportunities for their daughters. This certainly wouldn't be the last move but, all things considered, it was a good one and they would manage it well, and also the others still to come.

Here is Kathy's comment about how generous and selfless John is in relation to the several necessary family moves. "He was willing to sacrifice to be sure that his family was well-situated." Of course, that's John.

Ending and Beginning

The decision to leave Indiana for Boston was pivotal. It opened doors that neither John nor Kathy could have imagined at the time. It was the ending of a highlight time for them and also an unbelievable beginning. The terrible 9/11 terrorist attacks were two years away. That would change everything for the United States and thrust John into the world of counterterrorism, which in turn would lead rather quickly to leadership roles beyond any of his dreams.

John and Kathy left Fishers in 1999 for him to become the second man in the Boston office as Assistant Special Agent in Charge for White Collar Crime, Cyber Crime, and Civil Rights Investigations in four New England states. Circumstances somehow soon mixed with divine providence to lead by 2004 to his becoming the second man nationally, the Deputy Director of the FBI! Along the way to such a surprising destination, John and Kathy had faced several faith-straining experiences over the years, as most families eventually do.

One was losing their first child by miscarriage while living in New Jersey and on a skiing trip to Colorado with friends. John's shifting work assignments took the couple from home to home in places near Minneapolis, New York, Indianapolis, Boston, and Washington. Naturally, there was considerable stress and disruption, finding affordable housing, the changing schools for the girls, some danger for John, and touches of occasional depression for Kathy. Life could be complicated and demanding, but this family was comprised of overcomers.

In 2005 and 2006, for instance, there was another unwelcome ending. John's aging parents each became seriously ill back in Indiana. In the late 1990s John and Kathy had moved back to Indiana for him to assume an FBI position in Indianapolis, motivated in part by wanting their girls to be close to the Pistole grandparents and their aunts in Anderson. But now, as final illnesses set in for Hollis and Elizabeth, John was heavily involved as Deputy Director at FBI headquarters in Washington. This distance was hard for John to bear.

John's sisters, Cindy and Carole both living near the parents in Anderson, Indiana, kept in close touch, and did everything possible to help the ailing parents on a daily basis. John wished he had been closer so he could have given his sisters "a break" occasionally. When funerals became necessary, daughters Lauren and Jennifer were concerned about missing time away from high school, and John would have to wrench himself away from pressing national matters. No matter. Family was crucial. Hollis and Elizabeth, so typical of them, had planned their funeral services in detail. Kathy recalls this planning "as a huge gift" and the services themselves wonderful, remembering, healing, quality closure events. They were in the home Park Place congregation.

The Pistole parents had invested richly in their four children, all of whom have been successful professionals. The youngest, John, helped always by his wife Kathy, has made an impact nationally and internationally. In his remarks at his father's funeral, he praised his sisters for being so loving and loyal in the final months of life for both parents. He spoke of his father as a hero who had laid a great foundation for the future. Many present viewed John as doing the same thing.

Can She Be Comfortable?

It's not easy for a wife to find the freedom to become all that she desires when her husband is very prominent in the public eye. This is especially true when he is constantly being called away on urgent business, sometimes shrouded in secrecy, sometimes to other countries, and with young children in the home. Kathy Harp faced this for many years and is most gracious in her assessment. Despite everything, she reports, "my husband has been fully committed to the well-being of his family despite his responsibilities."

At crucial times of pending transition, this exceptional couple has managed to talk things through and go on with a minimum of disruption, at least in their relationship. The move from Minneapolis to New York in the 1980s involved financial strain that they found ways to handle. The possible family moves to Italy and then to Israel in the following decade brought excitement and then needed adjustments when circumstances derailed both pending plans. Having to leave Fishers, Indiana, in 1999 was particularly difficult for Kathy, but she found wise counsel in their beloved church congregation and worked through the questions quite well.

The situation that came along in 2014 was especially demanding. John certainly had been forced to stretch to be the FBI Deputy Director in 2004 and then the TSA Administrator in 2010. But now he was being asked to move away entirely from the Washington scene and federal government and attempt to apply his experience and skills in the very different world of higher education. Years of living on the East Coast had the benefit for Kathy of being relatively close to where her parents and two sisters lived. All became threatened by an unexpected phone call.

Family friend Bob Coffman from back in Anderson, Indiana, had earlier tested John's potential interests in possibilities after his federal service concluded. There was some clear openness to significant change and that filtered its way back to the presidential Search Committee of Anderson University being chaired by Pat Bailey.[33] Now on the telephone for John was Lou Gerig, Chair of the Board of Trustees of Anderson University, undergraduate alma mater of both John and Kathy. Would John entertain an invitation to move back to his hometown in Indiana and likely complete his career in the Mid-West as the university's new president?

As he now looks back years later, John admits his initial surprise to the idea of his being President. Sure, he immediately recognized that his values aligned well with those of A. U. but, with no background in higher education administration, at first he reacted privately with this humorous thought. "When I was there as a student it was a dry campus. I wonder what they're now smoking back in Indiana that would lead them to consider a person like me!"

Leaders of the Board of Trustees were very sensitive to the possible reluctance of Kathy to make such a dramatic move. This was especially true of Lou Gerig who is a cousin of Kathy. He knew that her parents were aging and retired in Deleware and that her sisters still lived in Virginia and Maryland. While Kathy was highly supportive of John's calling, she also is an independent individual whose concerns had to be considered. It was made clear to Kathy by the Search Committee that any necessary assistance would be able available to her so that she could visit her family as often as necessary once a relocation to Anderson was complete.

And what would be expected of her in campus life? After all, previous first ladies had played prominent roles. Gerig spoke to Kathy personally about this on behalf of the Board. She would be allowed to find her own way. Board Vice-Chair Dennis Carroll was aware that John and Kathy each have "a strong appreciation for individuality." Given this, he recalls the significance for the overall call process when Kathy expressed willingness to go wherever John decided. "I will do what's right for John, and his people will be my people."

Coming back to Anderson would have the awkwardness of being invited to attend virtually every banquet and special event where John would be. Previously, she had been invited to only select occasions where John was to attend, with no expectation that she be there. No matter. Kathy would have many friends in Indiana, a life of her own as desired, and soon she would find pleasure in hosting in the President's home various groups of faculty, staff, and students, especially enjoying the Life Groups (students).

Many relationships on campus would turn out for Kathy to be "satisfying and invigorating." Once the relocation was complete, she acknowledges that John "found that he had much heavy-lifting to do." Standing faithfully beside him, whatever the challenges, she confesses with emotion, "I love and respect John so very much!" She would shower love on many in the campus community and her extended family already had expressed much love for the Anderson campus. Kathy's paternal grandparents, Rev. Harry and Mrs. Henrietta Harp, are namesakes of an endowed memorial fund in the School of Theology. Kathy, as noted previously, is also the niece of Drs. James and Elizabeth York whose generosity can be seen across the Anderson campus.

John and Kathy did wind up serving back in Indiana and attending John's home congregation, Park Place Church of God. They certainly knew how to adapt to new settings, and Anderson would be a good one indeed.

President Barack Obama, daughter Jennifer Pistole,
wife Kathy Harp, and John Pistole, 2015.

John Pistole, wife Kathy, daughters Lauren and Jennifer

The John Pistole family, with wife Kathy Harp,
daughters Lauren and Jennifer,
and the children of Uganda, Africa,
sponsored by John and Kathy through Children of Promise.

Chapter 12

Back Home Again In Indiana

I believe God takes the things in our lives--family, background, education--and uses them as part of our callings. I don't think God wastes anything. —Eugene H. Peterson

President Pistole's lack of background in how higher education works may be just what we needed in 2015. John doesn't get caught in looking only to the past. He is decisive and looks to a fresh future that's needed. —Janet Brewer, Anderson University librarian

In 2014 John Pistole was named the fifth president of Anderson University, assuming office in March of 2015. It was fortunate that by then, in addition to having a great family of origin, he had accumulated the considerable assets of an excellent education, a clear Christian identity, and lots of experience in administering large organizations and facing their often complex and urgent crises. His hometown university had nearly a century of marvelous service behind it and yet big challenges just ahead. They would require all that John had to offer.

Compared to the scale of things the new university president had been used to, Anderson University would be a relatively small organization, although one operating in territory relatively unfamiliar to John. Even so, as Eugene Peterson says, "God doesn't waste anything." John may not have been an experienced administrator in the world of higher education, but he would bring much that was relevant to the new task at hand, and God would allow little of his past to go unused.

The circumstance was much like Clarence Macartney's first time to meet Woodrow Wilson. Macartney, the beloved preacher/author after whom Macartney Library of Geneva College is named,[34] was a student at Princeton Seminary when Wilson was named its new President. Had he not been so named, "Wilson would not have been elected as Governor of New Jersey; and except for his record as Governor, he would not have been nominated by the Democratic Party for the Presidency of the United States. Thus do great issues turn on the hinges of apparently small events."[35]

Faithfulness to God's will in the things at hand often leads to unanticipated larger gifts and greater responsibilities. That raises the assertion made by a contemporary biographer about the heroic role Winston Churchill played on behalf of Great Britain in World War II. "The point of the 'Churchill Factor' is that one man can make all the difference."[36] A world war wasn't facing Anderson University in 2015, but there were dark clouds, big challenges, and the hopes of many that the "Pistole Factor" would manage to turn the tide toward a viable new future. John already had faced successfully several very big challenges for the whole nation and now sensed God's call for him to lead this campus forward in whatever its circumstances were and would be.

Missing DNA?

One question was being raised on occasion. Despite all his great gifts and professional experience, had John Pistole somehow been deprived of a key element of the DNA shared by his parents and three siblings? They all were dedicated teachers, covering the full range of elementary, middle school, high school, university, and graduate seminary settings. John hadn't headed that way early in life, instead choosing law and then government service. The family's extensive educational DNA report looks like this:

> Mother Elizabeth—was a highly respected counselor and teacher at Anderson
>
> High School for many years, retiring in 1983. She was an A. U. graduate, 1943.

Father Hollis—taught at Anderson University's graduate School of Theology for twenty-five years, retiring in 1984. He was an A. U. graduate, 1945.

Sister Cindy—taught in middle school and then at Anderson University from 1987 to 2011. She was an A. U. graduate, 1968.

Sister Carole—taught for many years in the Anderson Community School Corporation, also retiring in 2011. She was an A. U. graduate, 1972.

Brother David—served as a longtime professor of biology at the Indiana University of Pennsylvania, retiring in 2017. He was an A. U. graduate, 1977.

Brother John, the youngest of the Pistole children, apparently missed the memo explaining that he was supposed to be a teacher. This communication gap would be filled finally, although it took him thirty-seven years to find his way back to Anderson University. He had been an A. U. graduate, 1978, he same year his wife Kathy Harp graduated from the Anderson campus.

John would be the family's late bloomer in terms of being an educational professional. Despite the lateness, he would emerge as a superb teacher/administrator.

The lack of educational focus had begun to dissolve over time, even in the midst of John carrying so many other kinds of titles and roles. As a well-informed FBI agent and then executive, increasingly persons in governmental power had turned to him for briefings and detailed instruction on a range of national security matters. Sometimes it was explaining complex and controversial matters to a commission or congressional committee in Washington. Sometimes it was in the Oval Office of the White House where John prepared carefully and briefed U. S. Presidents of both political parties. Sometimes it came to involve his direct classroom instruction in investigative and security matters. His classrooms were primarily in the United States and Europe. Whatever hat he wore at given times, John had emerged as a skilled educator.

The FBI Academy was a very familiar setting to John. After becoming Administrator of the Transportation Security Administration in 2010, he continued his educating ways. The TSA was in considerable need of its large staff being professionalized. With his great appreciation for the FBI's Academy, John conceived and got Congress to fund a new TSA Academy in Georgia, complete with a mock airline terminal and other facilities for trucks and trains that could give new officers hands-on training experience in real-life surroundings. He then provided personal training videos for the many students who would benefit in coming years.

When agreeing to become President of Anderson University, none of John's administrative or educational expertise would be wasted. The administrative part would be central, of course, but he also would be a guest classroom lecturer in psychology, communications, and particularly cyber-crimes, criminal justice, and national security. Had he missed the Pistole teaching DNA? Not really!

Admittedly, John arrived on A. U.'s campus lacking much direct knowledge of the world of higher education. He would have to do some learning on the job. And yet, the comment of Janet Brewer, campus librarian, must be taken into account. "President Pistole's lack of background in how higher education works may be just what we needed in 2015. John doesn't get caught in looking only to the past. He is decisive and looks to a fresh future that's needed."

John and siblings Cindy, Carole, and David

Carole, David, Cindy, and John

Another Challenge Calls

John Pistole and his wife Kathy Harp were caught off guard at first. Initially a call had come to John from his friend Bob Coffman while John was head of the TSA. Now another came, this time not merely a friendly contact and general inquiry. This one was significant and maybe life-changing. Calls of an urgent nature were almost a daily experience for John. It would take something truly dramatic to shock him. This second call was of that sort. On the line this time was Lou Gerig, representing the Anderson University Board of Trustees.

John knew Lou, a relative of Kathy, but not the call's purpose. At first he thought Lou was asking for the names of candidates qualified for the presidency now opening on the Anderson campus, John's beloved alma mater back in Indiana. After he had asked for a day or so to come up with some names to help, Lou clarified the misunderstanding. "We are asking *you* to consider this position, John!" Eventually he would accept, bringing him full circle in life.

John was an experienced administrator of very large organizations and had strong academic credentials, but admittedly he wasn't familiar with the world of higher education administration. When he had initially shared the invitation from A. U. with his wife Kathy, she reports, "I had to pick myself off the floor!"

"John, you aren't a pastor, don't have a terminal degree in higher education—you're not qualified!" And yet, after a little reflection, she realized this. "John's capable and confident. He knows what he can do. If he decides to accept this big invitation, he'll do the job and do it well."

Bob Coffman, John's friend since their shared college and young lawyer days, had tested this presidential possibility informally with John in the months prior, learning at least that John had begun thinking about his post-Washington life. John had shared privately with Bob that he would have interest eventually in heading some large not-for-profit that served people well, preferably a church-related one. He was a Christian servant not necessarily tied to the government for his entire career. Further, given his strong Christian commitment, he would be open to something without a huge salary attached, something that surely would come his way if he wished.

In Bob's mind that interest spelled the possibility of Anderson University. Bob always had kept in touch with Dr. Larry Osnes, one of his college professors and mentor in the Center for Public Service on the Anderson campus. After founding the CPS in the early 1970s, Larry had served as President of Hamline University in Minnesota for many years. Now he was retired and, through a casual contact with A. U. trustee Bill Gaither, had become a consultant to President James Edwards late in his presidential tenure. Larry was now serving as a consultant to the A. U. presidential Search Committee after the retirement announcement of President Edwards.

The name of John Pistole finally had come up in the Search Committee's deliberations and members had keen interest in this possibility. Thus, Gerig's call to John. Yes, the world of higher education would be quite the change of settings for John, but the committee was looking "outside the box" for someone who saw the bigger world, had faced major issues with integrity, and could lead the school forward in challenging times. That certainly might be John.

John indeed would pray about and then accept this new challenge, but only after several consultations. He initiated a long talk with his brother David who was finishing a full career in higher education. John engaged his friends Jeff and Debbie Jenness as prayer partners. They knew how capable he was, especially when relying on God's help, and were excited at the possibility. Close friends John and Gwen Johnson visited John and Kathy in Washington, were informed of the impending decision, and also were encouraging.

At the time, John Johnson was a faculty leader at Warner Pacific University in Portland, Oregon, one of Anderson's sister schools. He told John and Kathy about the sometimes stressful relationships between a college faculty and its administration. Yes, that world would be different from the FBI and TSA, but the many skills John had developed in federal service surely would carry over. Organizational life is similar whatever its scale. The Johnsons made this point to John and told him that he had something special that would be a great advantage in the role of a campus president. "You value people and have a way of letting them know it."

John also consulted privately with various leaders in Washington about his pending decision. One was Janet Napolitano, former Homeland Security Secretary to whom the TSA reported. She knew public higher education well, having worked with the public universities in Arizona when governor of that state and now the President of a large university in California. She explained to John that the culture of higher education is much more "consultative and shared-governance" in nature than the "command and control" style of leadership of the Washington agencies. "Even so, John," she concluded, "knowing you well as I do, I'm sure you could make the adjustment." Soon Janet would herself be the President of the University of California and John the President of Anderson University.

The A. U. Search Committee interviewed John in the private office of Bill Gaither in Alexandria, just a few miles from the Anderson campus, to avoid any premature and awkward publicity. The only real question Board members had was whether John's exceptional experience would translate to higher education. Dennis Carroll, Board vice-chair, recalls this strong impression gained from the interview: "We loved his humility, his heart, how very tuned he was to the spiritual life of the university. Yes, this would work."

A senior Trustee on the Search Committee, Bill Gaither, was cautious at first. The Committee must not be too easily overwhelmed by John's considerable credentials in another field. He asked John, "You'd be coming in a tough time in our history. Do you really want this job?" The response was, "I will come only if God wants me to. Kathy and I will pray seriously about the matter." Gaither then said to himself, "Yes, he's our man. He loves his parents, the school's history, his Lord, and he can look at things through a new window." Shortly, the decision was made.

As John and Kathy were preparing to leave Washington, close friend Joe Bush set up a luncheon meeting with the President of Washington's Wesley Seminary where Joe taught. This was an opportunity for John to converse with an experienced leader in Christian higher education. The president's advice to John included, "Be sure you have a really good Chief Financial Officer—money will be tight and must be managed well." How right he was, and how fortunate that eventually John would have women and men like Dana Stuart, Jim Ragsdale, Dan Courtney and Brock Vaughters on Anderson's money-management staff.

Realities of Timing

The challenging situation being faced by Anderson University in 2015 was not hidden by the Trustees from its chosen presidential candidate. The circumstances had some ominous similarities with those of the TSA when John Pistole had become its Administrator in 2010.

No, the university was not a young organization like the TSA. It soon would celebrate its centennial. And no, it had not suffered a series of short-lived Administrators like the TSA. In fact, the university had been led capably by four outstanding men with long presidential tenures. Organizationally speaking, neither was Anderson University in its infancy. It was widely respected for its professionalism, quality faculty, and the placement of its graduates. Nonetheless, the challenge before the new president probably would be as difficult as it had been with the TSA.

The golden age of Christian higher education in general was losing its luster in the public eye and was facing increasing scrutiny. Was it worth the higher-cost of private schools that lacked significant endowments and were heavily student-tuition dependent? How valuable to a fast-changing society was a labor-intensive campus operation with numerous large buildings to maintain? The internet now was allowing alternative educational routes and methods. Becoming very popular was studying online, at home, more cheaply, while employed, at one's leisure. Demographics of high school numbers weren't encouraging and, for many church-related schools like Anderson University, the loyalty and support of their founding denominations were declining.

The Church of God Movement had suffered several new realities that had weakened the church's historic relationship with its four American campuses, Anderson being the oldest and largest. "Since the end of the Great Depression, benevolent constants had smiled on Anderson, but they were disappearing."[37] Most of the regional church gatherings of church leaders, where college presidents could relate and advertise, had ended their significant lives. The national ministries structure had been reorganized by the opening of the twenty-first century, with the Commission on Christian Higher Education eliminated. Ending also was the convening of the annual national convention of the church on the Anderson campus grounds, no longer introducing the school to many thousands of the church's faithful.

The Pistole presidency would have to begin in different circumstances than were enjoyed by its predecessor. In 1990 the City of Anderson had been looking for ways to recover from the dramatic downsizing of General Motors locally. By then the university that carried the city's name was a standout of local pride and had partnered with city and state leaders in founding the Flagship Enterprise Center as a new business incubator and accelerator. President Edwards, John's immediate predecessor, had provided leadership in a wide range of city, state, and national organizations.

He had raised the presidential office of the university to a new level of civic maturity and respect.

Nonetheless, in his final report as President to the Board of Trustees in 2015, Edwards had admitted that things were becoming difficult. He was managing to achieve a balanced budget at the cost of "significant reductions in faculty, staff, and programs." He insisted that Anderson University had not wavered in its "devotion to our founding church and to so many on whose shoulders we stand as we fulfill the stewardship of this mission, but we do so in a whirlwind of cultural change."

On the negative side, the years 2005 to 2015 had witnessed a steady student enrollment decline, budget cuts, and the resulting lowering of campus morale. Bob Coffman, Vice-President for Advancement for thirteen years, would be a vital source of background information and transitional support to his friend, the new President. He had planned to retire in 2015 but would agree to stay a bit longer if John accepted the presidency and desired his assistance. Campus donors must be met and the school's identity freshly established by a new and different leader. Once in office, John would readily accept this help.

Why John Pistole would value highly the historic mission of Anderson University goes back to his own undergraduate years. But why would he now fit well in this new challenge when his career had not been in higher education? The answer came in part from James Comey, former Director of the FBI, who spoke at John's Inauguration. He announced that "John is one of the finest men I have ever known." James had watched John serve for years as Deputy Director of the Federal Bureau of Investigation, "a job that usually burns people up and causes them to crack a little, and in frustration belittle the people around them. John didn't crack and wouldn't know how to belittle others."

Comey went on. John had been one of the rare ones in Washington who had avoided the constant temptation of those in power to bend the rules when convenient and break people as necessary. "Many cannot take the long view or understand the importance to the country of doing things the right way, no matter the inconvenience. Washington isn't known for men and women who have large souls and small egos, who manage to be successful while staying honest, kind, and full of integrity. John's naturally kind and tough, an effective combination in a leader."

Laughter erupted at the Inauguration when Comey added this to his glowing comments about John. "And at times he's a corny dude!" Turning quickly toward the Trustees seated on the platform, he added this reassurance. "Nothing to worry about—he's a good kind of corny dude!" John's brother David, clearly another admirer, sometimes calls John "a knucklehead." Quite the combinations—tough and kind, a decisive leader with a large soul who's also a corny dude and knucklehead, someone cranking out in a college dorm the crazy sounds of "The Three Stooges" and then also calmly responding to loaded questions before suspicious congressional committees.

Local newspaper columnist Jim Bailey played off John's last name and the firearm theme, titling his *Anderson Herald Bulletin* announcement "Pistole Takes Aim at Preserving A. U. Tradition of Excellence." Patricia Seasor Bailey, Chair of the Trustee's search committee, said in her introduction of the new president, "He's a humble man, one who walks among giants while staying grounded."

John had made his big decision. It would be going back home to Indiana. Meanwhile, his friends John and Gwen Johnson were also in transition from Warner Pacific University to becoming international pastors for the Church of God in a congregation in Hanoi, Viet Nam. They already had served internationally in Korea, Egypt, and Lebanon, true global citizens like John. It would be from their new apartment in a bustling Asian city that they would watch proudly via the internet John's Inauguration ceremony back in Anderson.

It would be a new day for John and Kathy and the whole Anderson campus community. Campus personnel and its governing Board were very excited.

Getting Started

The Trustees of Anderson University staged a major announcement and introduction event on campus in October, 2014. Crowded into Reardon Auditorium were excited students, faculty, staff, the press, church leaders, and others. After some rousing music by the campus jazz band, Lou Gerig, Chair of the Board, stepped to the microphone. He made the formal announcement of the Trustee's election of Dr. John S. Pistole to be the next President and then yielded to Patricia Seasor Bailey.

As Chair of the Board's Search Committee, Patricia acknowledged the presence of Drs. Robert Nicholson and James Edwards, former A. U. presidents, and lauded their marvelous legacy of campus leadership. Then she proceeded to outline the key characteristics that had been sought in a new president and how John Pistole was outstanding in them all. John sat in a prominent chair on the platform, squirming a bit, seeming almost embarrassed at all the fuss and high compliments.

President Pistole with former presidents Robert A. Nicholson (left) and James L. Edwards (right)

Even though the historic book *River of Change* was ready for printing in celebration of the sesquicentennial of the City of Anderson, the editors decided to delay to make possible the inclusion of this major new event in the story of city's long history. The eventual book lists forty "Famous Andersonians," with twelve chosen to comprise a photo gallery of the greats. One of the twelve would be John Pistole, identified as "Top administrator of the Transportation and Security Administration under George W. Bush and Barack Obama, former Deputy Director of the FBI, and newly appointed as Anderson University president."[38]

The Board's inauguration planners had engaged local artist J. David Liverett to prepare composite sketches of the presidents of Anderson University, John about to become the fifth. His work was unveiled at an inau-

Presidents James L. Edwards (left) and John S. Pistole (right) with first ladies Deanna Edwards and Kathy Harp.

gural luncheon just prior to the formal inauguration event itself.[39] Then, at the big event in Reardon Auditorium, several speakers sang John's praises before he was invited to deliver his acceptance speech. It began with, "I am humbled and honored." The big challenge, he said, was "how best to pursue excellence in all things." Quoting Richard Foster, one of his spiritual mentors, "superficiality is the curse of our age."[40]

What would be the new President's overarching goal for the university's future? It would be nothing less than "a quality education in a Christian environment among people who really care about each other." Reading Romans 12:1-2, John said that future success "will not be all about me but a demonstration of the love of God through me. We must be bold about who we are and *Whose* we are." The faith tradition of the campus would be more than retained. It will be featured as central.

John was new but, as one would expect, he had made some careful preparation. Before actually assuming his new responsibilities, John and his wife Kathy had attended the annual meeting of the Council of Christian Colleges and Universities, an excellent orientation for both. Soon he would participate in an annual meeting of the President's Network of the Wesleyan Holiness Connection (WHC). Its goal is to increase involvement of the associated institutions of higher education in their Christian mission to the needs of today's world, emphasizing particularly their Wesleyan-Holiness Christian heritage. John determined to emphasize relevance to our times as an absolute necessity for the future.

In the volume that introduces the WHC's history, denominational members, and affiliates, new member John Pistole identifies himself as a "non-traditional president." His career prior to Christian higher education had been as a lawyer, followed by thirty-one years in the federal government with the Federal Bureau of Investigation and the Transportation Security Administration. "I realized that being president of a Christian liberal arts college would have new challenges and joys. I would be totally dependent on God's discernment, encouragement, wisdom, and strength."[41]

One personal joy noticed immediately would be the dramatic change of John's daily commute to work. He was used to long commutes, especially in the New York, Boston, and Washington years. One holiday event hosted in the home of FBI Director Bob Mueller had seen John and Kathy leaving their home at 4:30 and not arriving at the seasonal celebration until 6:45. Now John and Kathy were moving into Boyes House, A. U.'s presidential home. From there they could attend all campus events by walking across the street.

The new President would depend on Provost Marie Morris as initially he had depended on Gale Rossides at the TSA. Marie had been in place on the Anderson campus since 2009. The Trustees, recognizing her significant expertise in academic affairs, were freed by her presence to think "outside the box" when seeking a new president. After working with him for five years, Marie's bottom line about John would be this. "He's a servant leader. That's his heart. He's a humble and transparent individual who always wants to learn. And one thing he's learning is that in higher education there is a process to be followed and 'shared governance' with the faculty."

Part of John's getting started, Marie reports, involved his "propensity to fix things himself. That, combined with his open-door policy, occasionally would lead to the undermining of reporting lines, something he's learning to respect." An example would be the beginning of the national security program on campus. John announced soon after becoming president that he intended such a program. The Provost's response was, "OK, but the faculty controls the curriculum, so I'll set up the process and you pitch your idea with the faculty. If they embrace it, we'll have it." He did and they did. It was an early learning moment.

Getting Acquainted

President Pistole would quickly make efforts to gain direct acquaintance with campus faculty and the curriculum's strengths, weaknesses, and possible points of valuable growth. He also tested the best ways to work in this more collaborative setting. Meanwhile, there were other fronts of urgently needed acquaintance.

One obvious front was in the vital arena of fundraising. Supporters of the university had to be honored, understood, and related to personally. There was a large alumni world to be nurtured and the necessary identification of new persons with considerable resources whose help could ensure the school's vitality and future.

The Board Chair would offer this comment after John's first five years in office. "The President spent considerable time rebuilding bridges among persons of means. There were instances where connections had been neglected or trust strained. Building relationships and trust is necessarily a slow and personal process." It is hoped that the President's second five years will begin to see the fruit of this behind-the-scenes work during the first five.

Another particularly crucial arena for relationship building was the sponsoring church body, the Church of God Movement. John had been out of touch for years. His family had been deeply involved with the church, particularly his father who was a leader in preparing many of its ministers through the Anderson seminary on campus. But direct personal knowledge of that link had been weakened by John's many years serving other pursuits in very different settings, and much of that time attending United Methodist congregations judged most suited for his family's immediate needs.

Getting reconnected didn't take long. John was his usual relational self and was assisted happily by good friends. Lifelong friend Jeff Jenness now was the chief executive of Servant Solutions, successor to the church's Board of Pensions that Hollis Pistole had led for two years back in the late 1950s. The presidents of the church's four universities required ratification by the church's General Assembly after their Board elections.

Jeff, widely known and highly respected in the church, gladly stood before the General Assembly and spoke on John's behalf. He said that John is "totally sold out to God and will make necessary decisions however he judges right regardless of people's opinions." Jeff then described the positive results this way. "John's genuineness and humble spirit immediately won the day."

Even so, the new President was facing an uphill climb. The church was providing only a tiny percent of the school's annual budget. The large majority of campus students now are not affiliated with the Church of God by family tradition or personal commitment. Many faculty members, while decidedly Christian and sympathetic, are not directly affiliated with the Church of God. The church's one seminary is still the graduate school on the Anderson campus, but the other campuses now are offering competing ministerial preparation programs, and the church still is not requiring seminary or even an undergraduate education for its ordination candidates.

There remains on the Anderson campus plenty of professional commitment and church concern on the part of an exceptionally well-qualified set of Anderson University leaders. What has weakened is a substantial and mutually rewarding relationship between campus and sponsoring church. Relations are clearly cordial in the main, although not as deep, numerous, or frequent as in the past.

John would have to find ways to relate directly to church leaders and take program initiatives that address the church's real and felt needs. The Board of Trustees sought to assist by asking James Lyon, General Director of Church of God Ministries, to bring greetings on behalf of the church at John's Inauguration. He did that gladly, speaking of the long and proud history of the Anderson campus and its great impact on so many of the church's leaders, past and present. Noting the outstanding five Presidents who had and now are leading the campus over its century of church service, Pistole being number five, Lyon humorously commented, "Now we have our own Mount Rushmore!"

However, being a stone face honored on a mountainside isn't nearly enough to make it with the church. That requires an obvious depth of Christian commitment, a wide circle of warm personal and trusting relationships, and a campus capable of producing graduates well prepared to serve the church and world of today. James Lyon was most pleased by John Pistole's fresh presence on campus and featured him as a guest on the church's radio broadcast, *Viewpoint*. Aired in August, 2017, campus centennial time, John had opportunity to share his personal testimony with the church at large and others in the larger listening audience.

"I didn't aspire to my last three jobs," John explained, "God opened the doors. God gave me the strength and wisdom to do those jobs and allowed me to be perfectly at peace with whatever worked out. It's been a great adventure. I've done things I never dreamed of doing!" Now he clearly was motivated to do whatever was necessary to improve campus relationships with the church on the way to a sustainable campus future.

Such improvement soon would include a new scholarship program for select Church of God students and three major publications coming from Anderson University Press. One would be a centennial history of the university (filled with positive references to numerous Church of God leaders), one a recounting and reassessment of the Church of God Movement itself, and the third a biography of the President himself.[42] The intent of the biography, these pages, is something John would be quick to explain. It would be less to celebrate John's many life accomplishments and much more to share the story of his life's struggles and overcoming faith in the hope of encouraging new generations in their spiritual journeys.

President Pistole addresses his Inauguration crowd in 2015.

The new president sits at his Inauguration with the very pleased Trustee Chair, Patricia Seasor (Bailey)

Chapter 13

Finding A New Day

Whatever good or bad fortune may come our way, we can always give it meaning and transform it into something of value. —Hermann Hesse

Life is less about waiting for the storm to stop and more about learning to dance in the rain.[43]

Each new crisis is another opportunity for success. —John S. Pistole

Robert H. Reardon was President of Anderson University from 1958 until 1983. He was an institutional father figure and the face of the campus for decades. His leadership style was commonly thought of as "shooting from the hip." He was wise, often went by instinct, and was right much of the time. "Uncle Bob" was respected if not always appreciated by the faculty. He had a definition of a faculty member. It's "one who thinks otherwise." They think of themselves as the heart of what the school is all about, classroom teaching, and accordingly judge that they have a right to criticize the administration for occasionally being out of touch with classroom realities and not taking them seriously enough.

Putting aside the classic faculty-administration tension, for President Reardon something else was more basic. It was being sure that the campus *stay on course*. He stood firm over his many years, including throughout the social upheavals of the 1960s that rocked the nation and its world of higher education.[44] Reardon gladly honored the saying often attributed to Abraham Lincoln, "Be sure to put your feet in the right place, then stand firm."

Now President Pistole knew that he and the campus were facing yet another new day. Some classroom experiences would need refreshing and even redirecting. Relevance to contemporary needs and sensitivity to the available marketplace of students would be vital. Feet would have to be placed in some new places and not be moved. The difficult task would be determining what basics would be non-negotiable.[45]

Various senior faculty members would comment by 2020 that John had walked into several difficult situations that had been neglected for years. He had faced adversity from the start, and it would be compounded in 2020 by something none expected, the COVID-19 pandemic that would dramatically force a new day for the university and whole societies around the world.

Faculty members soon learned that their new President really means whatever he says. He obviously had come to serve, not be served. Whatever the new day would have to be, John Pistole would be faithful to Christ in all he did, always making clear that "this is what I am and want us to be together." This clarity, with its energy and optimism, soon would become widely appreciated.

Abraham Lincoln's presidency suddenly had to manage a Civil War unexpected and unprecedented. Likewise, in 2020 President Pistole would face a wholly unexpected new enemy to the campus, nation, and world—the Covid-19 pandemic. He would report, "In this unprecedented time, the risk-based, intelligence-driven program we have developed at Anderson University has been informed by successes at my previous job, Administrator of the Transportation Security Administration."[46] Yesterday should never be merely duplicated, nevertheless some yesterdays are critical to a viable tomorrow.

Determined to Stay

Two important things would have become reassuringly clear after the very first years of the new President's service. First, someone like John Pistole naturally would relate well to multiple constituencies on and off campus. Second, someone like John Pistole, because of his previous prominence on the national scene, would likely have attractive offers to move on. His commitment to the campus role would be tested and remain firm. One example became well known to the public.

John received an invitation to consider moving to a high government position, the Directorship of the FBI. He earlier had been Deputy Director for nearly six years and had left behind in Washington many friends and admirers. The most recent Director had gotten caught in a difficult web of circumstances that led to his being removed from office by President Donald Trump.

Word broke on May 30, 2017, that President Trump had contacted John about an interview for the open Director position. John was flown to the White House, some fearing he was very open to this prominent possibility and hoping he was just being courteous in accepting an invitation to consider it. Before going, John alerted the University's Board of Trustees that at least he would participate in the interview. Aware of the chance that he might be gone quickly, the Board developed an emergency contingency plan. Fortunately, there would be no need to implement it.

John also had alerted in advance Rev. James Lyon, General Director of Church of God Ministries. James annually gathers the presidents of the church's four universities for times of retreat and enrichment. John called just before the annual meeting was to convene in Chicago and was most apologetic. "I can't be there, Jim, and I can't tell you why, but I'll explain shortly." As promised, John did call again to explain that he had been called to the White House in Washington and had no control over the timing. Jim was "struck by how respected and conscientious John is, highly disciplined and faithful in his commitments and relationships, whether church, government, or university."

Gentle by nature, John Pistole could be firm and decisive when necessary.

Mike Pence, Vice-President of the United States and former Governor of Indiana, and others sat in on the Oval Office interview with John. This was a serious and pivotal occasion. Later, John's friend Jeff Jenness was in Washington on church business and invited to a Bible Study in the office of the Vice-President. There Jeff heard a little about John's interview with President Trump. Apparently it had gone quite well, at least on the surface. President Trump was always hard to read or predict.

As one would expect, John had displayed his usual quiet confidence. He was pressed with the question, "Do you really want this job?" In response, he had made it clear that, as a Christian public servant, he was open to whatever God would want, although he already had a very satisfying and important position as President of his Indiana alma mater. Loyalty also was discussed in the interview. John, of course, would not hesitate to affirm his intent always to be loyal to the U. S. Constitution and the law of the land if he were to be Director of the FBI.

Rumor has it that President Trump was wanting more assurance of loyalty than that. After all, there was a series of dramatic public firings of key leaders judged not adequately loyal. However that was put to John, or maybe just strongly implied, John wouldn't hesitate to provide an honest answer. His loyalty would be to the nation's Constitution, the rule of law, and the mission of the FBI.

John had known Chuck Rosenberg since after 9/11 when this skilled lawyer had joined the staff of FBI Director Robert Mueller as Counsel for National Security. Rosenberg now reports that he and John had talked before this interview with President Trump. In Rosenberg's view, John would have accepted the high position of FBI Director had it been offered "because he is dutiful, a true public servant." We will never know.

When that Oval Office interview ended and a few days had passed, another highly-qualified candidate, Chris Wray, was chosen, for whatever reason. John, satisfied about this decision and maybe even relieved, would remain a university president in Indiana, to the pleasure of all on campus and in the city of Anderson. Since then, he has expressed no regrets about not being invited to be the Director, although additional speculation about other possibilities would emerge on occasion.

For instance, conjecture began in 2020 that Director Wray might be nearing the end of his tenure amid some controversy. Might President

Trump now be thinking that he had made a mistake back in 2017? The Anderson, Indiana, newspaper quickly assured its readers with this headline. "Pistole Not Interested in Being FBI Director." John was quoted as saying, with his characteristic touch of humor, "I have my hands full here at the university and I can't beat the local commute."[47]

A proper bottom line could well be the assessment of John by Jeff Jenness, lifelong friend, former basketball teammate, and leader in the church. "Here's a man who has traveled the world numerous times, met and dealt with world leaders over momentous issues of international security, and been courted by more than one U. S. President for high positions. Throughout, his Christian commitment always has been on display, never in a haughty way that upsets others, but with an integrity that tends to make people feel that he's the real deal." This real deal was back home in Anderson, Indiana, and apparently home to stay.

Dancing in the Rain

John Pistole became the new Anderson campus President in March, 2015, with plenty of experience testifying before committees of Congress in Washington. He knew how to deflect and diffuse difficult questions and say nothing when he should not speak, either for national security reasons or for the public perception of his national agency. He could testify and really clarify complex issues or, when appropriate, speak as necessary without actually saying much of anything.

Granted, now in a university setting, John at first faced being largely unschooled in the precise ways of campus life, although many of the organizational dynamics weren't all that different. He would adapt quickly, exhibiting on several sensitive occasions the belief that, as one writer has put it, "life is less about waiting for the storm to stop and more about learning to dance in the rain."[48]

John's sister Cindy characterizes her younger brother as having a "laid back" personality, a man "who never flaunts the fact that he's been everywhere, done so much, and known so many important people personally." Church leader James Lyon makes the same point a little differently. "John brings a calm and confidence to Anderson University in a time of stress. He really knows who he is because of his close relationship with God."

Jim and John had come to their present leadership positions in Anderson at about the same time, one as chief executive of the campus and the other chief executive of the church's national ministries. Their offices at first were across the street from each other and they quickly became friends as well as key colleagues. One day there was a sudden emergency.

A bomb threat was received for that immediate section of the city. Jim tensed, trying to think through just what to do. John personally appeared at Jim's office door to tell him that all relevant authorities already had been contacted. Jim should keep his people inside until John gave the all-clear, and that would come soon since all the things needing done were well underway. Jim later recalled, "John delivered the news with such calmness that I couldn't be alarmed. I came away assured that whatever mountain the campus must climb, John will lead it well."

There are times when human goodness is lacking, with justice unfortunately a rare commodity. What then? The classic Hesse quote above is paralleled by one that John Pistole had become known for in Washington circles. Whether in 2002 in Washington, with the feared likelihood of another 9/11 terrorist attack and John prominent in the nation's counter-terrorism effort,[49] or in 2020 in Anderson with John sitting in A. U.'s presidential office with COVID-19 forcing a shutting down of most of the school's normal operations, he was known to say this. "It's another opportunity to demonstrate character and succeed!" Chuck Rosenberg recalls John's constant attitude about turning a negative into a positive and observes, "It's a cool window into how John thinks and behaves."

President Pistole arrived on campus at an historic and difficult time. The centennial celebration lay just ahead and, along with other things, was forcing a key question. What is required for A. U. to be relevant to church and society in its second century? After all, the school had barely survived its infancy and soon John would face a new threat to its very survival.

The school's beginning was in 1917. Within a year the tiny educational operation, then known as Anderson Bible Training School, already had run up an unwelcome debt for its parent body, the Gospel Trumpet Publishing Company of the Church of God. Many ministers of the church were nervous about the possibility of a new institution of human learning replacing the biblical standard of divine gifting as the primary qualification for Christian ministry. They moved through their new General assembly to limit the fragile little school's potential significance in church life—and maybe even its continuing existence.[50]

But even more had soon threatened the brand new school. World War I was raging in Europe. Many young men were being drawn into the U. S. military, causing the school's modest enrollment to drop in its second year. Then swept in the "Spanish Flu," a terrible pandemic that soon infected an estimated forty percent of the world's population and killed as many as fifty million people, including Woodrow Wilson, the American President who apparently contracted the disease while negotiating the Treaty of Versailles in 1919.[51]

The first case of the Spanish Flu in the U. S. erupted in March, 1918. Soon Anderson Bible Training school had to suspend its operation temporarily. But its leaders, J. T. Wilson and Russell Byrum, refused to let it die.[52] While it didn't, things weren't that much better by 1934 and the terrible Great Depression.

These are the words in 1964 of President Robert Reardon as he reflected on those Depression years on the occasion of the school's half-century celebration. "Here was a college that lacked prestige in athletics, had no accreditation, was constantly in the throes of poverty, could boast only a small number of students, had little standing in the academic world or in the community, and yet had unbounded confidence in its mission, courage and endurance beyond imagining, and the sheer determination to succeed."

What, then, about President Pistole a full century after that 1918 time of world pandemic crisis? The university now did have prestige in the academic world, full accreditation, marvelous campus facilities, a great breadth of academic programs and qualified faculty, and more. But it was facing declining enrollments in the midst of a turbulent time of major change in the world of American higher education. And then, on top of that, reminiscent of the 1918 campus crisis, it happened again—another crippling pandemic!

This time it was Covid-19, the worst health crisis worldwide since the Spanish Flu of 1918. President Pistole acted decisively in March, 2020, closing the normal operations of Anderson University in the middle of semester two, classes going online as possible, most buildings vacated and locked, and virtually all scheduled athletic, music, and dance events cancelled, including the 2020 commencement. Whole American cities were being "locked down." The French president announced that his nation was "at war" again, this time against an enemy more invisible than Nazi Germany.

President Pistole called for caution, calm, and prayer. He recalled his earlier work with the federal government in response to the 9/11 terrorist crisis and judged that the long-term impact of the current pandemic likely would exceed that horrible event. Regardless, like his brave presidential predecessors in Anderson, he made clear that he would not let the Anderson school die! To the contrary, as he said to the extended campus community:

> Imagine our entire AU family, students, staff, faculty, trustees, alumni, and donors, standing one day soon in a huge circle in the campus valley, holding healthy hands and worshipping our Creator and Sustainer. Envision our being surrounded by a great cloud of witnesses, all those who have gone before us here at A. U. and have persevered, not in their own might, but in that of the Almighty.

He added more from his own deep faith.

> As a Christ-centered school, we know that God is bigger than any human problems, and my prayer is that we can find ways to live out our core values of Servant Leadership, Responsibility, Integrity, Generosity, and Excellence, to make a difference for good in a hurting world.

When the hill to be climbed is steep and the pathway lost in deep shadows, what should be done? John would counsel that we keep humble, be creative, and keep believing. Step out in faith not fear. Project toward others the best that is available, like once happened in the Revolutionary War of the American colonies.

As the Redcoats advanced toward the Elizabeth Town Presbyterian church in New Jersey, Pastor Cauldwell noticed that the colonial troops were desperately low on wadding for their muskets. Without wadding, the muzzle loaders couldn't fire, and religious liberty and a free nation might never be known in Boston and New York, let alone from sea to shining sea.

Racing into the church, Cauldwell began tearing pages out of hymnals, including a favorite of the congregation, "The Old One Hundred," the Isaac Watts rendition of Psalm 100. With a stack of paper pages now in hand, he went charging back into the thick of the fight. The pastor is said to have run from man to man, stuffing hymnal pages into their pockets and shouting, “Give ’em Watts, boys, give ’em Watts!” Psalm 100 begins, “On your feet now—applaud God!”

Only a few years into the Pistole presidency, it would seem like multiple enemies were gaining on the Anderson campus and church. Emerging from the 2017 General Assembly of the Church of God was the establishment of a two-year study known as “Project Imagine.” A “Roundtable” of church leaders had been addressing the perceived unsustainability of the then-present complex of assemblies and special groups and conflicting agendas in the Church of God in North America. The question was, “Can we imagine a better way?”

As one would expect, this process generated a range of competing views. The search was on for discovering God’s will and way ahead. Similarly, President Pistole insisted that, in times of major cultural change, we must seek to “reinvent” the university and imagine a fresh and sustainable future. “Fresh,” however, must not mean any abandonment of the university’s historic core mission for the Christian spiritual development of students.

In part to highlight this mission’s continuance, John would invite to campus a prominent fellow believer in Christian higher education, John Ashcroft, the former Attorney General of the United States. He was asked to address the campus identity question. Ashcroft spoke in Chapel and pictured for students his understanding of the biblical meaning of Christian higher education, an understanding he knew his longtime friend President Pistole would readily affirm. He used two scenes from the Bible, one from Malachi 3 and one from Luke 24.

In the first scene, people are together discussing their beliefs. God shows up and listens in, taking careful minutes of the meeting. In the second, two men are walking on the road to Emmaus discussing the horrible crucifixion of Jesus and trying to understand divine meanings in light of such an unbelievable happening. Then Jesus shows up and walks with them, enlightening their conversation and soon transforming their lives from stunned retreaters to unstoppable witnesses.

What’s the Christian university all about? What’s life at its best? Ashcroft said life’s best requires an act of faith enriched by a journey with God, an ongoing reasoning together about life’s deepest meanings. It’s about taking seriously the God who shows up, listens in, and brings great news. If engaged in sincerely, he went on, especially in a supportive educational community like Anderson University, God will show up again, look on, and take memory minutes of the meetings.

That had been John Pistole's personal experience when an Anderson student. Jesus himself had come along in the person of his teaching Spirit. His understanding had emerged over time as a relationship with Jesus grew. Who Jesus really is became more and more apparent, clarifying what life at its best, with God, should be.

Anderson University had been such a Divine-human conversation site for almost a century and, now as its new president, John would be determined to carry that spiritual tradition forward. Believing in the potential of student lives being truly transformed in more than intellectual ways, excellence in *all things*, including the spiritual, is why a Paul McNulty and a John Pistole both had left their prestigious positions in Washington to serve conversation-convening and life-transforming campuses, Paul to Grove City College in Pennsylvania and John to Anderson University in Indiana. They both were convinced that, as Hermann Hesse once said, whatever good or bad fortune may come, we always can give it meaning and transform it into something of value.

Climbing Uphill

John Pistole loves American history. Recently he read closely Ron Chernow's celebrated biographies of Alexander Hamilton and Ulysses S. Grant.[53] He's also keenly aware of the published life stories and rich wisdom of his presidential predecessors at Anderson University.[54] Wise counsel, he knows, can be derived from yesterday, although it must be tailored with new trajectories designed for today. A wise leader both highlights the goal and brings the whole community together in pursuit of a commonly desired new future, informed but not dictated by the past.

The years just before the new Pistole administration had witnessed a steady decline in campus enrollment. Faculty had become somewhat frustrated. When professors think of themselves as the heart of the enterprise but lack much ability to control the school's destiny, blaming the administration is easy. Faculty were naturally anxious about the future implications of the facts recounted by President Pistole in his first report to the Board of Trustees in April, 2015.

The number of undergraduates enrolled had dropped from about 2,000 in 2005 to under 1,600 by 2015. The university was facing about a $3 million budget deficit in 2015-2016. This financial weakness was further complicated by $5 million of deferred maintenance of campus facilities and the modest size of the school's permanent endowment. The reported amount of $36 million was actually about $9 million less when borrowing against it and unfulfilled pledges were taken into account. A further challenge was the needed repayment of over $40 million in long-tern bond debt that existed when Pistole took over.

Faculty were cautiously optimistic nonetheless. They had a strong desire for the university to succeed despite what the new President characterized as "the stark reality of our enrollment and financial situation." John had brought with him something important from his many years of executive leadership with the FBI and TSA. He knew that "every day is filled with challenges and opportunities." He was, as many say of him, "the non-anxious person in the room" despite the challenges at hand. John made clear to campus personnel that he was full of hope. "With God's guidance and discernment we will work our way through these challenges." There was no question in anyone's mind that John is a man of deep and abiding Christian faith.

Pistole's plan from the beginning was grounded in the perception that the university was "not as distinctive or compelling or relevant as we could or should be." He hoped to reverse this problem by stabilizing the campus in the first two years of his presidency, revitalizing it in another year or two, and then finally seeing it thrive again. But, into the fourth year of his presidency, he had to report that "we're still stabilizing."[55] A year later a pandemic exploded that destabilized the society as a whole, and further challenged campus progress.

Apart from the pandemic, why the great difficulty of stabilizing and then revitalizing? In part it was because the pool of high school graduates in Indiana had decreased while the costs of the school's operation kept rising. Given the modest endowment, the annual budget must be funded primarily by student tuition. Enrollment increase was critically important but difficult.

Specialists in higher education were reporting that smaller private schools were increasingly at risk of failing altogether. It already had happened in Indiana with St. Joseph's College in Rensselaer, an institution forced to close its doors in 2017 after operating proudly since 1889. This closing had left some 1,100 students in the lurch. President Pistole was determined to avoid any such disaster by making Anderson University freshly relevant to the times, partly by increasing the size of its public footprint and thus its enrollment.

President Pistole addresses his first convocation/chapel session in Reardon Auditorium.

John passionately made this statement to the students in an early chapel address. "God is at work at Anderson University, transforming and renewing minds for godly work. I believe our world is in desperate need of hardworking servant leaders who are committed to integrity and excellence in all they do."[56] The man now in Anderson's presidential office had vision. It was about the very best for student futures. Surely a way could be found into a sustainable future.

President Pistole began speaking often of a central campus goal. It was "lives transformed." Romans 12 speaks clearly of God's intent to "bring the best out of you, develop well-formed maturity in you." John is all about that for himself personally and for the students of the university. He had been "worldly" as a teenager and now was dedicated to student lives being transformed in the wonderful ways he had known himself.

Paul added this in his letter to the Romans: "Don't become so well-adjusted to your culture that you fit into it without thinking. Instead, fix your attention on God. Unlike the culture around you, always dragging you down to its level of immaturity, God brings the best out of you, develops well-formed maturity in you."

John Pistole was always open and vulnerable about the downsides in his own spiritual journey. He repeated the story of his high school car accident on various occasions. When asked in preparation of this biography if his Executive Assistant at Anderson University, Ronda Reemer, could be interviewed about who John really is, close-up, he said simply, "Great idea. It is what it is!"

When asked about John, Ronda responded privately with this. "John is professional, fast-paced, works with integrity, is task driven. I have learned not to approach him without doing my homework first. He asks a lot of questions! His expectation of faculty and staff is to work hard with intentionalism and professionalism and demonstrate 'excellence in all things.' He introduced that phrase when he came to A. U. It stuck!"

For John, excellence requires several things, one being adherence to the faith tradition of the campus. "We must stay grounded in our Church of God heritage," he said, "while launching those things that move us into the years ahead. Never ignoring yesterday, we can't simply duplicate it. Since there are no guarantees, I will keep seeking God's face." He has challenged students with Jeremiah 29:11, 13: "For I know the plans I have for you," says the Lord, "plans to give you hope and a future."

For evidence of the future-granting God, the President has recalled and celebrated the many dozens of A. U. grads now in public service. That also is true of many other fields of service. For instance, he noted that there are alums currently impacting the world of opera—Lawrence Brownlee, Lynelle Johnson, and Shelby Rhoades. Names like that could be listed for business, athletics, Christian ministry, and many other walks of life.

When asked about the hoped-legacy of his presidency, John said simply, "A new trajectory." His goal at Anderson University is to spawn major new campus programs especially relevant to the new day of student and societal needs. The campus must focus on identifying and serving well such a new day as this. To do this, he went beyond celebrating those many

A. U. grads serving well in public service. He brought one to campus leadership.

In 2020 John named Dr. Brock Vaughters the new Vice-President for Finance and Treasurer. Brock, a 2003 A. U. graduate on the Business faculty since 2014, had served the Defense Department, several businesses, and various campus committees that sought ways for the campus to do things differently and move forward. The President asked Brock to assist with envisioning and implementing needed campus changes. They agreed that, as Brock puts it, "we need to flip the script and learn what today's needs are, where the market is, and how we can serve, not just keep doing the many good things we've always done."

Faculty Perceptions

After John Pistole's first five years back in Anderson, faculty perceptions of his leadership were surveyed for this biography. There were a few concerns that will be noted in the next chapter, but they are limited and overwhelmed by the many positives, including these:

> John shares his faith openly and enthusiastically as an integral part of his personal identity and role as university president. His Christian faith clearly undergirds his major decisions. He's at A. U. because he truly sees it as a calling from God.
>
> John allows meaningful input from faculty in key decisions. Necessary position cutbacks, while emotionally loaded, have been done as fairly as possible. While his actions are well-informed, he's quick to admit a mistake if time demonstrates that. He's transparent, reports the hard facts, and is a "the-buck-stops-here guy."
>
> John clearly values the liberal arts, even though he's focused more on strengthening the disciplines that support the scientific and professional fields such as engineering, public health, and national security services. He has actively leveraged his own experience and personal contacts to enrich the curriculum and the public's perception of the growing national vision and relevance of the campus.
>
> John had worked effectively at the national level to handle the tremendous fallout of the 9/11 terrorist crisis, and thus was well prepared to help the campus deal with the disruptions that have come along, like the unex-

pected Covid-19 pandemic.

If anyone can lead the Anderson campus in finding the needed new day, it's John Pistole.

The negative faculty perceptions, relatively few in number, tend to come in relation to given programmatic shifts questioned by some. We now turn to the more detailed presidential actions of John Pistole's first five years in office, his various attempts at "a new trajectory" that can serve well a new day.

In his office, door often open, President Pistole listens carefully to colleagues and exchanges ideas in search of the best wisdom.

HONOR ROLL

Prominent Guest Speakers/Lecturers hosted by President John Pistole and Anderson University, Anderson, IN., 2015-2021.

Andersen, Kristian
Aschroft, John
Ayotte, Kelly
Brennan, John
Carraway, Melvin
Carroll, Charles
Clapper, James
Coats, Dan
Comey, James
DeVeydt, Wayne
Frieg, Jose
Hein, Jay
Hill, Alice
Hoekstra, Pete
Holder, Eric
Inglis, John "Chris"
Lim, Bernard
Malvesti, Michelle
Mason, Mike
Mayorkas, Alejandro
Mueller, Robert S. III
Olsen, Matt
Ostrognai, Jim
Quigley, Fran
Rosenberg, Chuck
Rowland, Lloyd
Rush, Loretta
Shedd, David
Stockton, Paul

PROVOST
Dr. Marie Morris

Marie Morris was providing superb academic leadership to the Anderson campus when President Pistole began his tenure in 2015, and she continued to do so by his side until her retirement in 2021.

Chapter 14

Our "PJP" In Action

"I have nothing but contempt for the kind of governor who is afraid to follow the course that he knows is best for the State." Sophocles would be pleased with John Pistole. —Sophocles in *Antigone*

Educating the mind without educating the heart is no education at all.
— Aristotle

The first president of Anderson University, John Arch Morrison, was in office from 1925 to 1958. Good as he was in many ways, the students never used his initials to affectionately call him "JAM."

John Pistole's presidential predecessor, James L. Edwards, loved students and often was referred to as "PEddy." John Pistole had been affectionately called *Juan Pistolé* by some in Washington. Soon after he became the President of Anderson University in 2015, students almost universally were referring to him affectionately as "Our PJP" (*P*resident *J*ohn *P*istole). They felt personally connected to an important man who seemed pleased to be personally connected to them.

The *PJP* came from the winsomeness of his personal style. Along with the nickname came his activism that began reshaping many aspects of campus life. For instance, President Pistole announced in late 2018 that "we've got the right people in place, we've got a great Board of Trustees, and we're in the silent phase of a focused fundraising initiative."[57] He was gathering the best around him to enable a quality thrust forward.

Two of John's early and critical tasks had been to strengthen the Board of Trustees and assemble a quality executive team through whom he could administer campus life effectively. Numerous other actions were taken during his first term in office, many judged by the campus community and wider public to be clearly positive and hopeful. A few others, natural for any president, gained mixed reviews. Following are the highlights of both categories of presidential actions.

Strategic Initiatives: Clearly Positive

Despite high respect for John Pistole's previous and substantial administrative experience in national government, and his clear commitment to A. U.'s future, one question lingered. Will he be able to take the necessary initiatives to stabilize the university's challenged present and introduce the desired future? Observes Dr. Deborah Miller-Fox of A. U.'s English faculty, "For at least a decade prior to John Pistole's arrival, the primary strategy seemed to be merely reducing institutional expenses. But most faculty agree that we cannot cut our way to institutional health." Would John come up with a better plan?

The faculty had gotten used to what many of its members perceived as the dead-end administrative approach of stabilizing by amputating. That was an understandable but not altogether fair perception. First, many institutions of higher education were being forced to "rightsize," a more positive word than "downsize." Second, there had been added before John Pistole's arrival two new programs with obvious fresh potential for success, engineering and dance. What the previous administration admittedly had not been good at was casting a compelling vision of where the institution was being taken by the multi-year rightsizing process.

Dr. Jerry Fox, senior member of A. U's business faculty and elected Faculty Chair pro. tem., spoke for the entire faculty at the Inauguration of John Pistole. He projected excitement about the fresh prospects of the coming new president. Soon, on that same historic occasion, John Pistole was himself at the microphone. After being greeted with standing applause, he proceeded to announce his intent to have launched some exciting new academic programs and other innovative developments, clearly projecting an aggressive approach to the future.

Such activism clearly would have to occur in the face of the significant limitations obviously at hand. The new President's goal was to stabilize the institution as quickly as possible and then help it to thrive again. This goal, as time would soon show, would prove difficult to accomplish since the limitations ran deep and were resistant to any quick solutions. Even so, in John's first term as the new President, he and his leadership team would oversee the accomplishment of several very positive developments. Here are several examples.

The Board of Trustees

A process was begun to reconstitute the university's governing Board. It included seeking new members who had national prominence, financial means and, along with a strong commitment to Jesus Christ, a clear understanding of what it takes to operate successfully an educational enterprise that also must be viewed as a sustainable business. The President and Board Chair, now Pat Seasor Bailey, acquaintances since their college and graduate school years, gladly teamed in this multi-year effort.

Some of the new Board members were interviewed for this biography. All were anxious to share and agreed that the task ahead for the university would be demanding but clearly possible, especially with President Pistole at the leadership point. One is John Wechsler, a successful technological entrepreneur who says, "Innovation is my strength and teaching the young to add value to the world my real thing."

John Sanders is another of "the new guard." He is a successful and generous Christian businessman known to John Pistole from their days together during John's years with the Transportation Security Administration. Wechsler, Sanders, Donna Harman, and others are now Board members in large part because of their respect for John and his vision for the university's future. As Wechsler puts it, "John doesn't vacillate with the market. He knows who he is and stays true to who he is. He provides calm inspiration to those around him. With this amazing group of Board members, anything is possible."

The Cabinet—the President's Executive Team

The Board of Trustees holds the President responsible for the entire operation of the university. From the beginning, John relied heavily on Provost Marie Morris in the academic arena and focused his direct efforts more on strengthening church and donor relationships. By 2018-19, however, he also was getting involved more directly in campus organizational life. He found that he had in house certain leaders, even some he had hired himself in the key enrollment and finance areas, who were not providing him with the depth of expertise the university needed.

The faculty, for instance, often was being provided with admission reports that were less than informative. These reports featured encouraging projections not clearly substantiated by clear facts. Even when pressed for more detailed explanations, the faculty had not been receiving the satisfying kinds of responses that congressional committees and U. S. Presidents had become accustomed to receiving from John Pistole.

A few personnel changes clearly were needed and the President was appropriately decisive. By 2020 John finally could say that his Cabinet, his executive leadership team, was now his team, and its functioning "outstanding." It now was comprised of Marie Morris, Provost, Brock Vaughters, Vice President for Finance and Treasurer, Jennifer E. Hunt, Vice President for Advancement, Heather A. Kim, Vice President for Enrollment, Marketing, and Communication, and Dan Courtney, a former CEO and now Special Assistant to the President.

Serving the City of Anderson

Early into the new presidency, Board Vice-Chair Dennis Carroll, longtime judge locally, took John Pistole on a tour of Anderson's city organizations and introduced him to key city leaders. John loved his hometown and soon became active as a prominent citizen of the Anderson. He joined the governing boards of the Madison County Community Foundation and the Ascension St. Vincent Hospital. On occasion he appeared on the local newspaper's front page when interviewed by a national news media on some pressing matter of the day. When "Black Lives Matter" became a major national movement advocating for the civil rights of African-Americans, John spoke clearly to the university's constituency on the subject and was one of the leaders in July, 2020, of a prominent statewide gathering of prominent leaders discussing how best to confront racism while maintaining community safety.

At that meeting that included the presidents of nine Indiana colleges and universities, all Christ-centered, there was a "lamenting of the brutal deaths of innocent African-American men and women that have created such pain, anger, and frustration for our communities." John introduced a panel consisting of Paul Keenan, FBI special agent in charge of the Field

Office in Indianapolis, Rodney Cummings, Madison County Prosecutor where Anderson University is located, Scott Mellinger, Madison County Sheriff, and James Burgess, President of the local chapter of the NAACP. Facilitating such important conversations among diverse leaders is a special skill of John's, and social justice is a life-long passion.

John also sent a letter to the campus community on June 2, 2020, explaining how he "as a Christ-follower" had been dealing with "the trauma of systemic racism and racial tension." He hoped "to offer salt and light to a hurting world." Addressing specifically "my African-American/Black sisters and brothers," he confessed that "I don't pretend to understand the racism you have been experiencing for a lifetime. What I do know is that I'm called, with God's leading, to help bring peace and biblical reconciliation to every situation I encounter. Where there's injustice, I'll work for accountability and change that helps bring about justice." Such a man quickly became a highly valued citizen of the City of Anderson, Indiana.

The Flagship Enterprise Center

The Flagship Enterprise Center associated with Anderson University is a business incubator and accelerator located on the growing edge of Anderson that faces the interstate highway running straight to the Indianapolis metro area. It's a partnership with the City of Anderson intended to create "the second-largest business incubator in the State of Indiana that creates the opportunity, parlaying the resources of the FEC and the adjacent A. U. Flagship Education Center, for Anderson University to become an increasingly major force in the economic revitalization of its home community and region, while producing experiential education, internship, and placement opportunities for students."[58]

President Pistole found the Flagship Enterprise Center to be "a greatly underutilized A. U. resource. He soon became more hands-on in seeking to alter that circumstance. He reconstituted its governing board, naming as its new Chair a senior Trustee of the University and longtime local judge, Dennis Carroll. John then applauded the Flagship Board's decision to name as its new CEO Dr. Terry Truitt, Dean of the University's business faculty. The FEC, John now judges, "is in good hands and will be better kept on its mission track."

New Academic and Sports Programs

When John Pistole was asked in 2020 about his future vision for campus programming, he said this. "We are at a crossroads. I'm trying to pivot the campus from being primarily a liberal arts school to also having strong new programs that offer studies beyond the traditional." Here's a sampling of such fresh and relevant developments to date.

Christian Spiritual Formation

Anderson University now allows students from any major outside ministerial studies to take an organized group of courses encouraging critical thinking about the integration of their faith with what they are learning from their academic disciplines. This program offers a formal exploration of Christian Spiritual Transformation and provides both broad, deep, theoretical, and practical understanding of Christian formation.

Studies in National Security

A campus program of longstanding was the criminal justice major that prepares students to enter employment in fields related to law enforcement, courts and corrections, victim advocacy and assistance, juvenile justice, as well as providing a foundation for graduate study. Now added are two important courses of study rooted in the unusual expertise of President Pistole.

> The *national security studies* program is interdisciplinary and uses Christian ethics as a foundation in preparing students for a career in public service. Coursework from history, political science, criminal justice, sociology, social work, computer science, math, Christian ministry, and psychology provides a well-rounded liberal arts education.
>
> The *cyber security* program is designed for students who seek to defend against cyber threats in industry and public service. Cyber-security majors are trained to be the "good guys," defending individuals, customers, and the public against today's numerous cyberattacks.

Studies in Engineering

They encourage students to become servants of the technical needs of today's society, and include mechanical and electrical engineering, quantum mechanics, electromagnetism, and computational and statistical physics. Students work with smart machines, factory assembly robots and autonomous vehicles, and human computer interaction to solve high-tech problems through automation.

The engineering programs had been launched initially toward the end of the previous administration. While young and active when President Pistole arrived, by the end of his first term in office there were four majors addressing this growing field of study: Computer Engineering; Electrical Engineering; Mechanical Engineering; and Mechatronic Engineering. Also, accreditation had been achieved for the first three.

Public Health

The public health degree, within A. U.'s School of Nursing & Kinesiology, can be paired with almost any major and presents an opportunity for students to combine their unique skills and passions with serving the world's needs.

New Sports Teams and Facility

Partly in the attempt an increase student enrollment, two new programs of intercollegiate athletics came into being, men's and women's Swimming & Diving and Lacrosse. The Soccer program was upgraded with fencing and seating for fans.

Prominent Campus Guests

National leaders of prominence began arriving often on campus at President Pistole's invitation. By bringing such significant persons for extensive student and public exposure, John intended to leverage his many federal contacts for the enrichment of the educational experience of the student body and the public's perception of the growing prominence of the campus locally and nationally.

Among these guests, in addition to James Comey who spoke at the President's Inauguration, have been Robert Mueller, former Director of the FBI under whom John Pistole had worked as Deputy Director, the Assistant Secretary of Homeland Security, John Hill, former Attorneys General of the United States John Ashcroft and Eric Holder, former CIA

Director John Brennan, prominent FBI veteran Michael Mason, and more (see page 184). Reported Mueller when on campus, "John is a leader people want to follow. He has left an indelible mark on every institution he has served. From the dedicated faculty and staff to the inquisitive students, my visiting the serene Anderson campus has been a memorable experience."

These national leaders were featured in campus chapel, classrooms, and a public lecture hall, and their works published were cited for student attention. They include *Never Again: Securing America and Restoring Justice* (Ashcroft, 2006) and *A Higher Loyalty: Truth, Lies, and Leadership* (Comey, 2019). A "Situation Room" was constructed in Decker Hall for the use of students majoring in the new national security major. It's a replica of the White House "Situation Room" where John had spent considerable time in his prior national responsibilities. More development would be on the way soon.

Church of God leader James Lyon made clear on the church's radio broadcast *Viewpoint* in 2020 that John Pistole knows and brings to campus so many national and world leaders that he is enhancing the possibility of Anderson University influencing the future of world affairs. He's helping lead a new generation in understanding how Christian faith can and should inform individual spiritual journeys and life in the public square."[59]

This effort at bringing prominent leaders to the city and campus was aided greatly in the summer of 2020 by a $1,000,000 grant from the Lilly Endowment of Indianapolis. It is intended to help establish on campus a new "Center for Security Studies and Cyber Defense." Beyond the quality education of students and attraction of celebrated guests, this Center will provide cyber security services at reduced cost to institutions neighboring the campus, possibly even free to select non-profits. It also will send informed and motivated students into local civic, social, and service organizations. Behind such initiatives was obviously the person and federal security experience of campus President John Pistole.

The Indianapolis Colts

Here's one seeming negative that actually was a positive. For many years the Indianapolis Colts professional football team had staged its preseason training camp on the Anderson campus. John Pistole authorized the end of this relationship. Personally, he is a big Colts fan, in fact a fan of sports in general,[60] but there was a hard fact to be faced. As opposed to some other teams, the Colts organization wasn't giving much back to its host campus and city. Sure, it paid its way, but that was about it.

The campus and city of Anderson did get some good publicity from the Colts' presence each year. The tradeoff, however, was considerable campus distraction and inconvenience with no discernable boost in student recruitment or facilities enhancement for related student athletic programs. Further, the city had to come up with about $100,000 annually to help A.U. break even financially. John weighed all this and the plug was pulled. Anything distracting and draining no longer could be retained, pleasing as it might be in itself.

Facing a Pandemic

As noted earlier, the social and educational scene in 2020 turned dire quite unexpectedly. A pandemic suddenly blanketed the world, forcing Anderson University and most public and private schools to take drastic actions for safety purposes. A. U. temporarily closed its campus facilities, went online with most instruction, refit classrooms, even postponed intercollegiate athletics to the Spring of 2021, and rescheduled a modified Spring, 2020, Commencement to be part of a virtual Homecoming weekend in October, 2020.

On March 18, 2020, President Pistole sent out a video message to the A. U. community explaining these actions. He grieved for the many students who had worked hard to sharpen their athletic, music, and dance skills and would not be able to present the fruit of that work publicly as originally planned. He especially apologized to the seniors for the great loss of their graduation celebration, although all degrees of course were awarded as earned.

That apology to seniors was followed by the President offering something very personal. When the health crisis was over, he invited any senior to come back to campus and to his office. There he would put on his cap and gown, present the diploma, and smile his best as selfies were taken. That was "PJP" at his finest!

Meanwhile, across the summer of 2020 extensive plans were made for the beginning of a new fall semester. So much about the pandemic was still unresolved in the nation. The campus task force guiding the emergency

John, always the athlete, poses by the statue of the first AU President, John A. Morrison. Both are wearing their masks because of the COVID pandemic.

planning was led by nursing professor Dr. Sarah Neal. That body reported, "It's like flying a plane while it's still being built!"

The best of health-screening technology would be employed. The prohibition of alcohol use on campus would help—student parties featuring alcohol already had forced some universities to cease on-campus operations. The steady hand of the President was a clear positive. He admitted to being a little apprehensive. "This is all new territory." Even so, "My passion, whether in government or now in academia, is unchanged. It is to inspire and empower people to do their absolute best in transforming, adding value, and making a difference in the lives of others." A pandemic could cloud the path of John's mission but only temporarily obstruct its journey.

Strategic Initiatives: Mixed Reviews

Beyond overseeing fresh program thrusts and dealing with a pandemic, President Pistole had faced several hard decisions and didn't fear to make them. Some traditional ways of doing things were perceived by some as not working well anymore, and they were changed, although with lingering questions in some instances. Any President lauded for her or his successes also will face a few detractors. Following are four examples of actions taken between 2015 and 2020 that had opponents and questions not yet fully resolved.

Faculty Size and Salaries

President Pistole inherited years of flat faculty salary levels. Initially circumstances would force him to continue the inherited pattern of reducing total faculty size, eliminating positions that had inadequate student enrollments to support them. The institutional profile developed by the Trustees in the presidential search process had presented this to candidates in 2014: "It is exceedingly important for a new presidential leader to be a consistent and vocal advocate to find ways to appropriately compensate A. U.'s exceptional faculty and staff and add new strength to their numbers." The harsh reality was that there would need to be more pain before realizing such desired gain.

In March of 2019 a letter of faculty concern was sent to the administration and Board leaders over the signatures of Dr. Doyle Lucas, Faculty Chair, and Dr. Scott Borders, Faculty Affairs Committee Chair. It had been processed through an ad hoc faculty forum and expressed an understanding of the demanding need to stabilize university finances. However, faculty members wanted it to be clear that lack of support for the faculty causes "fear that we are on the precipice of becoming a mediocre institution."

According to the letter, the continuing stagnation of faculty salaries had led to "diminishing morale" and the impression "that we are an institution in decline." Senior faculty member Dr. Michael Collette, however, wants noted a common faculty perception about President Pistole himself. "He's doing all he can to rebuild the institution. He brings us a sense of hope every day. Everybody respects him." Scott Borders had alerted the President to this coming letter, fearing no reprisal from a man like John.

John acknowledged in the next faculty meeting that he had received the letter and promised that, if money became available, the faculty would receive priority consideration. In fact, some money did become available, presumably through special gifts from some concerned Board members. The President, in the form of a one-time 2019 Christmas bonus, distributed these funds to the faculty and staff. While this did not raise the base of salaries, it was a welcome gesture in the right direction. Even so, this important concern area remains.

Leadership of the Falls School of Business

This prominent school within the University had grown in recent years to be one of the larger ones. It also had been hit hard when select faculty positions had been eliminated for cost-savings reasons. Then came an additional problem that strained feelings. Its respected Dean, Dr. Terry Truitt, accepted the invitation to become the CEO of the Flagship Enterprise Center associated with the university. Had Dr. Truitt been "encouraged out?" The confusion resulted from some wrong or partial information received by the school's faculty. Some faculty made wrong assumptions and inappropriately approached directly the President's office for assistance. The President had responded directly, wanting to fix the situation while unintentionally violating administrative protocol between his office and that of the Provost's.

The Provost, Marie Morris, explains that a clerical error in her office helped fuel the situation and the President, with his open style of working, and still learning normal processes in higher education, had acted too quickly and thus unintentionally added to the confusion and misunderstanding. She quickly adds however that, after the fact, John heard her concerns, acknowledged his error, and said his wife has to tell him that "sometimes you jump into things too quickly in an attempt to fix them."

It should be said that Dr. Truitt's moving to the FEC was at its initiative and was his decision—no forcing out. The move now is seen generally as a good one for him and the FEC, and thus for the university. It's a good example of how an administrative process, despite the involvement of exceptionally good and well-intentioned people, can get distorted and problematic, and yet lead to a positive outcome. Two other examples of this kind deserve noting.

The Adult Studies and Admissions Programs

The long-standing Adult Studies program was suspended and the staff forced to find a new and more efficient way for the university to serve an adult population. Many came to judge that this program's ending was premature and had been caused by a combination a the lack of understanding by President's Cabinet and its being informed less than helpfully by key staff about the program's operation and outcomes. A loss of income quickly resulted, probably more than the savings from the program's elimination, and an alternative program eventually would be developed. Looking back, the President admits that the elimination may have been a mistake. Whatever later hindsight shows, John Pistole rarely fails to act when present circumstances appear to warrant, or to admit a mistake if future developments clearly warrant such.

The second example of possible error in judgment involves the several admissions programs of the university. The main operation was focused on traditional undergraduate students, and success had been generally poor in the years prior to President Pistole arriving on campus. Some of the professional programs did their own recruiting, including the School of Theology and the Falls School of Business. It was determined that combining these admission programs into one office operation would bring cost efficiency and better results.

Again, in hindsight, this determination appears to some to have been wrong. The School of Theology and the Falls School of Business actually suffered, with the combined operation not prepared to do recruiting among these specialized constituencies. The Provost now observes, "We may have missed the key issue, which was having ineffective leadership in enrollment." That problem now has been addressed separately.

The School of Theology

A second major step related to the School of Theology and may have weakened it further. This campus graduate school, the one seminary of the Church of God, had existed since the 1950s as a relatively independent unit within the larger university structure, with its Dean reporting directly to the President. Part of that time it was viewed and funded separately by the church and accredited separately by the Association of Theological

Schools, which at first required a separate library and cataloging system for the seminary. In more recent years, that relative independence had lessened considerably and the seminary's enrollment now was suffering.

A pivotal decision had been made by the previous administration and was implemented by President Pistole. The graduate school was merged with the undergraduate Department of Religious Studies, another move in the name of efficiency of operation and a more financially sustainable enterprise. It was a merging of the administration, housing, operations, and faculties of the seminary with the undergraduate Department, and a cutting of the combined faculties by several full-time positions. Judgments of the results are mixed. The seminary clearly had been in difficulty, and now appears to be even more so.

Was there some other way to go? Apparently not, unless the church that originally parented the campus would take a different stance toward the necessary educational requirements of ordained ministers. This isn't likely and the future of the graduate seminary now is in question. This is difficult for John Pistole who is committed to the quality academic preparation of ministers, and his father had given so much of his professional life to this seminary. Curricular efforts were made, especially by Dean Mary-Ann Hawkins, in attempts to bolster the serious enrollment picture. For instance, a joint masters program was developed (M.Div./M.B.A) since congregational leaders now often are expected to perform business as well as spiritual and theological guidance.[61] A five-year track also was designed for achieving both an undergraduate and graduate degree.

To date, these curricular initiatives have not brought significant results. The merger has not been reconsidered, even though some judge that the combined operation, except for cost savings from faculty reductions, has not brought increased benefit to the university or church. The resulting dilemma is voiced by a senior business faculty member, Dr. Doyle Lucas, elected Chair of the university faculty and a strong advocate for the importance of the university's church relationship.

"As a Church of God guy," reports Lucas, "I like having a distinct, stand-alone graduate seminary for ministerial preparation. As a business guy, I understand the realities of dollars, enrollments, and unsustainable operations. The university over the years has seemed to want the seminary more than the church does."

This merging move in the area of religious studies and ministerial preparation is part of a larger picture. To realize the mission that the university still has under God, John Pistole is generally perceived to be more "data-driven" than his predecessor. He has found himself initially having to "right-size" the university in general, and he has acted to do that. An educational institution must be a viable "business." On the other hand, as Dennis Carroll, a leader of the Board of Trustees puts it, "we must protect our core as a Christian liberal arts institution, and we also must know where the market is. While some cutting has been necessary, the university must retain the same DNA that graduates have so loved over the years."

President Pistole applauds this judgment, difficult as it is to implement. Given all of his actions in his first years as President, many clearly wise and a few with mixed judgments in hindsight, he has managed without question to retain the confidence of the faculty and Board of Trustees. As one faculty member puts it, "He doesn't panic and isn't easily thrown off track."

John's Relationship with Students

The new president quickly went well beyond saying the right things about the importance of students on campus. He began modeling his words, actively relating to students and often doing it in their campus spaces and with a naturalness that students loved. John's fine words were supplemented with believable actions, explaining the quick rise of the "PJP" nickname. President John Pistole loves students and they love him back. His approachable style was welcomed. Rather than the "aloof man at the top," he chose to function as their readily available "PJP."

John officially became President on March 1, 2015. Spring break came shortly after and already John was on the road in Florida with Bob Coffman, the university's Vice-President for Advancement and longtime friend of John. They were meeting donor friends of the university but took time out to visit the university's baseball team then playing in the area. During warm-ups, John went right out on the field to meet the A. U. players. He was excited to make personal connections. Bob recalls that the players were equally excited to meet him and wanted pictures taken. That was only the first of many such warm and spontaneous president-student connections, athletic and otherwise.

The love for PJP hung prominently outside on a student dorm wall.

Take one evening in the student dining hall back in Anderson. Campus guest Chuck Rosenberg had taken time off his demanding role as head of the nation's Drug Enforcement Administration to come and do an interview with the new president, his close friend. As they went through the line together to get their trays filled "with chicken fingers and French fries" and then sit at a rather noisy table, Chuck quickly realized something he considers very important. Just like in John's many years in federal service, he was doing it again. He was "treating everyone the same way, Board member, janitor, student, faculty, kitchen staff, it doesn't matter. They, of course, *are* the same, but many in positions of power don't know it and act that way. I saw that 'PJP' was home in Anderson where he is loved."

Many students have put their feelings into words of their own. Mariah Murray worked in the Student Life Office and says that "President Pistole has always been inviting, charismatic, and a man of God." It was obvious that "students could come to him anytime and he'd be open to talk." Rebecca Peach was President of the Student Government Association. She found the President "clearly leading from a posture of humility."

Emily Callen, a senior nursing student, reports this: "I was walking through the campus valley and saw President Pistole walking toward me. I was like a fan girl about to pass someone I knew was famous. Much to my surprise, he actually spoke to me. 'Good morning Emily, how are you?' It was all I could do to get a basic sentence out of my mouth. He actually knew MY name. Not only that, he genuinely wanted to know how I was and what class I was headed to in case we could walk together. I'm pretty sure my heart didn't stop racing for ten minutes. He almost made a fan girl faint! I called my roommate immediately to tell her I had just run into PJP and HE KNEW MY NAME!"

Ian Leatherman was a mechanical engineering major active in the university's cross country and track programs. After noting that the President "wants to glorify God in all he does," he shared a telling example of the power of a leader's gracious presence. Once PJP was offering words of encouragement to the track team just before a conference meet. His phone rang. He glanced at it, put it back in his pocket, and said to us students, "Oh, it's just some reporter from CNN. I'll call him back later." Ian thought to himself, "I just witnessed a man say, 'not now' to a national news network because he thought we were more important at the moment!"

Alexander Certain expected a college president to be a "big shot" who usually is cooped up in his office. "But not our PJP. He exhibits the best meanings of community and hospitality. When I was a sophomore, my girlfriend and I were walking arm in arm toward Reardon Auditorium for some weekend event. The President was walking close by and alone. He joined us and asked me if it would be alright if he took her other arm for the rest of the walk since his wife wasn't with him that evening. "I said she and I would both be honored!"

And there's Carter Haupt, a Political Science and National Security major. He's so grateful for the significant guests the President had been able to bring to campus, people who greatly enrich the academic experience and add realism to what expected careers are really like. But, more personally, Carter had eaten in the President's home, sat near him in several fireside chats in Dunn Hall, and seen him at numerous student events. "He's so real and personal that students want to hear his stories and learn from his life."

February 22, 2020, saw a perfect example of John Pistole as a student-centered university president. John was standing in the university's Lewis Gym at center court. It was half-time of a crucial men's basketball game. The loudspeaker explained that John would draw one name from a hat. The lucky person would be invited to the floor with the dramatic announcement that he or she would have two chances to make a basket from center court. If successful, there would be awarded a full year's free tuition! John, a former basketball star himself in earlier years, still trim and athletic, handed the ball to a nervous young man, a prospective student, and showered him with vigorous encouragement. Isn't education designed to open doors of possibility?

New student Rylan Metz won a full year's free tuition for his miracle shot at halftime of the AU basketball game. Most remember President Pistole, who loves basketball and students, being more excited and pleased than the big winner.

Attempt number one actually made it clear to the backboard but bounced away harmlessly. John gave the student the second ball with his own body language making clear that success could be real. "Believe and go for it, son!" Away it flew. In about two breathless seconds, the threads of the distant basket snapped as the ball went into and through with a shocking perfection. John waved his arms with an uncontrolled excitement as a crowd of students swarmed onto the floor to hug the amazed young man. A president, struggling to raise funds to keep the school solvent, had momentarily lost himself in the pure thrill of giving money away to a prospective student who likely needed it badly. What was on the outer edge of possibility had actually just happened. A loved president, a "pistole," had just fired another volley of exceptional student encouragement and achievement.

John's Executive Assistant, Ronda Reemer, observes that "John has an open door policy with students. He listens to their stories and provides appropriate guidance and direction. Students may not always get the answers or decisions they are seeking, but *they do feel heard and loved.*" Yes, John is present to students in ways they can understand and appreciate.

There's more. An early chapel address to students had John emphasizing the importance of "hardworking servant leaders who are committed to integrity and excellence in all they do." For students to be motivated to become such themselves, they would need direct exposure to actual persons who modeled this ideal. Here's one instance of quality modeling.

John and his wife Kathy have many dear friends, among them John and Gwen Johnson. Soon into the Pistole presidency, the Johnsons returned to Anderson after three years pastoring an international fellowship in Hanoi, Viet Nam. At one point in their transition, the Pistoles invited them to live with them in the president's campus home, Boyes House. There was plenty of room and surely for a few months the four of them could figure out how not to interrupt each other's normal routines.

Reports John Johnson, "they were so gracious to us!" Often the two Johns had little talks about biblical meanings and spiritual formation. They were both eager learners still on the grow even after many years of maturing and serving the nation and world. Then came that eventful morning. John, the president, was out in the community very early for his daily run, almost like he was still in training for an upcoming basketball season. John, the missionary pastor, was in the kitchen making coffee when his friend returned. It was an odd return. The president seemed to be almost quietly sneaking in the back door. One side of his face was scraped and bruised badly.

The athlete president had made a misstep a few blocks away and fallen on his face while running. "He looked like he'd been in one of those Rocky movies and the president had gotten the worst of it!" The wounded warrior didn't want Kathy alarmed, although she was all over the situation as soon as she knew. The problem? It wasn't just the embarrassment of the accident. Later that morning John was scheduled to do an interview with CNN, and it wouldn't be audio only. With all the facial repairs possible, John made the interview, trying to position his head to avoid the camera highlighting a somewhat mangled façade.

John Pistole was still on periodic call for interviews about national events and, while the busy university president, also was serving as a member of an advisory group for Dan Coats, Director of National Intelligence from 2017-2019. John would meet the interview demands even with an emergency facial patch-up and whatever other inconvenience presented itself from time to time. John Johnson makes this observation: "He does all of this so humbly and with a level of integrity that is impeccable." So says one John about another, both faithful world servants of the same Lord.

Again, what is the view of Ronda Reemer, Executive Assistant and Secretary to both John Pistole and his presidential predecessor, James Edwards? On a daily basis she functions as the one between the President and the entire community of campus people, many of whom want to communicate with, meet, and get something from the President. Also on a daily basis, she handles his busy schedule and orchestrates the many tasks he needs to place on her desk. She sees him up-close in both the pressured and lighter times.

Ronda describes John with words like "whirlwind," "professional," and "integrity." His constant expectation is that "all faculty and staff work hard toward the overarching goal of 'excellence in all things'." Who is John? "He's a God-fearing, humble, and gracious man. It's an honor and privilege to work with him." Note Ronda's "with" instead of "for." John is a team leader who cares deeply about the integrity and enhancement of those around him. He's their activist "PJP."

Chapter 15

JUSTICE, EDUCATION, AND "MINISTRY"

I pray that, according to the riches of God's glory, he may grant that you be strengthened in your inner being with power through his Spirit, and that Christ may dwell in your hearts through faith as you are being rooted and grounded in love. —Ephesians 3:15-18

We do not follow Jesus if we maintain a dualism between our Sunday experiences and the experiences of the rest of the week. Jesus has sent us all *into the world.* —William E. Diehl

By 1983 John Pistole was ready to live the rest of his life as a champion of knowledge and justice, first through a local law practice, then through the Federal Bureau of Investigation, the Transportation Security Administration, and finally Anderson University. But how was this to be done and why? For an answer, John's Christian identity sends him to the Book of Ephesians.

It's been said that justice is love made evident in public. John had personally come to know the life-transforming love of God early in his life. Soon he had found himself very much in public and was determined to make God's love as evident as possible in the pursuit of knowledge and justice in that wider arena.

John had learned quickly the reality of a common observation. A nation can have the worst laws, but if it has good people you don't have to worry much. But be in a country with great laws and bad people and there's lots to worry about. Culture often appears stronger than laws in actually controlling behavior. John was blessed to live in a country with numerous good laws. He would come in touch with numerous people who were in great need, often having been victimized by truly bad people. "Ministry" would be an essential element of his life's mission, whether at the FBI, TSA, or A. U.

Foundational to his ministry would be seeking personally to "be strengthened in his inner being with power through God's Spirit" (Eph. 3). John Ashcroft reports that he and John were "teammates," especially in the first three years after the 9/11 terrorist attack. They were Christian colleagues in public service facing a dark culture indeed. Many around John Pistole were under his authority and being enriched by his influence. His goal remained justice, love being made evident in public.

When Anderson University came back into John Pistole's life and "ministry," he remembered quickly that this campus had a rich history of making evident in public a love that sacrifices for the needs of people. One clear instance is seen in an earlier time of presidential transition. When Robert H. Reardon was assuming campus leadership in 1958, he had in hand a set of ten-year goals. The first was "to exalt the spiritual and train for responsible Christian citizenship."[62]

This goal was reflective of the famous motto of Geneva College, undergraduate alma mater of an A. U. historian and former Dean. The motto had first been adopted in 1881 when the Church of God Movement was just beginning and decades before A. U., its first educational institution, was founded. The motto is *Pro Christo et Patria* ("For Christ and Country").[63] Both Geneva and Anderson would mature as Christian educational institutions across the twentieth century, both maintaining the symbol of an open Bible and believing that its divine revelation has serious implications for public life in all its dimensions.

John Pistole began his Anderson presidency in 2015 with *Pro Christo* deep in his heart and *et Patria* defining his previous decades of public service. Christian ministry and justice in the public square are central pieces of the puzzle of life at its best and the university's mission at its highest. As John sees it, and has lived it, the pursuit of justice for all is part of the "ministry" of love intended for all true believers.

After a New "Pearl Harbor"

St. Paul, writer to the first-century Ephesians, had found himself a prisoner in Rome for his faith. This was the imperial capital, the center of world power at the time. John Pistole, a careful modern reader of Paul's letter, found himself in the midst of the federal government of the United States, a country claiming to be the one remaining super-power of today's world. Paul's new-found faith in Jesus Christ was considered an oddity, something persecuted in the Roman Empire of his time. That's a risk Christ-followers today, like John, may soon face again.

As the twentieth century wound down and the twenty-first began, John's strong faith was again becoming an oddity, maybe not exactly persecuted in Washington, but often not respected and certainly not followed except by certain outstanding individuals. There was in process a social shift away from Christians being the dominant faith community in the United States. Historically, biblical values had been embedded in the U. S. system of justice and its definitions of the good were honored in public laws, practices, and rhetoric. Now Christianity was becoming merely tolerated and even ignored. The nation was becoming more pluralistic and less sure of the relevance of its historic roots or the certainty of its future safety.

The "9/11" tragedy became the new "Pearl Harbor" of a nation suddenly aware that it was under siege and no longer secure just because there was an ocean on either side. Nuclear bombs, climate change, and international terrorism were shaking the foundations of a proud and rich United States. In the midst of such dramatic forces, John Pistole went to Washington to serve as a Christian gentleman. History, government, and law were subjects he'd studied with care. His family, college, and faith backgrounds all had inclined him to agree with an observation made by Christian philosopher D. Elton Trueblood just after World War II.

Announced Trueblood, the great Quaker philosopher-theologian, "The Ten Commandments constitute the most memorable and succinct extant formulation of the ethical creed of the West. The most profound argument for democracy is the realization, fundamentally biblical in origin, that the love of power is so pervasive that democracy, a system of mutual checks, even upon the ruler, is the only alternative to injustice and oppression."[64]

John Pistole embodied this viewpoint. For him the challenge came particularly after the new Pearl Harbor in 2001. In Trueblood style, he warned the Anderson University graduating class of 2006 of something he had learned in his service through the FBI up to that time. "Complacency can be far more dangerous than any enemy." He called on graduates of his beloved alma mater to be active Christian persons, intentionally infusing their coming careers with the goodness and justice that radiates from the person of their Master, Jesus.

Such a call to a new generation came out of a particular religious tradition in which John had been reared. The Church of God Movement (Anderson) is part of what now is called the broad "evangelical" stream of Christianity. That stream, however, needs careful definition. Decades ago a groundbreaking book by Donald Dayton looked at the nineteenth-century roots of this tradition.[65] He argued persuasively that the original "evangelicals" had a more publicly relevant view of their Christian faith than many do today.

The original evangelicals combined personal and social transformation, reaching out in the name of Jesus to engage peace, civil rights, and justice issues, like the abolition of slavery, temperance, and women's rights. Many neo-evangelicals now focus primarily on being "saved" and going to heaven, judging the public wrongness of today beyond repair and politics a dirty business. The Church of God Movement, originating in the late nineteenth century, tackled issues of personal and public transformation, including racial and gender bias. It also focused on the abolition of faulty church institutions that block the current work of God's Spirit.[66] Justice must be love infusing institutions where evil is embedded.

That was John Pistole's church home. His professional life reflects deep appreciation for the older evangelicals. The gospel of Christ is to be what the word "gospel" means, good news. If, as Jesus announced, it isn't good news for the poor and justice for all, then how can the news be very good? Christians are called to experience changed lives and then work to change the world for the better.

When second in command of the FBI and at the point at the TSA and then A. U., John was joining a Christ-crusade for justice and life-transforming knowledge. He was and is a conscious spreader of good news to the poor as Jesus did and instructed his disciples to do. He is a Christian "minister," as all believers should be.

Justice in an Imperfect World

John Pistole often has faced the sometimes dangerous and often heartbreaking world of public corruption and violent crime. Always, he has understood himself to be both a public servant and an agent of the kingdom of God that is seeking to become evident in the hearts of humans and in halls of power. In the process, John came to know firsthand that this is a very imperfect world where justice doesn't come easily.

The former director of the environmental program at the University of Vermont put it well when commending a published social history of recent decades in the United States. This book, he said, "reveals that rampant greed and avarice have a formidable adversary that lies in the good hearts, deep faith, and perseverance of those who would create a better world."[67] John has been one of these adversaries. Reverence for the law, especially when infused with love, has been an assumption of John's parents, college professors, and above all his Lord. It also became his.

There was in John's formative circles a deep belief that faith in something (Someone) beyond the individual and the moment appears essential if there's to be real community and shared values that nurture the best in humanity. Reaching this goal is always an unfinished journey. It's a journey John has been taking his entire adult life. As a soft-spoken Midwesterner, son of a seminary professor of applied Christian theology, he has found himself near the center of world-shaping events and life-transforming possibilities.

Many of us during our seminary years were introduced to the writings of Christian philosopher and theologian Reinhold Niebuhr. He helped us see the power of evil in the world, and also the Christian obligation to seek justice.[68] John Pistole arrived at a similar envisioning, in part by coming from a strong Christian home featuring a father whose primary ministry was educating Christian ministers, including making them well aware of great Christian thinkers like Reinhold Niebuhr and his equally articulate brother Richard.

Dr. Hollis Pistole believed deeply in St. Paul's call to be "strengthened in your inner being with power through his Spirit" (Eph. 3) and then to make that strength relevant where people actually live, hurt, and hope. Hollis was a professor of *applied* theology. Son John has continued that application task in arenas his father never had opportunity to address, but was so proud that his son did.

John soon came to share his father's deep belief, spiritual quest, and determination to be a practical servant of public justice. He became committed to making real at least a measure of justice in this very imperfect world. How? Hardly through pastors alone. John was deeply impacted by the work William E. Diehl, who laments that so many Christians are largely passive in impacting the world with their faith.

Diehl announces, for a variety of sound sociological reasons, that the ministry of the Christian church in the twenty-first century "will fall on the shoulders of the laity." The good news is that non-clergy Christians already are located in strategic social positions, thereby able to carry out the needed ministry—in offices, factories, homes, schools, government, in short, in the world. "We do not follow Jesus if we maintain a dualism between our Sunday experiences and the experiences of the rest of the week. Jesus has sent us all *into the world*."[69]

John Pistole believes this deeply and has embodied it effectively. He explains. "There are parallel worlds of work and faith and they should intersect. We each are called to a unique congregation, and I felt that powerfully in my government work. God gave me a congregation of FBI agents and NYPD officers. I was called to minister to them in an unordained way—as Jesus did with everyone he encountered." That ministry also extended to officers of the TSA, and now to the faculty, staff, and students of Anderson University.

TSA colleague John Sanders watched John Pistole live his faith each day in Washington. Without shame, he would pray caringly for an ill staff member. "I was blown away by John's open display of faith. When a TSA officer was killed in the line of duty at the Los Angeles LAX Airport and John saw the video, "I watched him cry and have to leave the room." John then visited the family of the slain officer, truly mourning their great loss and offering comfort. Later, in the midst of his presidential reception speech at Anderson University, when all attention was to be focused on him, John paused and asked some guests to stand and be welcomed by the crowd.

What he was doing was spontaneous and so natural. John wasn't recognizing a few of the many robed dignitaries in attendance, but members of that deceased officer's family who had traveled from California to celebrate with their "minister" friend on this great day. John Sanders, fellow leader in the TSA with John, was deeply impressed by such Christian compassion. "That's why I stayed in contact with him after our government service and was open to his invitation for me to become an A. U. Trustee. I give thanks that John's still in my life."

Combining justice and ministry is difficult and rarely done well or comfortably. John's father had pioneered the effort for him. What should be the limits of a government's right to control life and death? How can government be an agent of justice without violating the human rights of its citizens in the process? Such questions would be the daily dealings of John Pistole for more than thirty years.

Hollis Pistole once gave a "B" grade to a seminarian in a required field experience. Having never received that low a grade as a graduate student, the young man asked for an explanation. "Where did I fall down in my course performance?" Dr. Pistole readily admitted that he had not fallen down at all. There were about twenty in this class and evaluating their field experiences was difficult. So John's father had given a "B" to everyone, one approach to fairness. But the student with his first "B" winced, now knowing that the lower grade had been the result of a grading system completely beyond his control.

It's an imperfect world. Justice, even in instances of good intentions, sometimes is impersonal and more understandable than satisfying. Dr. Pistole approached the school's Dean and sought permission to up this student's grade to an "A." The responding question was, "Are you willing to up all twenty?" To which Dr. Pistole responded, "No, I'm sure some of the others don't deserve it as much." He was told to leave things as they were, unfair as that might be. Any change would introduce more unfairness. He did, reluctantly, explaining this to the student and actually asking forgiveness—not that he'd done anything wrong. Grading systems and social organizations are what they are. One of Reinhold Niebuhr's great books is *Moral Man and Immoral Society*. Justice in the public arena never comes easily.

In the long run, of course, this little grading incident meant virtually nothing. But it did to the soft-hearted Dr. Pistole. He didn't forget. Soon that "B" student was Dean of the seminary while his former teacher remained on the teaching staff. When Dr. Pistole's autobiography was released shortly before his death, he handed a gift copy to his former student, saying that he'd written something personal inside the front cover. There were found exceedingly generous lines. This sense of justice, mixed with a Christian pastoral caring, even when caught in unyielding circumstances beyond his control, was passed on to Hollis's son John.

Patricia Bailey, now Chair of the Anderson University Board of Trustees, thinks stories are the best way to convey real meaning. When asked to tell a few about John, she hesitated. In John's case, she explained, they are hard to come by, especially from the FBI and TSA years. John will tell a few without many details—national security is always a limiting factor. Another limitation is just that John "is so humble about it all."

Even though strapped by these limits, Bailey makes plain what comes through loud and clear to her. John is on mission and not afraid. As a life-long overcomer, he's capable of taking decisive action, even against public or faculty opinion. "He's willing to wade right into difficult issues and invite frank discussion. He listens and communicates well. He then combines courageous action with a gentle and very relational style. That's a rare integration, a mixing of Christian ministry and executive leadership at their best."

Resourced from Above

The in-depth spiritual identity of John Pistole prompts a little theology lesson. We all know "unders" that can limit and frustrate our lives. Sometimes we are under resourced and undermined. What about the availability of some wonderful "over"? John would come to know such an overarching when many never do. With assistance *from above*, he would manage to overcome negative circumstances. He believes strongly that there is Someone over us, God, graciously superintending life's flow and our loving ministry efforts.

If an atheist is one with no invisible means of support, John Pistole is anything but an atheist. During his entire adult life he has leaned on a gracious source beyond him whom he has sensed lovingly above him and lingering nearby on his behalf. Matthew 28:20 promises that this Presence will remain always and wonderfully sustain those who align themselves with God's mission among lost, lonely, and needy humans.[70] John has sought to be so aligned and on a mission of justice in an imperfect world. He has joined Jesus in pursuing the higher goals of the divine kingdom. That's real ministry, even if of the unordained kind.

Elizabeth, John's mother, was a high school psychology teacher and counselor. Sometimes she would test things at home on her kids. John recalls a time of hypnotizing, an "experiment" that dealt with the power of suggestion. How, Mom explained, could others influence us with their words and suggestions? An example was something like, "You're getting sleepy, very sleepy . . . and you'll bark after you awaken and I clap my hands." Then came her key question. How might our words be able to influence others, especially for good?

Over more than three decades, John Pistole would move up through the ranks of the FBI with surprising speed, and then head the TSA and finally Anderson University. What would help make this all possible? Always present, of course, have been John's own natural giftings, a quality education, and strong motivation leading to hard work. Above all that, however, he insists that there has been more. Beyond surrounding resources and sometimes favorable circumstances have been the guidance and enablement of a gracious God.

John's close friend Jeff Jenness would visit him in Washington on occasion and develop this telling perspective. "I watched John *overachieving*. Don't misunderstand. I would never question John's unusual giftedness and intelligence. My point is that John has a way of being calm and thinking clearly in the most stormy of circumstances, and his discernment seems to be more than his own. He's an *Over*-achiever because there's Someone *over him* preparing, calling, and guiding."

Success for John is never to be separated from the relationship with his loving Lord. He knows two things, who he is and *Whose* he is. John reports this. "I've told more than one recruiter that I wasn't qualified. Especially for my last three roles as Deputy Director of the FBI, Administrator of the TSA, and President of Anderson University, I clearly wasn't qualified. But God was preparing the way, opening doors, and equipping me. My role has been to say 'yes' or 'no' to these callings and this resourcing, and fortunately I have kept saying 'yes'."

A. U. Trustee Bill Gaither was impressed in the key interview with candidate John Pistole and then the first Board meeting with President Pistole. "He took prayer very seriously for himself and us. I liked that." Ministry as a Christian necessarily involves the practice of prayer. An almost daily spiritual resource for John has been his praying a classic covenant prayer of another John, Mr. Wesley of England:

> I am no longer my own, but Thine.
> Put me to what Thou wilt, rank me with whom Thou wilt.
> Put me to doing, put me to suffering.
> Let me be employed by Thee or laid aside for Thee,
> Exalted for Thee or brought low for Thee.
> Let me be full, let me be empty.
> Let me have all things, let me have nothing.
> I freely and heartily yield all things
> To Thy pleasure and disposal.

Ministry from the Beginning

Coming out of college, John Pistole was strongly motivated by his deepening Christian faith. His choice of law, he judged, could be an expression of such faith and the natural outcome of his collegiate studies and experiences. Early vocational choices were motivated by a combination of personal interests, presenting opportunities, and what might offer an adequate way to earn a living. In those ways, John always has been very human indeed. So, a man who began at the bottom and would rise to the top of his several professional callings surely had something going for him beyond his human capacities and favorable circumstances.

John, at first an "ordinary kid" from Anderson, Indiana, would serve under two U. S. Presidents and be interviewed for a major federal Directorship by a third. He would rise to near the top of the Federal Bureau of Investigation and begin at the top as Administrator of the Transportation Security Administration and as President of Anderson University. Through it all, John would readily witness to something extra-ordinary. God was calling and providing and he was being guided by the philosophy of "servanthood in public service." This is the philosophy of the Center for Public Service at Anderson University where John was an undergraduate CPS fellow. It also is basic to living a relevant and productive Christian faith.

John hesitates at the word "ministry" for himself, but his wife Kathy doesn't. She says, "He's been in ministry wherever he's been." John's commencement speech at Anderson University in 2006, while still the Deputy Director of the FBI, would feature his call for all graduates to enter ministry with their whole lives, regardless of differing career paths. His advice was for the new graduates to step out in faith, serve others, and do all the good possible. He recalled for the new alumni his own college experiences on the Anderson campus, like TRI-S trips, internships through the Center for Public Service, and participation in the Model United Nations program.

These campus programs had opened his eyes to the need for and value of public service flowing out of a servant's heart. "Each of you," he announced with strong conviction to that graduating class, "is called to be a minister for a unique congregation. If service becomes your primary vocation, regardless of how you're making a living, God will bless you."

Bill Gaither, icon of Christian gospel music and longtime A. U. Trustee, loves to tell the back story of Stuart Hamblen's famous song "It's No Secret." Stuart was a radio cowboy celebrity in Los Angeles when he attended a Billy Graham crusade in town in 1949. He went forward and was converted to Christ. Shortly after, Stuart was home in his backyard having a casual chat with a neighbor, John "Duke" Wayne.

Duke teased Stuart about a rumored religious "going forward" in public, and he got this response: "It is no secret what God can do, what He's done for others he can do for you." Duke's response was, "Sounds like you need to write a song about that." The song was written quickly after their simple exchange and became a beloved standard. John Pistole, not yet born and hardly ever prominent in the gospel music world, nonetheless also would become quite experienced at witnessing casually to people in high places about his personal faith.

John's own life makes something quite clear. Being an effective leader who also is dedicated to ministering on behalf of a Jesus-like goodness and justice throughout the world doesn't mean being the "preachy" one whom others easily push around or mostly ignore. Despite his humble spirit, John has not lacked inner certainty and readiness to share the deepest commitments of his life. In fact, mirroring his respected FBI "boss" Robert Mueller, John has modeled kindness and toughness, treating people well while not being open to cheap excuses for non-performance. Jesus may have been "meek" but hardly ever was weak. John is a Jesus follower.

Overcoming, But Not Alone

John Pistole readily acknowledges that something more has been at work in his life and career than just himself. There has been a pervasive *providential* element. It's true that John as a student would have preferred another college than Anderson, but his car accident took away that opportunity. He would have preferred a different law school than McKinney, but his bank account wouldn't allow it.[71] The tragic terrorist attack of 9/11 certainly wasn't his preference, but it did thrust him in completely unanticipated directions that would bring major professional promotions and life satisfactions.

John and Kathy once were vacationing with dear friends in Alaska. They would finish with an unannounced entrance into the Anchorage airport for their flight home. Jeff Jenness now reports that the whole demeanor of the airport staff quickly changed once word spread among the TSA officers that none other than John Pistole was present in the facility. Jeff says, "You could feel the love the TSA officers had for John. To them he was more than a consummate professional. He was an ambassador for Jesus Christ, one man who knows how to witness in a humble and non-offensive manner."

The former head of the Department of Homeland Security and recent President of the University of California, Janet Napolitano, offers a similar judgment. "We all knew John was very much a man of faith, but he didn't wear it on his sleeve. You could just tell by some of his references and how he lived his life. He is a straight-shooter. He doesn't sugar-coat or bluff, so you can take at face value whatever he says."

The general judgment about John would come to be this. John has a poise and personal centeredness that encourage those around him to gain such critical traits for themselves. That's leadership at its best. Napolitano adds, "He was a man to be trusted and even loved for his leadership and 'ministry'." Ask John how he managed the pressures, surprises, and frustrations over the years and likely he would flash a little smile and point upwards. He would manage with resources more than his own. He indeed has been an "Over-achiever." He has confidence that there is One above who reaches lovingly downward to assist faithful servants below.

Now John is regularly explaining the "secret" to the Anderson University students. It's the same one that was learned back in 1949. What God did for Stuart Hamblen "He can do for you." This secret was conveyed in John's January, 2020, chapel address as their President. "We practice to become accomplished in our studies, sports, and relationships. You tend to become what you keep practicing. It's the same in the spiritual journeys we all take. I recommend to you the classic little book by Brother Lawrence, *The Practice of the Presence of God*.

As John shared his wisdom with university students on a variety of occasions, always on display would be his personal modesty and a touch of subtle humor. For instance, as a way of connecting with a new generation still unsure of itself, he occasionally would recall some little incident from his personal past to make clear his own simple humanity. One example was the time he had become acquainted with a particular movie star immediately recognized by students. It was Harrison Ford who was featured in the *Indiana Jones* film series. He is an American actor whose films have grossed worldwide more than $9 billion.

John once was speaking at an aviation conference in Las Vegas, Nevada, where Ford was also being featured. Ford was an environmental activist and pilot as well as famous actor. After the speaking session, John and Harrison had opportunity to spend about forty-five minutes together walking through the convention center with a guide and enjoying each other's company. Reports John, "I was amazed at how many people came up to us and asked for *his* autograph and photo with them. He was very gracious and repeatedly accommodated. I was only the Administrator of the nation's TSA. Zero people recognized me and wanted my autograph and photo!"

No matter. John knew who he was, was comfortable with who he was, and could be genuinely happy when the spotlight was on another. There always was that awareness in John of a pervasive *providential* element in his life. God was present, God was guiding, and God is so very good! That is more than enough.

John with his beloved parents,
Hollis (d. 2006) and Elizabeth (d. 2005),
taken on their 60th wedding anniversary.

Chapter 16

AUTUMN LEAVES

Do not seek death. Death will find you. But seek the road which makes death a fulfillment. —Dag Hammarskjold

When faced with the challenge of a new role or crisis, I see two things and one result. Is God calling? If so, will I be obedient? If God is and I am, then I will be at peace regardless of the results. —John S. Pistole

The first holder of the presidency of Anderson University was John A. Morrison (1893-1965). Here are words of wisdom placed at the base of his statue on campus: "The purpose of life is to spend it for something that will outlast it." That first President John left behind a great legacy. His current successor, another President John, is in on the way, doing as Dag Hammarskjold suggests. He's seeking the road which eventually will "make death a fulfillment."

The Book of Genesis emphasizes the importance of direct sight. God looked at what had been created and saw that it was good (Gen. 1:31). We humans can't see all that God does, but we do tend to judge things by how they look to us. When we haven't seen them at all, we doubt their value or even their existence. Seeing, we claim, is believing.

How is John Pistole to be valued, judged, believed? It depends on what there is about him that you've actually seen. If you've only spotted him from a distance, only read the headlines, you're tempted to see someone who is bigger, better, and more important than most others. He's walked with the great and made decisions that have affected millions. That's true, of course, but hardly what God sees when observing John.

The Divine sees John looking beyond the immediate and short-term and valuing an eternal grounding for his decisions. He is seen as a man being committed to lasting values, to lives transformed, to the love of the Eternal shining from the face of the man from Nazareth. He is observed traveling the road which leads to death one day being a fulfillment.

Jesus made clear that God judges less by our outward actions and more by what's inside. Most significant are our motivations, intentions, and the lack or absence of love. Central is the degree of commitment to the upward way and the level of obedience to the calling from God. Again, a clear view of John Pistole is gained less by the prominent public actions on the outside, impressive as they may be. The true view is the inside one.

There, deep inside, beyond the awareness of many, one finds John as the active seeker after the mind of Christ. He intends constant obedience to his Lord in all of life, personal and professional. Apart from all that's so prominent about his career, John is actually a simple, modest, Christian man following his sense of God's calling on his life.

John Pistole's way of thinking follows what two former professors at Anderson University sought to make clear in their book *Work that Matters*. Drs. Kevin Brown and Michael Wiese seek to bridge the divide between work and worship, something John has done exceptionally well. "Our labor," they say, "if understood as a means to an end, risks making our value as human beings—as children of God—contingent on *what we produce.*" Does God value us merely because of what we produce and reward us because of what we have produced?

For Christians, what we are to do is be light to a darkened world (Matt. 5:14). We never produce this light, only reflect it. The source is the One who is light itself. "The purpose of our reflecting this light is not to draw greater attention to ourselves—it is meant ultimately to point others to God (Matt. 5:16)."[72] John Pistole has been a prominent leader, yes, quite a leader. Of more lasting significance is another fact. He also has been a pointer of others toward God, a light reflector that helps them find their way.

Any Regrets?

The 2015 move from the powerful and headline-laden halls of government in Washington to an economically struggling small Mid-Western city was a big one in many ways. Ask Kathy Harp, Anderson University's current first lady, about regrets and you'll get this. On the whole, she has grown comfortable back in Anderson, Indiana, although missing the diversity of cultures and her family members back East. She's the loving wife of President Pistole who joins him gladly in living forward, not mulling over some yesterday.

Kathy certainly doesn't miss the traffic in New Jersey, New York, Boston, and Washington. What she has come to love is that her husband now can walk to work and be home much more. And then there are the many college students who have "spoken life into mine." Much as her husband, the beloved campus "PJP," she has enriched the lives of the numerous students while carrying few regrets and being buoyed by many blessings. And her presidential husband? John has experienced the stresses of the large responsibility he has carried in Anderson since 2015, although that's nothing new to him. He also shows no signs of regret for having left prominent roles of service to his nation to serve in the prime leadership role of his alma mater. In fact, he views his current service as still vital to the nation and world. The campus catalog puts it this way, a reflection of John's very heart:

> Anderson University has always been about the business of preparing people for service to the church and the wider culture. As we enter our second century of impact, the challenge remains…and the need is as great as ever.

> Creation groans for more; it "waits with eager longing for the revealing of the children of God" (Rom. 8:19). What the world needs is a generation that has come to life--servant leaders who have been transformed by the Holy Spirit into the likeness of Jesus Christ.

The old saying has it that you can't bring someone back to the farm once having been to Paris. That's often true, but clearly not always. As Jesus said, it depends on what's inside a person. When God looks inside John Pistole and judges it good, what's being seen? After all, John is very human, a bit of a "knucklehead" as his brother David says or a "corny dude" as was announced at his Inauguration. He's somewhat reserved on the outside, but with a relaxed and even silly strain inside. Here's a quick glance inside.

The "Three Stooges" was an American vaudeville comedy team active from 1922 until 1970. Their hallmark was physical farce and slapstick, hardly John Pistole's outside demeanor seen by most. Jerome "Curly" Howard joined the hilarious trio in 1932 and became the soul of this comedy team. His "Nyuk! Nyuk! Nyuk!" laugh became widely imitated, as well as his excitable exclamation, "Woo, Woo, Woo, Woo!"

Surprising to many, John Pistole is a big Curly fan and a clever imitator. Put the usually reserved university president in a room without cameras or press, and with either his brother David or a close friend like Jeff Jenness or Stan Deal, and Curly can come alive! John's colleague Christopher Favo recalls the time when he and John were relatively new FBI agents on a skiing slope together. It was in the mid-1980s when the band "Jump 'N the Saddle" had a popular song called "The Curly Shuffle." A few of the words are:

> When me and my friends go out on the town,
> We can't sit still and we can't sit down.
> We don't like to fight and we don't like to scuffle,
> But we dance all night doing the Curly shuffle.

This song suddenly began playing on the ski resort speakers and, reports Favo, John joined in "with a spot-on great impression!"

John is an interesting, probably an unusual combination. He's a reserved and decisive executive with a fun-loving kid still lurking somewhere inside and anxious to come out. More importantly, in God's eyes John has become a dependable reflection of Jesus Christ in the street clothes of today. One characteristic of that reflection is the ability to be at peace regardless of the circumstance.

When facing a new crisis, as noted above, John sees two questions and one outcome. Is God calling? If so, will I be obedient? If God is calling and I am obedient, then I can be at peace regardless of the results. John isn't Australian by birth but he is by attitude. The Aussies have a common saying. "She'll be right, mate!" That is, when put in God's context, "Whatever's wrong somehow will be set right over time by our best efforts combined with God's pure grace."

This perspective on life goes well with John's general spiritual outlook. Reads the Old Testament, "God will never leave you nor forsake you. Do not be afraid; do not be discouraged" (Deut. 31:8). And there's this in the New Testament: "Rejoice in the Lord always . . . and the peace of God that passes understanding will keep your hearts in Christ Jesus" (Phil. 4:4, 8).

When asked about what's still on his "bucket list," John responded as few are able. "Kathy and I have no unfinished bucket list that I can think of. We have a deep contentedness and have been blessed beyond measure. There are too many blessings to spend time focusing on a rare regret."

Common Pistole Traits

The letters "PJP" (***P***resident ***J***ohn ***P***istole) form the nickname soon coined for John on the Anderson campus. It doesn't, however, quite fit the Pistole family that's infused with the letters "E" and "F." There are four Pistole kids and E-F has finally come to fit all of them, now even PJP.

The "E" is for "educator." Parents Hollis and Elizabeth both were teachers, one in a high school and one in a graduate seminary. The four children all became educators. They all are "pass it on" people. Their unusual intelligence and creativity are understood to be given by God for the benefit of coming generations. That's just who they are, givers, leaders, and custodians of yesterday for the sake of tomorrow.

This "E" is enriched by the four educator Pistoles fulfilling their individual callings in the contexts of two "F"s. The first is for ***F***amily. From their earliest years, the young Pistole four all were privileged to be reared in a home that was nurturing and loving and stimulating. As explained above, Hollis and Elizabeth were both "green" people. They encouraged a "go forward" attitude toward life. They insisted on taking the academic pursuit seriously. They also opened their children to the wider world with travel and cultural exploration.

And there's the other "F." ***F***aith was central always for the Pistole parents and was actively and creatively nurtured in their children. Close to the Anderson home, there always was Park Place Church of God. Later, the four young Pistoles would encounter congregations that were less than ideal in several ways. This was especially true when they remembered the home congregation, Park Place.

John humbly receives the communion elements from his sister Carole (Pistole) Greenwalt and her husband Ed.

This congregation was and still is a nurturing community of faith where opportunities abound and honest questions are entertained constructively. The children's choirs and bell ringers of Pastor David Coolidge were an avenue for early involvement for John, and there were other ways for the children to make contributions to corporate worship, even in early and immature ways.

Decades of life now have come and gone for Cindy, Carole, David, and John. The "E" and both "Fs" remain very much alive for them all, even with the beloved Pistole parents now gone and some difficult life challenges having been faced. There has been a miscarriage, a divorce, a near economic disaster, the death of a spouse, and more. While all have lived in the very real world, the four have stayed in touch, different as they now are in many ways. Three are retired educators while the youngest, John, is the unretired President of Anderson University.

And the status of Christian faith for the Pistole four? All are Christian believers. In fact, Carole and John are active members of today's Park Place Church of God in Anderson, Indiana, where they began. Older sister Cindy is a dedicated member of Central Christian Church in downtown Anderson. David is no longer involved actively in the institutional church, but still cherishes what his father once told him. "Son, one's personal faith and faithfulness are what's ultimately important." Accordingly, David remains a believer even if not affiliated and active with any particular church.

John reflects back on his college years in Anderson and sees his own experience much like a goal he now is emphasizing for students at Anderson University—"Real Life Transformed!" He says he had come to college as a student focused on three people, "Me, Myself, and I." When he graduated, there were still three, but they had become "God, Jesus, and the Holy Spirit."

For John, college had been a great beginning of a long spiritual journey to gain and live out "the mind of Christ." That journey goes on. Now, much later in life, John has managed to embody this spiritual wisdom: "We begin, slowly at first, to live simply before God. Increasingly we come to see things in the light of eternity and, as a result, successes and failures no longer impress us or oppress us."[73]

One way or another, the four Pistoles never escaped Indiana. Three currently live in hometown of Anderson. Although David's the exception, ironically he's been located for years in Indiana, Pennsylvania, teaching at a public university there. He made attempts at formal church life across the years but found those congregations hardly Park Place Church, and less than helpful to educated professionals, especially when he and Renee lost their beloved little Christopher. The decision to turn off life supports to an infant is life-wrenching indeed. God was not blamed. To some extent, however, the church was at fault, not being helpfully present for them as the understanding and healing community of faith they very much needed.

The church experiences of John and Kathy have been several, of course, since they have moved so often. Although mixed, most of these have been somewhat to very positive. They have served and been nurtured well by various congregations in their own times of personal crisis. John, having begun his church-going as an infant at Park Place Church of God in Anderson, is now back in the same congregation as a loved layman and active Sunday school member. His boyhood home on nearby Walnut Street is now gone, replaced by a lovely community of student housing. His parents are gone, although in some ways not really. Very present indeed is his home church.

John and Kathy attend the Crossroads Sunday school class. They are regulars, at least when John's in town. To Kathy's dismay, often when the weather is good, they barely make it to the class on time. John takes great physical care of himself. Early Sunday mornings are usually his big bike-riding times in the earliest daytime hours. He has a tendency to squeeze in every possible mile before heading home for a quick shower and then over to the church with Kathy. While he usually makes it, it's sometimes a bit later than how Kathy would prefer to schedule things.

Once present in the class, however, and despite his public prominence over the decades, John remains a learner and seeker, intellectually and spiritually. He never dominates the group, several of the members being A. U. related. The teacher is Janet Brewer, A. U. librarian. In fact, Janet reports, John's actually rather self-effacing, the one honoring those around him and occasionally asking for prayer on behalf of times of stress for the campus across the street.

John would hesitate to say the following about himself, but his biographer has no hesitation. This special man is a straight shooter, a decisive and yet humble and loving representative of Jesus Christ, much as the Master would want. His Christian friend Stan Deal describes John this way. "He's an up-front truth-teller whose primary characteristic is integrity."

It's like Jesus instructed in Matthew 5:37. "Let your 'yes' be 'yes' and your 'no' be 'no'." The world around John tends to be changed for the better when he thinks, envisions, prays, and then acts. Although John has been in the driver's seat of very large institutions, he always has had a great quality in his steering style. He's pleased to give credit to others and prefers to nurture rather than manipulate those accountable to him..

Much credit for who John is goes to Hollis and Elizabeth, both now deceased. They were Anderson University people in the 1940s before their four children became A. U. graduates in the 1960s and 1970s. The Pistole family has been involved closely with this campus for eight decades. To date, the two daughters of John and Kathy, Lauren and Jennifer, have no children. Lauren was divorced in 2018 and Jennifer is still single. Since Mom and Dad have no grandchildren so far, they manage by treasuring their "grand cats." And they relish relationships with their siblings and the extended family of Anderson University.

Passing It On

John Pistole hesitates to be thought of as a Christian "minister." Even so, as the above chapter makes quite clear, the work of his life shows ample evidence of following in the ministry steps of Jesus. His interaction with the young prostitute in Minneapolis reflects well the conversation Jesus had with the woman at the well. There was no condemnation or condoning of the evil life, just a gentleness, insight, listening, and caring that brought that woman of old, and now the more recent thirteen-year-old prostitute, at least to an awareness that they were understood, even loved by a very different kind of man. That man was Jesus and now John, who is a Jesus man.

Then there was that Mob arrest in New York City that John led. We see in that an FBI agent in action, reflective of the Jesus who was meek but hardly weak. When he entered the Temple and saw the money changers at work, he saw organized crime working against his Father and kicked over their tables of ill-gotten gain. And when Jesus came to the home of Mary and Martha after Lazarus had died, he cried with them and comforted them. Justice requires action and human hurt cries out for deep empathy.

With God's help, John has nurtured in himself both the decisiveness and the gentleness, seeking to mature in and reflect the mind of Christ.

John Pistole sees in Robert Mueller a Jesus-like loving tenderness. A strong and demanding national leader, Bob kept on his office wall in Washington the photos and names of the FBI agents who had died in the line of duty on his watch. On occasion, John and Bob, professional colleagues and close friends, FBI's number one and two for years, would go together to the home of someone recently bereaved and share a genuine compassion.

When Hollis Pistole died, John's sister Cindy called immediately. The secretary put the call straight through to John who was meeting with Director Mueller. When the news was repeated to Bob, recalls Cindy, John said there were tears in the eyes of this "crusty Marine."

Later, when John was being inaugurated as President of Anderson University, he paused among the formalities to recognize the presence in the large crowd of members of a family who had traveled from California to Indiana just for this occasion. Why had they come? They had been bereaved on John's watch and he had visited them with tenderness and care. Now they wanted to celebrate with their admired "minister."

Since the beginning of his university presidency in 2015, John has made himself available and vulnerable to scores of students. He never hesitates to tell his personal story, good and bad, with its long journey of faith development. He's seeking to pass on through the stories of his own experience an overcoming faith so needed by today's new generations. In this way John is carrying on the example of his father.

In the early 1960s, Hollis had accepted a call to the faculty of Anderson School of Theology because he desired to nurture young men and women into Christian ministry. A half a century later, son John now desires much the same, accepting the presidency of that same campus to assist young women and men to have their lives transformed and find their own servant places in the world of today.

John also has followed his father (mostly) in this life testimony: "I have gained no fame, fortune, or greatness to speak of. God took the bits and pieces of what I had and made something wonderful out of me."[74] The "mostly" qualification, of course, is that John has achieved considerable "fame." He would prefer, however, that this testimony of his father be applied to him fully, without any particular note of the fame business and stress on the active goodness of God that has made it all possible.

A question was posed to John about the legacy he desires to leave behind someday. "It's less about me," he responded, "and more about what of value I will have been able to pass on to others. Since people forget so easily, the verdict of history is inconsequential. It's the verdict of eternity that counts." His parents would loudly applaud that testimony.

When asked about "Eternity's" desire for the future mission of Anderson University, he said this. "It's to grow young people for lives of faith and service to church and community. The preferred university future is for it to be unapologetically Christian, with particular commitments to holiness and unity, the core of the Christian gospel as understood by the Church of God tradition."

He continued, not wanting to seem narrowly focused on students of the Church of God tradition. "This university encourages the presence on campus of students with various Christian identities and also others who are unaffiliated serious seekers."

Autumn Leaves

Many close friends of John Pistole were asked to identify a theme that best represents their friend. What speaks the most important truth about his person and public life? The word "integrity" often came up, as did the phrase "straight shooter," a conscious play on his last name.

Jeff Jenness spoke of "*Over*-achiever," explaining that John has achieved much, no doubt, but always with the "*Over*"—God—providentially superintending and leading the way. Bob Coffman said much the same thing: "God has had his hand on John's journey and John always has sought that presence, guidance, and strength. He prays regularly for discernment. He's dedicated his life to being obedient to what he understands to be God's will."

President Pistole speaks of his often praying *DEWS*, that is, seeking *discernment, encouragement, wisdom, and strength.* Such seeking has made all the difference, he reports. John hopes that all people will learn to pray this way and then live accordingly. We, readers of this life story, probably should add a "*G*" to the *DEWS*, *gratitude* both for who God is and for God having blessed our troubled world with the person, life, and "ministry" of John Pistole. He certainly had his challenges growing up, as most of us do, and now he has met the challenges of adulthood much as God intended, and as many of us have not.

John has served while being on a life-long journey of Christian growth and witness. It's been like John Ashcroft's father told him. "I want you to know that even Washington can be holy ground. It's a place to hear the voice of God, and wherever you hear His voice, that ground is sanctified, set apart. It's a place where God can call you to the highest and best."[75]

Ashcroft claimed that holy ground during his significant federal service. So did John Pistole while following a life journey similar to that of Nathan Foster,[76] son of one of his spiritual mentors, Richard Foster.[77] So should we all wherever we find our places of divine calling.

John's spiritual journey has been a modern-day, monk-like quest for the deeply spiritual. In his case, the quest has been anything but one with Medieval-looking robes, celibacy, and isolation from the rough and tumble of our very real world. Over time, if faithful to this kind of prayerful journey of faith, God's grace will enable the enrichment of character that increasingly comes to be reflective of Jesus, no matter the ugliness encountered along the way.

Autumn leaves in front of the
Olt Student Center of Anderson University.

John Pistole would hesitate here, insisting that he has hardly arrived at the goal. Who has, at least while existing in this world? Even so, his life is clear evidence of a person truly formed into the likeness of Christ's character. John carries with him daily the witness of St. Paul: "Not that I already have obtained all this, but I press on to take hold of that for which Christ Jesus took hold of me" (Philippians 3:12).

This Christian journey enables a person to be loving and bold, open and vulnerable. One becomes willing to put the whole of self on the line, being very concerned about the truth and meaning of biblical revelation and equally concerned with being involved personally in the implications of the faith. Being with Jesus and becoming like Jesus requires being part of the ongoing mission of Jesus Christ. God's grace understands our humanness, gives the space and time needed to grow and mature, and provides the passion to actually be the hands and feet of Jesus in this world. That's who, what, and where John Pistole has been for decades and still seeks to be.

We've much to learn from John's journey. We "moderns" are slaves to achievement, even in our spiritual lives. John has learned to "stop viewing the Bible as a book I need to understand, manage, or defend." Then what is it? It's "the personal stories of a loving Father reaching out to his children."[78] Once realizing that, there's no need to achieve or be perfect or prove to God that we are worthy of forgiveness and eternal life. We are not. No matter. Our sin is covered by loving grace. People who know they are loved deeply by God become free to love others deeply as well.

Along this journey's way, the faithful learn to be careful about the spirit in which they hold others—honoring them, preferring them, loving them. This lesson brings a freedom from self-pity and self-absorption. It enables an inner serenity that allows an acceptance of people for who they are rather than for who we want them to be. John knows well that this attitude is critical when dealing with the young on a university campus.

We humans, because of our fallen nature, are slaves to power, approval, and self-seeking. God calls us to another slavery, a truly liberating servitude. We are invited to chain ourselves to God's rule of love. Only in such submission can we find real freedom. Increasingly, through submission and obedience, we can become able to see things in the light of eternity.

Daily successes and failures no longer impress or oppress us. We are free to live selflessly. We become life givers rather than life takers.

Hollis and Elizabeth Pistole were givers to the very end of their lives, key models for their children. Elizabeth died the day after daughter Cindy's birthday and Hollis the day after Carole's. Both daughters are convinced that these timings were intentional, each loving parent holding on an extra day to avoid burdening the future with unnecessary sadness.

And what of death, the end of life's journey, at least as we know it here? John Pistole has reached a retirement age, but not that ultimate point of life's ending. When he does, having stayed faithful to the upward trajectory of his life, inevitably the road will lead to the image of autumn leaves.

Here's how Nathan Foster describes this final process in his *The Making of an Ordinary Sain*t. "The leaves prepared for death, revealing their glory, shown bright and dull, yellow and orange. An occasional tree was bold enough to display a red as rich as blood. Patiently they waited for just the right moment, and then, one by one, they answered the call of the wind and leaped into the air, their first and only great flight. I watched their ballet as they dove to their deaths with freedom and grace."

That final journey will come one day for John Pistole and the rest of us. If we follow John's example, it's likely that the departure will have those ballet qualities of freedom and grace. It may mirror that of the departure of John's father, Hollis. John's sister Cindy was with their beloved Dad in his last moment of life. She watched in amazement as he reached his arms forward, looked far away, smiled, and appeared to be seeing Jesus and his beloved Elizabeth beckoning him home. May we all one day join that joyous journey home.

Endnotes

1. Statement made by Rev. James Lyon, General Director of Church of God Ministries, in an interview conducted on July 10, 2020.

2. David's "Straight Shooter" suggestion is reflected in the colored arrows in the headers of the chapters. Jeff Jenness suggested that the word "trajectory" might be used as the title of this biography.

3. See Dr. Hollis Pistole's autobiography titled *My Story* (Anderson, IN: Chinaberry House, 2004), 6.

4. Ibid, 33. Hollis Pistole was highly appreciative of the prayer ministry and writings of Dr. Charles Whiston, participating in his summer retreats for theological faculty and later bringing him as a guest to the School of Theology of Anderson University.

5. See Isabel Wilkerson, *The Warmth of Other Suns: The Epic Story of America's Great Migration* (Vintage Books, 2011).

6. Of course, in their student days it would have been "AC" (Anderson College).

7. James Earl Massey, *Aspects of My Pilgrimage* (Anderson University Press, 2002), 195.

8. Robert H. Reardon, *The Early Morning Light* (Warner Press, 1979), 14. Much later Anderson University Press would publish the celebrated 2005 volume by James Earl Massey titled *African Americans and the Church of God.*

9. Hollis Pistole, *My Story*, 43.

10. This was in the 1960s when Bill and Gloria Gaither had begun writing music that soon would become very popular in the Christian world. Bill would be a Trustee of Anderson University with an unusually long tenure, allowing him decades later to participate in the calling of Elizabeth's son John to that school's presidency.

11. See more in *River of Change: The Sesquicentennial Story of Anderson, Indiana* (The *Herald Bulletin*, 2014), 21.

12. A musical album of the young Park Place ringers was produced in 1967, featuring on the cover a photo of the ringer group that includes John Pistole.

13. James Comey, a prominent friend of John's in later years, had a similar experience at about the same age. He and his brother had gotten caught alone in their home by the gun-toting "Ramsey Rapist." James explains in his memoirs how they managed to escape death. The awful experience "in its own way was an incredible gift. It made life seem like a precious, delicate miracle. As a high school senior, I started watching sunsets." John also had received an incredible gift and was much aware of his miracle. He began listening more closely for the quiet voice of God in his life.

14. Barry L. Callen, *Guide of Soul and Mind* (Anderson University and Warner Press), 1992.

15. In his autobiography, *My Story*, Hollis Pistole records his international travels, many with TRIS, including a rickshaw in India, camel at the pyramids, elephant in Thailand, donkey in Greece, gondola in Venice, and bullet train in Japan.

16. For full perspective and detail, see the chapter "Enriching the Journey" in Barry L. Callen, *Guide of Soul and Mind* (Anderson University and Warner Press), 1992.

17. Robert K. Greenleaf, *Servant Leadership: A Journey into the Nature of Legitimate Power and Greatness* (Paulist Press, 1975).

18. See the Reardon biography by Barry L. Callen titled *Staying on Course* (Anderson University Press, 2004).

19. Hollis Pistole, *My Story*, 39–41.

20. On one occasion when John Pistole had risen to significant leadership of the FBI, Bill Gaither, American gospel music icon who once was the supervising teacher of John's mother back in Indiana, visited John in Washington. Bill reports, "I tried to get my hands in the cookie jar by digging gently for a little inside information on a current event." The result? "John was kind, didn't say it wasn't any of my business, but left me realizing that I had not gotten inside his jar! What I learned was that he's a real professional."

21. For considerable detail on the FBI work of John Pistole in his New York years, consult the podcast of Jerri Williams, episode 190.

22. Such drama was portrayed in the popular TV series "The Sopranos" (1999–2007) featuring mob boss Tony Soprano. The FBI investigations of Vincent Gigante were featured in season one, episode six of the *FBI Files* titled "The Crazy Don" (first aired in 1998).

23. See chapter eleven for detail on how and why Kathy changed her mind.

24. John Ashcroft, *Never Again* (2006).

25. Much later John Pistole would become the President of Anderson University where Gloria Gaither had been an occasional guest and classroom instructor and her husband Bill a prominent trustee for some forty-four years. Bill would be a member of the search committee that would decide on John as the chosen candidate for the university's presidency in 2014. A brief sketch of their ministries is found in Barry L. Callen, *The Wisdom of the Saints* (Anderson University Press and Warner Press, 2003).

26. Another who excelled physically was John's good friend Chris Favo.

27. This Renovaré Covenant prayer reads: *In utter dependence upon Jesus Christ as my ever-living Savior, Teacher, Lord, and Friend, I will seek continual renewal through spiritual exercises, spiritual gifts, and acts of service.*

28. David Rohde, *In Deep: The FBI, the CIA, and the Truth about America's "Deep State"* (W. W. Norton & Company, 2020).

29. Years later, with John the President of Anderson University, the "York" family name would be prominent on the university campus.

30. This philosophy of Christian lay penetration into all sectors of society would be shared in 2020 by Dr. Brock Vaughters, newly appointed by President

John Pistole to the role of Vice-President of Finance and Treasurer of Anderson University. Says Brock, "Each group of A. U. graduates is a maze of many fingers being put out into the world."

31. See Barry L. Callen, ed., *The Holy River of God: Currents and Contributions of the Wesleyan Holiness Stream of Christianity* (Aldersgate Press, 2016), including an entry by John Pistole on the WHC's president's fellowship.

32. These words are Kathy's way of expressing appreciation for John's high sensitivity to her concerns at times of key decision. His heart, as hers, is always to seek and then follow together the will of God, whatever the apparent immediate impact on his professional life.

33. Lou Gerig, Chair of the Board, had declined to head the Search Committee because of his family relationship with John Pistole's wife Kathy. He knew early that John might become a candidate and his family tie would be a conflict of interest.

34. Yours truly was an undergraduate at Geneva College. I honed my academic skills in that classic library facility.

35. Clarence E. Macartney, *The Making of a Minister: Autobiography*, 1961.

36. Boris Johnson, *The Churchill Factor* (Riverhead Books, 2014), Introduction.

37. Merle D. Strege, *The Desk As Altar: The Centennial History of Anderson University* (Anderson University Press, 2016), 363.

38. *River of Change*, published by the local newspaper, pages 124–125. The river in question is the White River that winds through the city's downtown area.

39. The sketches of the five presidents by J. David Liverett appear on page vii.

40. Richard Foster, *Celebration of Discipline* (HarperOne, 20th anniversary edition, 1997).

41. Barry L. Callen, ed., *The Holy River of God: Currents and Contributions of the Wesleyan Holiness Stream of Christianity* (Aldersgate Press, 2016).

42. See *The Desk As Altar* by Merle Strege, *Forward, Ever Forward!* by Barry Callen, and *John S. Pistole: A Biography* by Barry Callen.

43. Quoted in Barry L. Callen, *God in the Shadows* (Emeth Press, 2018).

44. For the life story of Robert Reardon, see Barry L. Callen, *Staying on Course: Biography of Robert H. Reardon* (Anderson University Press, 2004).

45. President Pistole's philosophy in higher education programming is similar to what Winston Churchill's was in politics. "Churchill was radical precisely because he was conservative. He knew that the only way to keep things the same is to make sure your change them. A state without the means of some change is without the means of its conservation" (*The Churchill Factor*, Boris Johnson).

46. John Pistole as quoted in *USA TODAY*, August 13, 2020.

47. Anderson's *The Herald Bulletin*, May 19, 2020.

48. Quoted in Barry L. Callen, *God in the Shadows* (Emeth Press, 2018).

49. This huge anti-terrorism effort is detailed well by Garrett M. Graff in his *The Threat Matrix: The FBI at War in the Age of Global Terror* (Little Brown and Co.).

50. This early action of the General Assembly of the Church of God, and all its future actions related to higher education, can be found in Barry L. Callen, *Leaning Forward!* (Emeth Press, 2019).

51. See John M. Barry, *The Great Influenza: The Story of the Deadliest Pandemic in History* (Viking Press, 2004).

52. For the full story of Anderson University's beginnings, see Barry L. Callen, *Guide of Soul and Mind* (Anderson University and Warner Press, 1992).

53. Ron Chernow's biographies, *Alexander Hamilton* (2005) and *Grant* (2017).

54. John A. Morrison's autobiography, *As the River Flows*, Robert H. Reardon's biography by Barry L. Callen, *Staying on Course*, Robert A. Nicholson's autobiography, *So, I Said "Yes,"* and Barry L. Callen's edited volume, *Faith, Learning, & Life* (select wisdom writings of these presidents of the Anderson campus).

55. John Pistole in the *Indiana Business Journal*, November 29, 2018.

56. President John Pistole in a university chapel service, as published in the alumni magazine *Signatures*, Spring 2020.

57. John Pistole in the *Indiana Business Journal*, November 29, 2018.

58. Quoted from the institutional profile prepared for presidential candidates in 2014.

59. James Lyon, General Director of Church of God Ministries, on a summer broadcast of *Viewpoint*, based on a recorded interview with John Pistole in July, 2020.

60. John Pistole on occasion would go to Indianapolis with Bill Gaither to enjoy a Pacers basketball game. It was a relaxing diversion away from the daily professional pressures faced by Bill and John. John, of course, had enjoyed years as a gifted player himself and could really "get into" such games.

61. This joint degree is being discontinued for lack of interest. In its place is a "Taste and See" initiative, an online course taken by pastors as part of a cohort.

62. See Barry L. Callen. *Guide of Soul and Mind* (Warner Press, 1992), 246.

63. See the history of Geneva College, *Pro Christo et Patria*, authored by David Carson, 1997.

64. D. Elton Trueblood, *Foundations for Reconstruction* (Harper & Brothers, 1946), 8, 10, 104–105.

65. Donald Dayton, *Discovering an Evangelical Heritage*, available in various editions.

66. For a compilation of the many policy statements of the General Assembly of this Movment on a wide range of issues, see Barry L. Callen, editor, *Leaning Forward!* (Emeth Press, 2019).

67. Words of Dr. Ian A. Worley on the back cover of Barry L. Callen, *Seeking the Light: America's Modern Quest for Peace, Justice, Prosperity, and Faith* (Evangel Publishing House, 1998).

68. Two of Reinhold Niebuhr's more famous books are *Moral Man and Immoral Society* and *The Nature and Destiny of Man: A Christian Interpretation.*

69. William E. Diehl, *Ministry in Daily Life* (The Alban Institute, 1996), 92.

70. See E. Stanley Jones, *Abundant Living* (Abingdon Press), 1.

71. In addition to this 2009 honor, Indiana University's McKinney School of Law further honored Dr. Pistole in 2020 by granting a Bicentennial Medal "in recognition of distinguished and distinctive service in support of the mission of Indiana University."

72. Kevin Brown and Michael Wiese, *Work that Matters: Bridging the Divide Between Worship and Work* (Aldersgate Press, 2013), 48–49.

73. Nathan Foster, *The Making of an Ordinary Saint* (Baker Books, 2014).

74. Hollis Pistole, *My Story*, 7.

75. John Ashcroft, *On My Honor,* previously published as *Lessons from a Father to His Son* (Thomas Nelson, 1998).

76. Nathan Foster, *The Making of an Ordinary Saint* (Baker Books, 2014).

77. See Richard Foster, *Celebration of Discipline,* and other works.

78. See Barry L. Callen, *God As Loving Grace: The Biblically Revealed Nature and Work of God* (Evangel Publishing House, 1996, Wipf & Stock, 2018).

Index

CPSIA information can be obtained
at www.ICGtesting.com
Printed in the USA
JSHW021117300321
12766JS00001BA/1

9 781609 471682